HUMAN RIGHTS AND EUROPE

HUMAN RIGHTS AND EUROPE

by

DR. RALPH BEDDARD

Senior Lecturer in the Faculty of Law
Southampton University

THIRD EDITION

CAMBRIDGE
GROTIUS PUBLICATIONS LIMITED
1993

SALES &   GROTIUS PUBLICATIONS LTD.
ADMINISTRATION   PO BOX 115, CAMBRIDGE CB3 9BP
ENGLAND

British Library Cataloguing in Publication Data

Beddard, Ralph
   Human Rights and Europe.—3 Rev. ed
   I. Title
   341.481

ISBN 1-85701-014-0

Typeset by Carnegie Publishing Ltd., Maynard St., Preston
Printed in Great Britain by Gomer Press, Llandysul, Dyfed

TO
JUDI, LA VINIA,
HONOR AND BELLA

TABLE OF CONTENTS

PREFACE

The aims of the three editions of this book have remained identical; to provide an introduction to students and others who wish, or need, to know about the European Convention on Human Rights. The task involved in the pursuit of this aim, however, has changed significantly each time. When the first edition appeared the operation of the Convention was virtually unknown to practising lawyers and the number of admissible cases was small - the Court was about to deliver its third judgment. More cases had been decided by the time of the second edition but these were concentrated in certain areas of litigation and were as such uneven in their spread. In the long period which has elapsed until this present volume the European Convention has become a feature of European public law. The Strasbourg machinery has, at times, staggered under the weight of cases so that reforms to the procedure have become necessary and more are under discussion.

In order to maintain my objective of being brief, selections have had to be made and this has not been easy. No doubt I shall be accused of ignoring important cases but I have tried to choose those decisions and judgments which best give a picture of how the Strasbourg machinery operates and the way in which the jurisprudence is built up. A full analysis of the case-law would take a much larger volume - or even several volumes - and would not fulfil the need which this book is designed meet.

Europe changes and grows - even its notional boundaries are uncertain - and as a result the Council of Europe and the other organisations dedicated to its peace and stability need to react to these changes. This exciting movement does not, however, facilitate the writing of books. Since the manuscript was delivered to my helpful and understanding publishers several states in Central Europe and the Baltic have become Members of the Council of Europe while, amoeba-like, Czechoslovakia has divided and rejoined as two. The Council of Europe no longer, therefore, has twenty-six Members, as the first page says but any attempt by me to correct this is likely to be inaccurate by the time it appears in print. The figures, therefore, are those for the end of 1992. The point to be made is that the membership of the Council of Europe and the case load of the Commission and Court continue to grow.

This book is offered in the sincere belief that every lawyer operating within Europe has an obligation to those persons whom he or she advises to be familiar with the human rights provisions of the European Convention which have, sometimes surprisingly, found their way into all sectors of daily life.

May I extend my thanks and appreciation to all those who have helped, in no matter what way, in the publication of this new edition.

Southampton
July 1993

Ralph Beddard

TABLE OF CASES

ALPHABETICAL

CASES FILED WITH THE EUROPEAN COMMISSION OF HUMAN RIGHTS ARRANGED BY APPLICATION NUMBER

TABLE OF ABBREVIATIONS

All ER	All England Law Reports
Bull EC	Bulletin of the European Communities
BYIL	British Yearbook of International Law
CD	Collected Decisions of the European Commission of Human Rights, Volumes 1-46, Council of Europe
Cmd Cmnd	Command Papers
CSCE	Conference on Security and Co-operation in Europe
D&R	Decisions and Reports of the European Commission of Human Rights, Volumes 1-60 (replaces Collected Decisions, above)
ECOSOC	United Nations, Economic and Social Council
ECR	European Court Reports
EEC	European Economic Community
EHRR	European Human Rights Reports
FAO	Food and Agriculture Organisation
HRLJ	Human Rights Law Journal
ICLQ	International and Comparative Law Quarterly
NATO	North Atlantic Treaty Organisation
Series A	Publications of the European Court of Human Rights; Judgments and Decisions
Series B	Publications of the European Court of Human Rights; Pleadings, Oral Arguments and Documents
UKTS	United Kingdom Treaty Series
UNESCO	United Nations Educational Scientific and Cultural Organisation
UNTS	United Nations Treaty Series
YB	The Yearbook of the European Convention on Human Rights

CHAPTER ONE

The European Convention and the Individual

The European Convention for the Protection of Human Rights and Fundamental Freedoms can be described as one of the greatest achievements of the Council of Europe. It is, indeed, often spoken of as the major contributor to human rights law not only regionally but at a global level. The Convention, signed first in 1950 and now in force, to some extent or another in all the twenty-six member countries of the Council is held as a standard of achievement in its own right of a unifying Europe. If the criterion of success is to be the signing and ratification of a treaty and the bringing into being of complicated machinery of judicial adjudication, then the European states do indeed rank high in the international "league table".

The European Convention is important to the student of international law for the contribution it makes to the status of the individual in the international legal system. More than 450 million persons in Europe may bring before the European Commission of Human Rights allegations that their rights have been violated.[1] Twenty-five out of the twenty-six Contracting States have lodged an optional declaration allowing this individual petition.[2] Such applications will be considered by the Commission and well-founded ones will be passed to the Court of Human Rights or the Committee of Ministers of the Council of Europe for a decision on violation.

One of the explanations for the success of the Convention is that European states make up a culturally identifiable unit and their like-mindedness has meant easier agreement on what are considered to be basic human rights. Since 1990, states from Central Europe - Hungary, Czechoslovakia, Poland, and Bulgaria - have also become Members and participation by the Baltic states is expected. A condition of

---

[1] The total population of the Member States of the Council of Europe is approaching 520 million people.

[2] Poland is the only Contracting Party not yet accepting the right of individual petition.

the membership of these Central European states has been the restoration of democracy, and indeed Polish accession was delayed until full elections had been held. Some concern has been expressed, not that these Central European states are inappropriate parties to the Convention, but that their differing social traditions over the last forty years may distort attempts, formerly limited to Western Europe, to achieve a "European" standard. Levels of expectation in social and welfare matters, for example, may be higher in these states than in some of the less socially developed western states.

During the forty years since the inception of the Convention there has been a noticeable lack of success or enthusiasm in extending the list of rights it contains to embrace more sophisticated rights and freedoms where, it might be thought, Europe should lead the way.[3] The complementary European Social Charter purports to encourage the progressive guarantee of social and economic rights but, up to the present time, has operated somewhat disappointingly. Similar attempts within the European Community to cover social rights have met with some resistance, although it may be argued that the mechanism for enforcing such rights is appropriate in that context.

Thirteen Articles of the Convention, together with three in the First Protocol, contain the rights which the Contracting Parties undertake to secure for everyone within their jurisdiction. Four further rights are contained in the Fourth Protocol to the Convention which came into force in 1968 but which has so far been ratified only by seventeen states and not by the United Kingdom.

The rights and freedoms take as their starting point the Universal Declaration of Human Rights of the United Nations, although the drafting processes have produced some provisions defined in ways which render them wider or more restricted than the parent instrument.

The Convention's provisions broadly cover the individual's personal life and the need to live life to the full, according to personal wishes, together with those rights which are involved in instances of conflict with the authorities and the law.

Life is to be protected by the law and the European citizen is to be

---

[3] There have been four Protocols extending the Convention's guarantees to further rights but these have, in general, excited little enthusiasm and have attracted a varied and middling number of ratifications.

brought up in the privacy of the home surrounded by family and possessions. Education should be guaranteed, or at least not prevented, and where it is provided by a system of schools, the wishes and beliefs of parents should be respected. Everyone who is of age has the right to marry and found a family. The Fourth Protocol would also give freedom of movement, the right to choose a place of residence and the right to leave any country and to enter one's own. No one should be expelled from his or her state of nationality, either alone or collectively. Although the Convention does not guarantee the right to work, it does offer protection from forced or compulsory labour, slavery and servitude.

People exist as members of a society, and in the highly populated region of Western Europe a glance at literature will show what rights in this sphere the individual would demand. The Convention secures the freedom of thought, conscience and religion and the right to manifest religious and other beliefs. Whilst freedom of expression is a right befitting the effective political democracy to which the Convention is dedicated, in fact it has been found that modern technology has rendered such protection no easy thing. The "common heritage of political traditions", identified in the Preamble, requires the rights of assembly and association to be respected, and the latter, of course, must now include the right to form and belong to trade unions. Finally, in this context, the First Protocol secures the right to free elections by secret ballot.

Liberty and security are valued next to life itself and the Convention's provisions protecting the individual from arbitrary arrest and imprisonment are, as we shall see, much cited by individual petitioners. The European prisoner, when lawfully detained, is not to be tortured, inhumanly treated or punished and, furthermore, he must be brought to trial expeditiously and only for offences which were offences at the time they were committed. The concept of a fair trial is, to many, the very heart of justice and it is not surprising that much of the jurisprudence of the European Commission centres on the interpretation of Article 6 which embraces it.

Neither the Convention nor any other Council of Europe instrument guarantees the general right not to be discriminated against. Article 14 of the Convention declares only that the enjoyment of the rights and freedoms set forth in the Convention shall be secured "without discrimination on any ground such as sex, race, colour, language, religion, political or other opinion, national or social origin, association with a national minority, property, birth or other status".

Originally, it was held that since the principle of non-discrimination was to be applied in "the enjoyment of the rights and freedoms set forth in this Convention", it could not be construed to operate independently but only in relation to the violation of one of the other rights and freedoms.[4] Later, however, the Commission and Court revised this view, recognising that the insistence upon the specific violation of another Article before Article 14 could be invoked deprived the non-discrimination provision of practical value,[5] and holding that there could be a violation of Article 14 in association with another Article of the Convention, even where that other Article had not itself been violated. One might also speculate whether racial or sexual discrimination might, in some circumstances, amount to degrading treatment and thereby constitute a violation of Article 3 of the Convention.

The non-discrimination provision is relevant also to the limitations which states may impose, under the Convention, upon certain of the rights and freedoms. Thus, for example, although the freedom to manifest one's religion or beliefs may be limited for the protection of, *inter alia*, public order, health or morals, the law imposing those limitations must not be discriminatory.

Article 14 has not been interpreted by the Commission and the Court to impose absolute equality. Different treatment has been held to be acceptable when there is objective and reasonable justification. The Court has said, however, that Article 14 *is* violated ". . . when it is clearly established that there is no reasonable relationship of proportionality between the means employed and the aim sought to be realized".[6]

It will have been noticed that these rights contain no innovations and that their equivalents are to be found in the majority of constitutions and Bills of Rights. It is, indeed, of passing interest to note that the European Convention was used as a model by the United

---

[4] See, for example, Application 808/60, *ISOP* v. *Austria*, 5 *YB* 108.

[5] See the Commission's Report in the *Belgian Linguistics Case (No. 1)*, (1967) Series A, No. 5 at p. 11. 1 *EHRR* 241 p. 244.

[6] *Supra*, note 5, para. 10.

Kingdom in the early 1950s in drawing up constitutions for some of the newly independent African states.

A former Secretary to the European Commission, Mr A. B. McNulty, in reviewing the results achieved under the Convention up to 1971, remarked:

> It is a reasonable deduction that the Commission has substantially established itself in the confidence both of the public and of the parties to the Convention. It is particularly this basis for co-operation between the Commission and Governments, rather than a relationship of prosecutor and accused, which has brought this about and generally made the Convention workable at this first stage of its existence.

It is and always has been obvious that winning the confidence of the parties and the public would be a first step in any attempt to establish judicial determination of the protection of human rights. The last forty years have not been free of difficulties, however, and the confidence of the parties was won by the Commission, particularly in the early days, only by very careful treading. There are cases which, if presented to the Commission today, would probably make greater progress than they did at the time of application. However, a Commission leaning heavily in favour of governments would have lost the confidence of the public. This is hardly borne out by the increasing number of applications which the Commission has continued to receive from individual petitioners, and by the greater seriousness of the subject-matter with which a large proportion of those petitions deal. It is clear that the Commission and Court work; that the protection of human rights in Europe is successful is far more difficult to establish. The answer, of course, cannot be found in a book of this size, nor, indeed, in any work which considers only the working of the European Commission and Court. Human rights is not a study for the lawyer alone but also for the sociologist, economist and politician, not to mention the theologian, philosopher and ecologist.

What we can attempt to do here, accepting that the machinery of the European Convention has now been established, is to seek an answer to the following question: how far, if at all, does the Convention contribute to the quality of life of the European citizen? Any answer will inevitably concern itself with analysis at two levels, if not more. It is possible to see the Convention, in its context of European integration, as a kind of constitutional document for a united

Europe. Together, as far as some of the states are concerned, with the instruments and machinery set up by the European Communities, it provides a regional frame of reference, a European instance of review. What it is also providing – and this may be deemed to be more important in the long run – is an extensive jurisprudence on the interpretation and level of human rights standards in a *global* context. The agenda of international human rights law has been set by regional organizations.

The contribution of the European Convention to the European way of life, through the decisions at Strasbourg, through its influence on the European Court of Justice in Luxembourg and, more importantly, by its application in the national courts, has been immense. The confidence of states has been put to the test. The increasing use made of the Convention seems to show that the faith of the individual in the championing of rights is not dwindling. The end of the Cold War and the reintegration of Eastern and Central Europe pose new challenges, and throughout the chapters ahead we must not lose sight of the Convention's international dimension.

In a volume of this size, we cannot give any analytical study to the decisions of the Court and Commission.[7] Instead, we shall attempt to concentrate on examining events leading up to and surrounding the birth of the treaty and the machinery it sets up, and then try, by looking at the working of the Convention in the context of modern Europe, to elucidate what contribution it has made, or has still to make, to the quality of life of the European citizen and to the creation of a unified Europe.

To the end of December 1991 just over 19,000 cases have been through the machinery of the Commission, as described in Chapter 3. Thirteen inter-state cases have been considered, although concerning only six situations of international disagreement. The number of applications registered in the early years was between three and four hundred per year. This has grown steadily as the number of eligible applicants has increased, either because new Member States have joined the Council of Europe, or because the right of

---

[7] The leading English language text on the Convention (translated from Dutch) is *Theory and Practice of the European Convention on Human Rights* by P. van Dijk and G. J. H. van Hoof, 2nd edition, 1990, Kluwer. The Dutch-language third edition is also available. Other practitioner-orientated books have been announced by English publishers.

individual petition under Article 25 has been recognized by more states. In 1991, there were 1,648 registered applications. In the same year, over 5,500 provisional files were opened. Most of the communications received from individuals are hopeless of success or are not pursued further by their writers. Out of a total of over 19,000 individual petitions since 1955, less than 3,000 have been communicated to governments for their observations, whilst of those a little over 1,000 applications have been admitted. A majority of these applications have been disposed of by means of a friendly settlement or a decision on the merits by the Committee of Ministers. A total of 345 applications have been referred to the Court, which has handed down 307 judgments.[8] In over two-thirds of the cases decided by it, the Court has found a breach of the Convention[9] and in twenty cases it has found violations of more than one Article. Just satisfaction by the payment of compensation and/or costs has been awarded in 143 instances.

These figures do not, of course, amount to a sum of the success of the Convention. Its mere existence, and the prestige with which it is regarded, put pressure on states to avoid acting against its provisions, while in many states it has become part of the municipal law, and decisions of domestic courts have also to be considered. On the other hand, the prime object of the Convention was to set up international machinery to protect human rights in Europe, and as there has been no shortage of complaints, the question is bound to be asked whether that machinery in its operation, or the jurisprudence being accumulated by the Commission and Court, does in fact provide a means whereby an individual can obtain respite from oppressive acts of the Government under whose jurisdiction he or she happens to be.

THE CASES

In practical terms, therefore, what have the decisions of the European Commission and Court produced? It has been noted above that

---

[8] These figures, and an analysis of them, are to be found in: *Survey of Activities and Statistics, 1991*, European Commission of Human Rights, Council of Europe and *Survey of Activities 1959-91*, European Court of Human Rights, Jan. 1992, Council of Europe.

[9] In 174 cases.

there have been thirteen inter-state applications alleging violation of the Convention. In 1956 and 1957, Greece brought two applications against the United Kingdom concerning alleged mistreatment of prisoners in Cyprus.[10] These cases were later withdrawn by request of both governments, following a political settlement of the Cyprus problem. Since neither country recognized the right of individual petition at that time, there was no right of action for the victims to continue the fight for relief after the Commission had agreed to withdrawal, even though it had been established that there had been mistreatment. It is doubtful whether European public opinion would approve the withdrawal of such a case today.

The first of two similar cases brought by Ireland against the United Kingdom, in 1971 and 1972, alleging similar behaviour by the British authorities in Northern Ireland, was eventually referred by the Republic's Government to the Court, which ruled there had been a violation of Article 3 of the Convention for activities characterized as inhuman and degrading.[11] Cyprus, after independence, became a Contracting Party to the Convention and between 1974 and 1977 lodged three applications against Turkey, complaining of violations of the Convention brought about by Turkish intervention in Cyprus. The Committee of Ministers decided in 1979 that there had been violations of the Convention, but that the protection of human rights could be brought about only by the resumption of peace and confidence between the two Cyprus communities. It therefore urged the Parties to resume inter-communal talks.[12]

Five applications were submitted against Greece between 1967 and 1970 by Denmark, Norway, Sweden and the Netherlands, alleging, *inter alia*, violation of Articles 3 and 7 of the Convention and Article 3 of the First Protocol.[13] No friendly settlement was reached, and while the Report of the Commission was with the Committee of Ministers, the Greek Government withdrew from the Council of Europe and denounced the Convention. A new Greek Government

---

[10] Applications 176/56 and 299/57, *Greece* v. *UK*, 2 *YB* 182 and 186.

[11] *Ireland* v. *UK*, (1978) Series A, No. 25 and 2 *EHRR* 25.

[12] Applications 6780/74 and 6950/75, *Cyprus* v. *Turkey*, 18 *YB* 82, and 22 *YB* 440. See also Application 8007/77, 20 *YB* 98, and 21 *YB* 100.

[13] Applications 3321-3326 and 3344/67, *Denmark, Norway, Sweden and Netherlands* v. *Greece*, 25 *CD* 92 and 11 *YB* 690. Application 4448/70, *Denmark, Norway and Sweden* v. *Greece*, 34 *CD et seq.* and 13 *YB* 108.

ratified the Convention again in 1974 and, after it had furnished information to the Commission concerning the remedies available to victims of persecution under the former régime, the Parties agreed to close proceedings in those applications which were still pending.

Similar concern about the harsh treatment of individuals, this time in Turkey, led to an application against that state by France, Norway, Sweden, Denmark and the Netherlands in 1982.[14] That case was concluded by a friendly settlement wherein the Applicant States accepted amnesties promised by the Turkish Government and vague assurances that martial law would be lifted shortly. That case, permeated by the sensitive relations between the two sets of Parties, perhaps illustrates the unsatisfactory nature of inter-state petitions.[15] Finally, an inter-state application was brought by Austria against Italy in 1960 which concerned criminal proceedings leading to the conviction of six young men for the murder of a customs officer in the German-speaking South Tyrol.[16] The Commission, upheld by the Committee of Ministers, concluded that there had been no violation, but recommended that clemency be afforded to the prisoners. In fact, by this time, the youngest had been pardoned.

The inter-state procedure was bound to be founded, for the greater part, on unfriendliness in the relations between states, and the cases, in the main, bear this out. Although the applications against Turkey and those against Greece were brought by states with little economic or cultural contact with the Respondent States, and were occasioned by the seriousness of the violations, they illustrate the weakness of the Commission within the arenas of large-scale politics and diplomacy. The application by *Ireland* v. *United Kingdom* seemed, to a great extent, to be politically motivated, whilst the *Cyprus* v. *Turkey* application was a direct result of hostilities between the two parties. However, one should not dismiss such inter-state applications as serving no purpose, since one of the objects of the Convention is to publicize atrocities and, accordingly, motive is not entirely relevant.

---

[14] Applications 9940-9944/82, 35 *D&R* 143 and 26 *YB* 1.

[15] Turkey did not at that time recognize the jurisdiction of the Court, thereby rendering the solution of the dispute subject to political and diplomatic niceties.

[16] Application 788/60, *Austria* v. *Italy,* 4 *YB* 116.

A much clearer guide to the practical effects of the Convention might be expected to emerge from consideration of the petitions of individuals. The *Ireland* v. *UK* case, in 1976, is the only inter-state petition to be referred to the Court, whereas, to the end of 1991, a further 344 cases initiated by individuals under Article 25 have been submitted to the Court. Under the Convention as it now stands the individual applicant cannot refer his case to the Court; this must be done by the Commission or by an involved Contracting State. A large majority of referrals have been by the Commission alone, but in over ninety cases the Government too has asked for the case to be heard by the Court. In six cases the Government has acted alone. Frequently, Government referrals have indicated that the Government is convinced that its interpretation of the Convention – either of the content of one of the substantive rights or, more commonly, of the legitimate reasons for interference with the rights of the individual – is correct and that it seeks confirmation of its position by the Court. The Court is, after all, the largest international tribunal created under international law and its opinions on questions both of law and fact carry a great deal of weight both regionally and inter-nationally.[17]

In about two-thirds of the cases referred to it, the Court has found a violation of one or more Articles of the Convention.[18] The majority of violations have occurred under Articles 5 and 6, relating respec-tively to freedom from arbitrary detention and the right to a fair hearing. Article 8, protecting private and family life, home and correspondence – a wide range of rights – has been the next most frequently violated. There have been fewer breaches of other Articles. Chapters 4, 5 and 6 will survey the main trends in the juris-prudence of the Commission and the Court.

One test of the success of the Convention would be to examine the effects which the judgments of the Court have had. It should be remembered, however, that these are not always easy to calculate. A brief analysis of the applications which reach the Strasbourg organs reveals that many are sponsored by pressure groups. Quite often, a

---

[17] On important legal questions the Court may sit in plenary session and has done so in over eighty cases.

[18] A *Survey of Activities* is published by the Court. This is updated annually and provides a wealth of statistics and information.

particular group seeking legislative change will select a "victim" with a view to persuading the authorities that a change in the law is necessary. Following an adverse decision of the Court, the state will need to react to the judgment, but may often do this in a "minimalist" way, remedying the mischief responsible for the particular violation while ignoring the basic reforms which are necessary. The pressure group then needs to begin the process again in a further sector of the problem. It is obvious, for example, that many of the cases on prisoners' conditions and the treatment of deportees have been part of an on-going process of this kind. In many instances the Government may be willing to carry out reforms only to find that it is impossible for political reasons. We shall see that the decision-making powers of the Committee of Ministers, if used sensitively, can recognize the internal, political and social problems which the authorities may face in striving for perfect compliance with the Convention. There are instances where Government response has been tardy, or where an initial legislative reaction has failed to materialize. For example, in 1979 the Netherlands was found to be in violation of Article 5 in the *Winterwerp* case;[19] as a result, the Dutch Government submitted to the Second Chamber of Parliament a Bill on committal to psychiatric hospitals in special cases,[20] but by the end of 1991 this had still not been adopted. On the other hand, an adverse judgment may have an effect on practice, and render legislation otiose. Another example from the Netherlands concerns the case of *Engel et al.*[21] Before the judgment of the Court had been delivered an Act had been passed to standardize the range of disciplinary sanctions meted out by military commanders and to abolish the category of "strict arrest" about which the application had complained. Even before that, however, a ministerial directive had been published which resulted in such sanctions falling into disuse.

It is often difficult to calculate the effects of the judgments of the Court in isolation from the particular circumstances surrounding a case, or from the political events which may have preceded it.

The United Kingdom features second to Italy[22] in being the state

---

[19] (1980) Series A, No. 33, and 2 *EHRR* 387.
[20] Bill No. 11270.
[21] (1976) Series A, No. 22, and 1 *EHRR* 647. See below, Chapter 6.
[22] Many of the cases against Italy concern the length of court proceedings.

against which the greatest number of referrals to the Court has been made, and it is interesting to examine the effect which some of these judgments have had on United Kingdom law.

The first holding of a violation against Britain occurred in the *Golder* case,[23] and this led to an amendment in the prison rules to make it easier for prisoners to consult a solicitor. Further changes, this time with regard to disciplinary hearings by Boards of Visitors, followed the case of *Campbell and Fell* in 1984,[24] while the cases of *Silver et al* and *McCallum*[25] saw modification of the rules on prisoners' correspondence. All of this represents a long, hard slog for the prison reformers, and one should not forget the numerous applications rejected by the Commission at an earlier stage. In such cases concerned with treatment of prisoners, the authorities cannot forget their responsibilities for the prevention of crime and for the protection of others. We shall see later, in Chapter 6, that prisoners' correspondence can be restricted when it proposes the commission of further crimes, or plots the escape from gaol. Similarly, it may be necessary to isolate a prisoner from others for their, or the prisoner's own, protection. Failing a thorough review of prison procedures, which may be impracticable, such piecemeal responses may be justified. The sceptic may comment, however, that such an attitude keeps the prison reformer occupied, while economising on Government resources.

Freedom of movement is a right included in the Fourth Protocol, not recognized by the United Kingdom, yet immigration reforms have been achieved. Following *Abdulaziz, Cabales and Balkandali*[26] the Immigration Rules were amended in 1985 to avoid discrimination under Article 14. Extradition and deportation cases usually concern a specified individual and are often brought under Article 3, based on the fear that the detainee may be treated inhumanely if returned. These cases invariably involve the discretion of the Home Secretary or, sometimes, an immigration official. It has proved possible, if rarely, to prevent deportation.[27]

---

[23] (1975) Series A, No. 18, and 1 *EHRR* 524. See below Chapter 7.

[24] (1984) Series A, No. 80, and 7 *EHRR* 165.

[25] (1983) Series A, No. 61 and 5 *EHRR* 347. (1990) Series A, No. 183, and 13 *EHRR* 596, respectively.

[26] (1985) Series A, No. 94, and 7 *EHRR* 471.

[27] See the discussion of some of the cases below in Chapter 6.

Judgments of the Court against the United Kingdom have also, however, required legislative reform. The *Malone*[28] case led directly to the *Interception of Communications Act* of 1985, while the law of contempt of court is now more statutory in form since *The Sunday Times* case in 1979.[29] The abolition of corporal punishment in state schools in the *Education (No. 2) Act* was a direct response to the decision in *Campbell and Cosans*.[30] It is interesting to witness the discussions that appear to have taken place in the Ministry of Education before this solution was adopted. In the *Brogan*[31] case, however, the British Government reported to Parliament that, in view of the terrorist threat in Northern Ireland, it was not prepared to repeal any part of the *Prevention of Terrorism (Temporary Provisions) Act* of 1984, which had been found to involve a violation of the Convention. Instead, it took the dubious step of re-establishing its derogation under Article 15 with respect to the Province.[32]

An important point is that a great amount of benefit to the individual has often occurred in cases which have not, in fact, reached the stage where the Commission or Court has pronounced a violation. This may be either because a friendly settlement has been achieved through the mediation of the Commission, or because the Government has been alerted to a violation and wishes to comply with its international legal obligations. Sometimes the Government will offer compensation on the basis of similarity to cases which have already passed through the Strasbourg process.[33] Very often, a failure in domestic law is remedied by legislation and it is possible to withdraw the matter from the Commission with the consent of all. It is, of course, important that neither the Commission nor the Court should agree to a case being withdrawn unless it is satisfied that the principles embodied in the guarantees of the Convention have been

---

[28] (1984) Series A, No. 82, 7 *EHRR* 14.

[29] (1979) Series A, No. 30, and 2 *EHHR* 245 Following the judgment Parliament enacted the *Contempt of Court Act* 1981 c. 49.

[30] (1982) Series A, No. 48, and 4 *EHRR* 293.

[31] (1988) Series A, No. 145-B, and 11 *EHRR* 117.

[32] The legality of the UK's derogation has since been challenged by the case of *Brannigan and McBride*, heard by the Court in November 1992.

[33] For example, Applications No. 8476-81/79, *Eaton et al* v. *UK*, 39 *D&R* 11, where compensation was offered on the basis of the European Court of Human Right's judgment in *Young, James and Webster*.

met. It is essential that a Government should not be seen to be "buying off" the applicant.

In the early days, a state would often wait before changing its law until it sensed that an adverse report from the Commission was likely, but now that states realize that the Commission rejects all but genuine cases, the Convention's effects and influence are clear to be seen. This is, of course, the way, or an extension of the way, in which the Commission as a conciliatory body was intended to work. The Secretariat of the Commission works with a careful eye on events taking place in the state concerned following the decision on admissibility. Where it seems likely that a government is not prepared to take notice of the Commission or the Court, little time for stalling tactics is granted. On the other hand, where, as in the case of certain applications against Austria concerning "equality of arms" in appeal procedures, it is apparent to the Secretariat, and hence to the Commission, that the Government is concerned to remedy any shortcomings in the law, then the procedure before the Commission (or Sub-Commission according to the former procedure relevant in the Austrian cases) seems to have been kept at a slower pace. While this has obvious advantages by providing a settlement agreeable both to the Commission and the state, it is submitted that such an approach can, if taken to extremes, have the result of providing little relief for the individual.

In the Austrian cases, the law was changed to allow those prisoners whose sentences had been increased without their being represented to be granted a rehearing if the facts of their cases were such as to render them admissible under the European Convention. In most cases sentences were reduced, but in some of these applications an unjustly excessive period of imprisonment had been served before the rehearing could be held. In the *De Becker* case,[34] the second case to reach the Court, Belgian law was changed before the Court's decision was made, and Mr De Becker, and others in a like position, were granted relief. Members of the Evangelical-Lutheran Church of Sweden complained that parents of children belonging to the Church were prevented from giving their children appropriate religious instruction in accordance with their own denomination, as the children were obliged to receive religious instruction of the

---

[34] (1962) Series A, No. 4, and 1 *EHRR* 43.

Swedish Church at school. After admitting the case,[35] the Commission, hearing that a settlement seemed probable, adjourned consideration of the merits, and some time later the King-in-Council ordered that pupils of the Church should be exempted from compulsory religious education if their parents so requested. Similarly, in the applications of *East African Asians* against the United Kingdom, concerning the consequences of immigration restrictions, it was noted that during the currency of the case the United Kingdom Government had doubled the number of entry vouchers, had issued 1,500 "once-for-all" vouchers, and had allowed into the country 25,000 United Kingdom passport-holders expelled from Uganda. The Committee of Ministers felt that in many cases this disposed of the problems which had given rise to the application.

The *Boeckmans* case[36] against Belgium provides an example of how, in an isolated incident which would have amounted to a violation, the government made amends by giving compensation (in this case 65,000 Belgian francs) negotiated by the Sub-Committee as a friendly settlement to the case. Similarly in *Poerschke* v. *Federal Republic of Germany*[37] the applicant's sentence was reduced to conditional release on probation following talks between the Sub-Commission and the Parties. In the *Alam* application against the United Kingdom[38] an air-ticket to Karachi was accepted as part of the friendly settlement for what might have been a violation of Article 8 (right to family life), but the fact that new Immigration Appeals Tribunals had been set up was also a consideration in reaching the agreement.

A friendly settlement was also secured in the case of *Gyula Knechtl* v. *United Kingdom*[39] in March 1972. The applicant had complained that, following the amputation of his leg while serving a prison sentence in England, he was not allowed to consult a solicitor with a view to bringing an action in the courts for alleged negligence on the part of certain prison doctors and consultants. Under the terms of the settlement, the United Kingdom Government, while not admitting that the applicant's rights under the Convention

---

[35] Application 4733/71, *Karnell and Hardt* v. *Sweden*, 14 *YB* 676.
[36] Application 1727/62, 15 *CD* 57 and 8 *YB* 410.
[37] Application 2120/64, 9 *YB* 328.
[38] Application 2991/66, 24 *CD* 116, and 10 *YB* 478.
[39] Application 4115/69, 36 *CD* 43, and 13 *YB* 730.

had been violated, agreed to make an *ex gratia* payment of £750 to the applicant in settlement of his case before the Commission. This did not prejudice his right to continue his current action in the courts. In agreeing to the withdrawal of the case, the Commission also noted a White Paper, *Legal Advice to Prisoners,* laid before Parliament on 10 December 1971. Again, the United Kingdom Government, in an application brought by Harriet Harman,[40] paid Ms Harman's legal costs and undertook to reform the law of contempt which had criminalized the release to the Press of documents compulsorily disclosed in court hearings and read out in court. In the *Neubecker*[41] and *Liebig*[42] cases, against the Federal Republic of Germany, the applicants alleged that although criminal charges against them had been dropped, they had been left to pay costs, which raised an implication of guilt contrary to the presumption of innocence secured by the Convention. In return for withdrawal, in both cases, the authorities issued declarations that no finding of guilt should be derived from the conduct of the courts and, in the *Liebig* case, paid the applicant's expenses incurred before the Courts and before the Commission. The Commission noted that the Federal Government intended to draw the attention of the judicial authorities in the *Länder* to the need for courts to respect the principle of presumption of innocence when setting out reasons for decisions relating to expenses under the Code of Criminal Procedure.

In general, however, it is difficult to know what part, if any, the Commission's acceptance of an application plays in speeding up legislation. For instance, in Britain, the Immigration Appeals Tribunals proposed by the Wilson Tribunal and the Immigration Appeals Bill, accepted as part of the friendly settlement in the *Alam* case, cannot really be said to have been hastened by the imminence of a decision by the Commission in that case. How far, too, did the findings of mistreatment in Cyprus help in the provision of a political solution? In the early days of the Convention, Dr Hastings Banda was released from detention after members of his Party enjoyed a sympathetic reception from the Icelandic Government which, it is alleged, was

[40] Application 10038/82, 38 *D&R* 53 and 29 *YB* 121.
[41] Application 6281/73, 8 *D&R* 30 and 19 *YB* 304.
[42] Application 6650/74, 17 *D&R* 5 and 19 *YB* 330 and 21 *YB* 540.

being urged to bring an application against Britain, but we cannot tell how relevant this was. It is true that Norway saw the need to change its constitution, to admit Jesuits into the country, before it could ratify the Convention fully, but in most cases the Commission has played only a small role in marshalling the public opinion which is responsible for bringing about change. However, it is true to say that, at least in Britain, the possibility of using the Convention's machinery of enforcement is now recognized and accepted by the public at large, and that the case law of the European Court is treated with respect.

Before leaving the topic of the effects which the Convention has had, it is important to point out that in the majority of Member States the Convention is in fact part of the domestic law, and can therefore be applied in the national courts. This enables many potential applications to be dealt with at local level and in many cases, particularly those where a friendly settlement is likely, facilitates a cheaper and more efficient solution.

There are, and have been, movements to incorporate the European Convention into English law. The position in the United Kingdom is that international treaties concluded by the Government, under powers conferred by the royal prerogative, cannot become part of British law unless so incorporated by Act of Parliament. The European Convention requires states to "secure" the rights in *Section I* to everyone within the jurisdiction; it does not lay down the manner in which this shall be done. If the Government maintains, therefore, that treaty obligations are already to be found in national law, as it does with the rights found in the Convention, it is correct in affirming that it is under no legal duty to incorporate that treaty into the law. The present position seems unsatisfactory, however, not least because the English judges seem confused as to the weight that they should give to the Convention when interpreting English law. Undoubtedly, where there is ambiguity in the English statute, recourse should be made to the Convention, together with the International Covenant on Civil and Political Rights, to provide an authoritative interpretation.[43] Where there is no ambiguity, however, the Convention can be ignored and then any victim of such a decision can seek redress only through the Strasbourg

---

[43] See, for example, *R.* v. *Secretary of State for Home Affairs, ex parte Bhajan Singh,* [1975] 2 *All E.R.* 1081.

procedure [44] - a long and possibly costly process. Similarly, because the Convention is international law, it is binding only at governmental level, and is not operative to bind those enacting secondary legislation or exercising day-to-day discretions.[45] Incorporation of the Convention into United Kingdom law would have the effect of integrating the jurisprudence of the European Court of Human Rights, and perhaps other European national tribunals, into English law. It would also operate as a frame of reference, if no more, for the legislator and legal draftsman, and would find its way into more official decision-making procedures. It is arguable that, in the interests of justice, the Convention should find its way into United Kingdom law, irrespective of any decision to enact a Bill of Rights or to move towards a written constitution.

[44] See, for example, *Malone* v. *the Commissioner of Police for the Metropolis* [1979] 2 *All E.R.* 620 and thereafter *Malone* v. *UK* (1984) Series A, No. 82.

[45] See, for instance, *R.* v. *Chief Immigration Officer, ex parte Bibi* [1976] 3 *All E.R.* 843 and *R.* v. *Secretary of State for the Home Department, ex parte Brind,* [1990] 1 *All E.R.* 469.

CHAPTER TWO

The Background to the Convention

That the European Convention was part of an overall political plan for the unification of Europe, or at least a first step towards such an ideal, is shown most strongly in the background to its signing and the history of its drafting. If we are to discover the true nature of the Convention it is essential to examine it in this context and in the general setting of European political unification.

Many organizations had sprung up after the Second World War, with European unity as their objective. Mr Churchill was chairman of the United Europe Movement in Britain; M. van Zeeland's Economic League for European Cooperation grouped together prominent economists, industrialists and trade union leaders from many Western countries. These, together with other groups such as the French Council for United Europe, the European Union of Federalists, *Nouvelles Équipes Internationales* and the Socialist Movement for the United States of Europe, united in 1948 to form the International Committee of the Movements for European Unity. A Congress of the International Committee was held in The Hague in May of that year. The resolutions and the "Message to Europeans" which issued from that congress of 713 delegates were bursting with the two concepts of "democracy" and "human rights". The Political Resolution talked of a union or federation open to all democratically governed European nations which would undertake to respect a Charter of Human Rights, and resolved that a Commission should be set up to undertake the double task of drafting such a Charter and of laying down standards ". . . to which a state must conform if it is to deserve the name of democracy". In these early post-war days, European unity was considered by many to be the only answer to communism which it was feared would spread to the whole of Europe. The last forty years have revealed what different images the uniting of Europe aroused in the minds of Western statesmen, but it is clear that they all saw in it an opportunity to join together, perhaps under the blatantly anti-communist arm of NATO, for the defence of an old way of life and to maintain traditional values. Perhaps in the minds of a few there really existed the dream of a new kind of unity surpassing the concept of the nation-state which, perhaps more than anything, had been responsible for two of the greatest and most terrible wars of all time.

Following the conclusion of the Hague Congress, the International Committee created the "European Movement" as a permanent unofficial organization to promote the union of Europe. In March 1948, the Brussels Treaty had been signed by France, Belgium, Luxembourg, the Netherlands and the United Kingdom.[1] This treaty had provided for the creation of a consultative council consisting of the foreign ministers of these five powers, who discussed matters dealt with in the treaty. Two months after the Hague Congress, M. Bidault, the French Foreign Minister, put forward a proposal to the Consultative Council for the creation of a European Parliament, and in the following October the Brussels Council set up a five-power "Committee for the Study of European Unity". We cannot relate here the full negotiations of that Committee. The United Kingdom proposed a European council of ministers which would be a purely intergovernmental consultative organ. The Continental countries wanted a European assembly and were very disappointed at Britain's attitude. At one point the talks broke down completely and the possibility of creating a European assembly without British participation was considered. The United Kingdom, realizing the strong feeling which existed among the other powers, finally agreed to the idea of a European assembly and, on 5 May 1949, the Statute of the Council of Europe[2] was duly signed in London on behalf of ten states. In the Preamble, the Contracting Parties declare that they are ". . . reaffirming their devotion to the spiritual and moral values which are the common heritage of their peoples and the true source of individual freedom, political liberty and the rule of law, principles which form the basis of all genuine democracy". According to its Statute, the aim of the Council of Europe is to achieve greater unity between its Members by discussion of questions of common concern and by agreements and common action in "economic, social, cultural, scientific, legal and administrative matters and in the maintenance and further realization of human rights and

---

[1] 19 *UNTS* 51; *UKTS* 1 (1949), Cmd. 7599.
[2] 87 *UNTS* 103; *UKTS* 51 (1949), Cmd 7778.

fundamental freedoms". It is interesting to note that references to human rights and the rule of law in the Statute are not mere affirmations of faith but, on the contrary, are enshrined as formal conditions of membership of the organization. Indeed, Article 8 provides that breach of such conditions may lead to suspension of membership and a request to withdraw representatives. In 1969, when it had become clear to all that torture and mistreatment of prisoners was occurring in Greece, and that the European Commission was likely to hold that there had been a violation of the European Convention, there was a political move within the Consultative Assembly[3] to call upon Greece to withdraw from the organization, which that state eventually did. It was, therefore, in this rarefied atmosphere of European *entente* that the European Convention on Human Rights was born. It is interesting to speculate whether at any other time in the history of this Continent, either before or since, such a step could have been taken.

The proposed Convention was one of the first items on the agenda of the first Ordinary Session of the Consultative Assembly which consists of parliamentarians of the Member States. A motion, recommending to the Committee of Ministers the creation of an organization within the Council of Europe to guarantee human rights by collective means, was put at the eighth sitting of the Assembly by Pierre-Henri Teitgen of France, Sir David Maxwell-Fyfe[4] and other delegates. They spoke eloquently for the motion and indeed probably expressed the views of the majority by calling for such international protection machinery. M. Teitgen outlined briefly the form he believed a guarantee of human rights could take. A Convention would create a court and a commission of human rights; petitions would be addressed to the commission, which would sift them and retain only those worthy of serious consideration. These would be investigated by a court of human rights, to be composed of nine eminent lawyers, appointed by the Committee of Ministers and the Consultative Assembly. Members of the Council of Europe, corporate bodies, and all individuals would be able to petition the court, which would either find rights to have been violated, annul

---

[3] The Consultative Assembly of the Council of Europe is now known as the Parliamentary Assembly. .

[4] Later to become British Lord Chancellor, Lord Kilmuir.

the offending action taken and, if necessary, prescribe measures for reparation; or decide that there had been no violation. There was already, he revealed, a draft Convention which had been prepared unofficially by some of the members of the Legal Committee of the European Movement. While he received general support, M. Teitgen failed to arouse the enthusiasm of all the delegates. Less than a year had passed since the adoption of the Universal Declaration of Human Rights by the General Assembly of the United Nations, and many delegates expressed the view that action should not be taken by the Council of Europe which might duplicate the work being done at that time on the second stage of the United Nations Human Rights Bill, namely, the Covenants. Suggestions issued from some sources that it would be better to wait until the Covenants were agreed upon before drawing up a European Convention. It was perhaps as well that these suggestions were disregarded, since it was to take seventeen more years to reach agreement in New York on the final form of the Covenants.

Two fundamental questions arose which were never satisfactorily resolved. First, what were the rights and freedoms which members of the Council of Europe should in common guarantee to all persons within their territories? Secondly, how could a collective guarantee operate? In both cases a compromise solution was accepted in order not to delay the signing of the Convention. Already the more astute were becoming aware of what was to happen to human rights in the United Nations.

The Committee on Legal and Administrative Questions agreed unanimously that initially only those rights and freedoms could be guaranteed which were defined and accepted, after long usage, by democratic régimes. Other rights and freedoms, including social rights, were to be defined and protected in the future, but it was necessary to begin with accepted, widely agreed principles, and to seek to guarantee, first of all, political democracy. The next stage in the quest for European union would then be the co-ordination of national economies, and not until after that stage had been reached could any attempt be made to generalize social rights. The history of European integration has shown how over-optimistic the delegates were at that first session.

Disagreement as to the rights to be included in the Convention first occurred in the Committee on Legal and Administrative

Questions and concerned the so-called "family rights", represented by the right to marry and found a family, the prior right of parents to choose the kind of education they wanted for their children and freedom from arbitrary interference with family life. Although some members of the Committee objected that these were not essential rights, their argument did not prevail, since the majority of the Committee thought that the racial restrictions on the right to marry, and the forced regimentation of children and young persons, both of which had been common under totalitarian régimes, should be absolutely prohibited. The draft provision protecting the right to peaceful use of possessions was also criticized as a further example of a right which was not fundamental.

The Committee's report ended with a draft resolution to the Committee of Ministers indicating the general lines of a possible Convention. Twelve rights were to be included and these were listed in Article 2 of the draft. An amendment put by Lord Layton of the British delegation which sought to delete from the list the right of parents to choose the education they wanted for their children and the right to own property, although defeated, nevertheless had the outcome that these rights were not included in the final Resolution.

Article 3, which was passed without amendment, read as follows:

The Convention will include the undertaking by Member States to respect the fundamental principles of democracy in all good faith, and in particular, as regards their metropolitan territory:

(1) To hold free elections at reasonable intervals with universal suffrage and secret ballot, so as to ensure that government action and legislation are, in fact, an expression of the will of the people;

(2) To take no action which will interfere with the right to criticism and with the right to organize a political opposition.

It is interesting to see that these rights were spelled out in much more detail than the others, which were merely listed – an indication perhaps of the general perception that the Convention should be a document which would prevent the rise of another Hitler, and an attempt, having rid Europe of the scourge of Nazism and Fascism, to prevent those similar evils which were seen to be thriving under Eastern European Communism.

Articles 4, 5, 6 and 7 laid down that every state signatory to the

Convention should be entitled to establish the rules by which the guaranteed rights and freedoms should be organized and protected within its territory, subject to the provisos that they were to be guaranteed without any distinction based on race, colour, sex, language, political or other opinion, national or social origin, affiliation to a national minority, fortune or birth. No limitations were to be imposed, except those established by law with the sole object of ensuring the recognition and respect of the rights and freedoms of others, or with the purpose of satisfying the just requirements of public morality, order and security in a democratic society. As Article 7 stated, the object of the collective guarantee would be to ensure that the laws in which are embodied the guaranteed rights and freedoms, as well as the application of these laws, were in accordance with the "general principles of law as recognized by civilized nations".

Article 8 established a European Court of Justice and a European Commission of Human Rights. Any signatory state would be able to appeal to the Commission regarding any breach of the provisions of the Convention by another Member State. Likewise, after all other means of redress within a state had been tried, any person or corporate body would be able to lay a matter before the Commission. By Article 13, the Commission was empowered to undertake an investigation of the petition with, if necessary, an inquiry. If the Commission did not find the petition irregular or manifestly ill-founded, it was required to try to effect a reconciliation of the opposing parties. Should this in its turn fail, the Commission would be able to refer the documents in the case to the proposed Court of Human Rights to obtain a legal ruling. Alternatively, any of the Member States could submit the matter to the Court for a judicial decision, in which case the Commission had to relinquish it immediately to the Court. It is to be noted that the Committee of Ministers of the Council of Europe did not feature in the draft, and also that the Court was given exclusive power to make judicial ruling not only at the invitation of the Commission but also at the request of a Member State. This would automatically take the matter out of the hands of the Commission.

It is apparent from these early stages in the drafting of the Convention that neither the draftsmen nor the Members of the Consultative Assembly were blind to the difficulties of their task. The Committee on Legal and Administrative Questions had realized from the start that comprehensive acceptance of a group of rights would always be impossible in a working democracy, and that occasions were bound to arise where the rights of the individual might) have to be sacrificed for the benefit of the community at large. In this first draft, their attempt to control restrictions on the fundamental rights was contained, as we have seen, in general form.

The Committee of Ministers, however, did not accept the draft, mainly because of the question, which had been hotly debated in the Legal Committee, as to whether the rights included in the Convention should be more precisely defined or left as general statements of principles. The Committee of Ministers instructed the Secretary-General of the Council of Europe to invite each of the governments of Member States to nominate one expert to a Committee to draw up a draft Convention which would serve as a basis for future discussion. The Legal Committee was disappointed but made no objection, except to ask that the matter be treated as one of urgency. The legal experts met in February 1950 and produced a draft containing alternative methods of enforcement which they felt needed a political decision which they were not competent to take. The Ministers agreed that the time had come when the political problems involved had to be defined, and accordingly called a meeting of government officials early in June 1950 to prepare the ground for the Ministers' decisions. It will be noticed that the legal experts decided the first question, namely what the guaranteed rights should be, whilst the problem of how then to enforce them was considered primarily by the Committee of Government Experts.

The fundamental difference, as regards the substantive rights, between the draft submitted by the Consultative Assembly in September 1949, and the Convention as debated in August 1950 following the work of the legal experts and government officials, was that in the latter the rights to be guaranteed were not merely enumerated but defined. This step was taken as a result of the influence of several countries, in particular the United Kingdom, which felt that since the Convention was to enforce human rights it was essential that the rights should be defined as precisely as possible. It will be seen that the effect of this, and perhaps the desired effect, was for many years to inhibit the Commission and prevent any substantial extension of the rights by interpretation.

The Convention had three omissions: the right of parents to decide the education for their children; the right to own property; and, perhaps more surprising, the right to hold free elections and to form an opposition. It had, however, been difficult to obtain agreement on the exact contents of these rights, and indeed further draft texts submitted by the Consultative Assembly itself were not accepted by the Ministers but were passed on to the Committee of Experts. These were eventually, of course, included in the First Protocol to the Convention, which appeared some sixteen months later in March 1952.[5]

The terms of enforcement of the guarantee proved to be no less difficult a subject on which to reach agreement. Again there was conflict between the Members of the Consultative Assembly and its Committee on Legal and Administrative Questions on the one hand, and the Committee of Ministers on the other. The idealistic views of the Assembly were tempered by the realization that to guarantee human rights would require surrender of sovereignty on the part of the states concerned to the extent even, it was envisaged by some, of setting up a court which might review and investigate the workings of domestic courts. Other members, notably the United Kingdom, believed that such an extreme solution was not justifiable and tried at every juncture to persuade the Members of the Assembly and its Legal Committee to draft a Convention much less bold in character. The discussions of the Committee of Ministers and the Committee of Senior Government Officials, although not published, make it apparent that states were not prepared to surrender sufficient sovereignty at this stage. Even in these comparatively early days of the quest for European unity, a certain boldness of approach appeared to be lacking.

Two points of disagreement on the subject of the machinery of enforcement, fundamental to the whole idea of the Convention, arose: the right of individual petition, and the clause whereby the Convention applies to the overseas or colonial territories of states. As regards the former, the Committee of Government Officials submitted two texts for the Ministers' consideration. The first gave to any person, non-governmental organization or any group of individuals the right, without more ado, of petitioning the Commission directly. Seven of the delegates at the meeting of Officials agreed on this text, but five wished the right of individual petition to be

---

[5] For a detailed summary of the negotiations on Protocol No. 1 see A. H. Robertson, "The European Convention on Human Rights: Recent Developments", 1951 *BYIL* 359.

suppressed. The right of individual petition in the European Convention was, even in its limited form, a unique contribution to international law. It was not an easy step for the states to allow individuals to arraign their own nations before an international tribunal. The compromise text whereby the right of individual petition was subject to the prior consent of the Contracting Party concerned, evidenced by a separate declaration of agreement to that effect, was finally incorporated into the Convention. It had proved acceptable to all the delegates except one, on condition that it should be unanimously approved by the Committee of Ministers. That Committee adopted it by 12 votes with one abstention.

The other serious disagreement related to the so-called "colonial clause". One view of this matter was that the Convention should be drafted in such a way as to apply automatically to overseas territories unless specifically excluded by a declaration to that effect; the other view was that it should apply to metropolitan areas only, but that it might be extended to overseas territories by express declaration. It was recalled that certain countries, in particular the United Kingdom, could not constitutionally apply the Convention to their overseas territories without first consulting the colonial legislatures, a procedure which would delay the ratification of the Convention by some of the principal signatories. This was something of an overstatement since there were few United Kingdom Colonial Territories in which that was the case. The Ministers chose the text which required express declarations by the High Contracting Parties before the Convention would extend to their colonial territories. They added a paragraph to the effect that the provisions should be applied in the overseas territories "with due regard to local requirements",[6] and a further clause adopted at the suggestion of the United Kingdom read:

> The Convention may be denounced in accordance with the provisions of the preceding paragraphs in respect of any territory to which it has been declared to extend under the terms of Article 63.[7]

It is true to say that many of the Committee of Ministers' alterations

---

[6] Article 63(3).
[7] Article 65(4).

to the Convention were received with disappointment by the Consultative Assembly; in particular, the limitation of the right of individual petition was not accepted without complaint. The original intention had been that the States of Europe would create collective machinery which would not only act as a watchdog over the status of human rights in Europe but which would be available to any individual who might call upon it. There was considerable pessimism as to whether any state would make the optional declaration allowing individual petition, thereby embarrassing itself by allowing those under its jurisdiction to apply to the Commission. Individuals in those states where the declaration had not been made could find another state to espouse their cause and in this way make application, but it was felt that it would be virtually impossible to gain such support since this would appear to be an unfriendly act on the part of such a state. The general feelings in the long debates in the Consultative Assembly were echoed by M. Lannung of Denmark, who stated that the Convention was now "considerably less rational, complete and effective". M. Teitgen, *rapporteur* of the Legal Committee, spoke during the second day of the debate. He urged the Assembly not to refuse to accept the Convention: "We know that the text drawn up by the Ministers includes some proposals on which they will not go back. Let us then bow our heads and accept them." These sentiments eventually prevailed. No matter how fiercely the argument rages as to whether there is in fact a common culture and a common civilization in Europe, it cannot be disputed that it is because the Governments of Europe had much in common that they were able to reach any agreement at all.

After the signing of the Convention on 4 November 1950, it was then open for ratification by signatory members. Even allowing for constitutional requirements, it could not be expected that states would ratify immediately or sign without reservation in respect of ratification, since this was at the time perceived as an important step towards what was hoped would be a steady, and even speedy, unification of Europe. The Council of Europe was an experiment to bring together states with a long history of self-determination. Hesitation on the part of some states may also be explained by the fact that certain rights drawn up by the Consultative Assembly had not been included in the Convention, although hope remained high that these would be included before very long in a Protocol. Apart from all this, it must be supposed that the disappointment voiced by many of the delegates in the Consultative Assembly with regard to the Convention reflected the views of their respective Governments.

The first ratification of the Convention came from the United Kingdom. The text of the Convention was laid on the Table of the House of Commons on 23 January 1951, and the instrument of ratification was prepared on 21 February. The actual date of ratification was 8 March 1951. Two explanations may be advanced for the comparative promptness of the United Kingdom ratification. Under the leadership of Winston Churchill, the Hague Congress had called for European unity and the foundation of the Council of Europe. The United Kingdom was imagined to be, and itself believed that it was, leading the way towards this goal, and hence set an example by ratifying the Convention with alacrity. Further, it should be noted that while the other states were awaiting the Protocol, and expected it to appear in a very short time, the United Kingdom was unenthusiastic about the way in which the drafting was progressing and the form which the Protocol was taking. For instance, it was stated in a parliamentary debate that the British Foreign Secretary did not hinder the rejection of a draft concerning free elections,[8] while Britain's unease over the subject of education is demonstrated by her subsequent reservation to Article 2 of the Protocol, which secures that right. By deciding not to wait for the Protocol, but to ratify the Convention immediately, the United Kingdom Government was perhaps stressing that it regarded the two instruments as separate, and that ratification of one did not automatically mean that the other would receive like treatment.

The United Kingdom did not make declarations under the Article recognising the Commission's competence to receive individual applications, nor under Article 46, giving the Court compulsory jurisdiction. In answer to a question in the Commons concerning the recognition of the Court's jurisdiction, Mr Ernest Bevin said, perhaps echoing the Government's general attitude to this kind of commitment:

We have not undertaken at this stage to sign the optional clause. We think that in this country, with our obligations not only at home but overseas,

---

[8] Hansard, *House of Commons Debates* 13 November 1950, Vol. 480, 1499.

our procedure for appeals stands very high, and we are not prepared, without further thought, to hand over these appeals to another body.[9]

The second ratification came from Norway, but not until ten months after that of the United Kingdom. This again contained no declarations on individual petition nor on the Court, but the Swedish ratification which followed on 4 February 1952, did contain a declaration recognising the right of individual petition to the Commission. By this time the Protocol had been prepared and was signed in Paris on 20 March 1952. Ratifications of the Convention followed at regular intervals after this, and on 3 September 1953 Luxembourg supplied the tenth ratification which was necessary for it to come into force. The Protocol followed eight months later, on 18 May 1954, having been ratified by the requisite number.

Even at this early stage of European unification, however, those people who saw the Convention as the first step in a European public law were not likely to be encouraged by the attitudes Governments were taking, nor were they to be so by the sequence of events during the next ten, or perhaps twenty years. In Britain the Labour Party was in power and, not seeing the emergence of a European federation of socialist states, was suspicious of the Conservative Party's enthusiastic support for the European idea. Ernest Davies, the Under-Secretary of State, accused the opposition party of hoping to control affairs at home through a reactionary federated Europe. The Conservative Party's attitude, when again achieving office, showed very little difference, however, from that of Labour. The British view of the Council of Europe was outlined by Ernest Davies in a debate in the Commons in November 1950, where he said:

The original concept of the Council of Europe was that this body should afford, in the first place, a forum of European opinion and that it should be a forcing house for ideas which would be taken into account by Governments through the Committee of Foreign Ministers which formed part of the organization. It was generally hoped that this exchange of ideas would create a European opinion and would contribute to the development of a sense of European unity which all Governments ... in Western Europe desire to establish in their own interests...

[9] *Ibid.* p. 1503.

As to the Consultative Assembly, it was never considered that it should be a parliament, that it should have in any sense legislative powers...

It [the Council] was conceived as a body for the formulation of European opinion; it was not designed as an executive authority which imposes its will upon Governments...[10]

Britain ratified the Convention without recognising the right of individual petition or the compulsory jurisdiction of the Court. It is ironic that the first inter-state application to be brought before the Commission should be by Greece, against the United Kingdom, with respect to affairs in Cyprus.

Eight further Protocols have been concluded since 1963, and a further one, Protocol 10, has been opened for signature.[11] The Protocols have been used for two purposes: either to reform or enhance the procedures laid down in the Convention, or to add further rights to the list of those in the Convention and first Protocol.

Protocols 4, 6 and 7 fall into this latter category. The fourth Protocol, signed in 1963, adds four new rights while the seventh, of 1984, lists five more. Protocol 6 abolishes the death penalty, thereby adding to the right to life guaranteed by Article 2 of the Convention.[12] All three Protocols are now in force, although none has been ratified by every Contracting State.[13] The United Kingdom, for instance, has refrained from ratifying all three.

The third and fifth Protocols provided for reform of the Convention's procedures; the third by abolishing the Sub-Commission, a conciliatory body whose role was to negotiate a friendly settlement but which proved unwieldy and unworkable, and the fifth by regulating the election of Commissioners and Judges. The increasing number of applications which ensued as the Convention became more familiar called for further reforms to the Commission's procedures, and this was provided for in Protocol 8 which, *inter alia*, permitted the

[10] *Ibid.* pp. 1392 and 1401.

[11] Protocol 10 will reduce the two-thirds majority of the Committee of Ministers, when deciding on a violation, to a simple one.

[12] Article 2 of the Convention allows the death penalty to be imposed following a conviction, Protocol 6 limits this to "...acts committed in times of war or of imminent threat of war".

[13] Protocol 4 entered into force on 2 May 1968. Protocol 6 on 1 March 1985 and Protocol 7 on 1 Nov. 1988.

formation of chambers.[14] Protocol 9, which appeared in 1990, has still to enter into force but will give, with certain safeguards, the right to applicants to invoke the Court.

Protocol 2, which was designed to give the Court the power to hand down advisory opinions, was concluded in 1963 and entered into force in 1970. Such opinions on legal questions may only be requested, however, by the Committee of Ministers. Since in most cases such legal questions will arise in connection with individual or inter-state applications, they can usually be brought to the Court by the Commission by referral of the contentious issue. Sadly, the Protocol remains unused, whereas the power to give advisory opinions on general legal questions referring to the interpretation of the Convention clearly would have its uses.[15]

OTHER COUNCIL OF EUROPE INITIATIVES

In 1961 the Member States of the Council of Europe concluded the European Social Charter. Its Preamble refers to the Convention, and the Treaty may be seen as an attempt to complement its provisions by providing social and economic rights to be secured. The Charter, which is strongest in labour and related matters, is of interest because it recognizes that even within the "common heritage" of Europe priorities may be differently allocated. It meets this in a novel way. Part One of the Charter takes the form of a declaration which lists those social and economic rights which all Contracting States must accept as the aim of their policies. Part Two consists of a breakdown of those rights into their component parts, which it then elaborates. States are required to consider themselves bound by such Articles, or Paragraphs of Articles, as they choose, subject to certain fundamental provisions and an overall minimum selection. This "pick and mix" approach to the Charter was seen to be innovative and exciting. The Charter is implemented by a reporting system and its provisions allow, ultimately, for recommendations from the Committee of Ministers. However, the procedures have proved long,

---

[14] Protocol 8 entered into force on 1 Jan. 1990 and, together with Protocol 5, which entered into force on 20 Dec. 1971, has now amended the Convention.

[15] The Inter-American Court has such a competence and is frequently called upon to exercise its advisory jurisdiction.

drawn-out and scarcely effective. A new amending Protocol was concluded in 1991, which should have the effect of improving the machinery of the Charter.[16] More developments, including a possible complaints system, are envisaged.

A further initiative taken by the Council of Europe in the human rights area is the 1987 European Convention for the Prevention of Torture and Inhuman and Degrading Treatment or Punishment.[17] This Convention, recalling Article 3 of the European Convention, sets up the European Committee for the Prevention of Torture and Inhuman and Degrading Treatment and Punishment, which pays periodic and *ad hoc* visits to places of detention in Member States and, with the help of experts, compiles reports on the conditions of treatment.[18] The reports, which are confidential, have in most cases been published by the Governments concerned.

THE CONVENTION AND THE EUROPEAN COMMUNITIES

The aim of the Council of Europe was to bring European states into closer association and thereby accelerate the process of European union. Many felt that this was, to say the least, a rather lukewarm approach to such a vital and important issue. Economic and political union, of which many had so long dreamed, meant more than mere close association, and implied a supra-nationalism brought about by the merger of institutions.

In 1950 Robert Schuman announced his plan for pooling French and German coal and steel production under a joint High Authority with executive powers. The plan also envisaged the setting up of a court of justice, a parliamentary assembly and a council of ministers. Other European states became involved in the idea and, once again, the enthusiasm for a united Europe was revived. The United Kingdom, however, was to remain unexcited by the prospect offered by the Schuman Plan and felt unable to participate. The other European

---

[16] See D. J. Harris, "A Fresh Impetus for the European Social Charter", (1992) 41 *ICLQ* 659.

[17] The Convention entered into force two years later in 1989.

[18] For a description and discussion of the European Convention on Torture and Inhuman and Degrading Treatment and Punishment, see Malcolm Evans and Rod Morgan, "The European Convention for the Prevention of Torture: Operational Practice." (1992) 41 *ICLQ* 590.

states went ahead and a treaty setting up the European Coal and Steel Community was signed by France, Germany, Italy and the Benelux countries in 1951.[19] It came into force the following year. A European Defence Community was next proposed and the United Kingdom was prepared to become involved more closely in such a scheme. This, however, was abandoned following the rejection by the French parliament of the motion to ratify the Treaty.

The next few years saw a proliferation of European organizations and plans for further regional co-operation. It was at this time, for instance, that such institutions as the European Conference of Ministers of Transport and the European Space Research Organizations were created. Despite the failure of the Defence Community, the six members of the ECSC continued plans to extend their organization and in 1957 they signed, in Rome, the Treaties establishing the European Economic Community[20] and the European Atomic Energy Community.[21]

It is not for us here to rehearse the history of the European Communities. Well known are the details of the applications of the United Kingdom to join, contrary to the wishes of President De Gaulle and to the wishes of some or all of British political parties at some time or another. The United Kingdom finally became a Member of the Community in 1973, along with the Republic of Ireland and Denmark, and the number of Members of the Community is now twelve.

The European Community is of interest to us mainly because it was shown in the earlier parts of this chapter that in 1950 many delegates to the Council of Europe saw the European Convention on Human Rights almost as a constitutive document of a European federation, a sort of *Magna Carta* of European political union. Since European Union has taken a different turn by the creation of the Communities, we should look at the European Convention in the context of these supra-national organizations, and also at the role given to human, fundamental rights in present-day European organizations.

The treaties setting up the European Communities were essentially

---

[19] 261 *UNTS* 140; *UKTS* 16 (1979), Cmnd 7461.
[20] 298 *UNTS* 11; *UKTS* 15 (1979), Cmnd 7480.
[21] 298 *UNTS* 167; *UKTS* 15 (1979), Cmnd 7480.

economic in nature and, as such, contain few fundamental rights. This is not to say that fundamental rights do not appear in the treaties, but those that were included were there because it was felt important to underline certain economic and social rights which were essential or fundamental to the carrying out of the Treaties' objectives. It was emphasized also that other rights of a social nature might follow upon the creation of an economic union. Article 7 (EEC), for instance, says that there shall be no discrimination on grounds of nationality, whilst freedom of movement is secured by Articles 48-52 of the same Treaty. Rights of association and collective bargaining are to be promoted, and equal pay for equal work by both sexes is to be respected (Articles 118 and 119, EEC). Further Articles of the EEC Treaty deal with the protection of industrial and commercial property and business secrets, and the protection of the existing systems of property ownership (Articles 36 and 214, EEC). As can be seen, these rights are scattered throughout the Treaties and are merely a consequence of the aspirations to the Common Market ideal. Nowhere are they laid out as a list of fundamental rights, nor can they be said to embrace all the fundamental rights of the individual in the context even of the social and economic ambience of the Community. Nevertheless, it was soon discovered that human rights in general could not be ignored in the application of Community law.

In the *Nold* case in 1974,[22] the Court said:

> In safeguarding these [fundamental] rights the Court is bound to draw inspiration from constitutional traditions common to the Member States, and it cannot therefore uphold measures which are incompatible with fundamental rights recognized and protected by the Constitutions of those states ... Similarly, international treaties for the protection of human rights, on which the Member States have collaborated or of which they are signatories, can supply guidelines which should be followed within the framework of Community law.

Where a matter in dispute does not affect Community law then Member States themselves are alone responsible, within the framework of their national systems, for the protection of fundamental rights. The Luxembourg Court does not have the power to apply the constitutional rules of Member States, but since it is obvious that

---

[22] Case 4/73, *Nold* v. *the Commission*, [1974] ECR 491 at 507.

states cannot be presumed to be Community members in contradiction to such rules, the Court has treated these rules as *principles* which underlie Community law.

Article 164 (EEC) requires the Court to ensure that in the interpretation and application of the Treaty the "law" is observed. Similarly, Article 215 requires the Community to make good any damage in cases of non-contractual liability ". . . in accordance with the general principles common to the laws of Member States." "Law", then, can be seen to include the general principles rather in the same fashion as is understood by the term in Article 38 (c) of the Statute of the International Court of Justice. It is to be noted that all the States Members of the European Communities are Parties to the European Convention on Human Rights.

In 1977 the European Parliament, the Council and the Commission issued a Joint Declaration in which they formally stressed the prime importance which they attached to the protection of fundamental rights ". . . as derived in particular from the constitutions of the Member States and the European Convention for the Protection of Human Rights and Fundamental Freedoms".

It was realized at this stage that a Community catalogue of fundamental rights might not only be difficult to draw up but also counter-productive in its effect. Some disagreement as to the speed with which an eventual political union might be achieved has led to a certain sensitivity with respect to attempts to enlarge the ambit of the Community institutions.

Nevertheless, it cannot be denied that the issue of individual rights is fundamental to the development of the Community, and successive documents have referred to it. The Preamble to the Single European Act of 1986 reaffirms that the Members are ". . . determined to work together to promote democracy on the basis of the fundamental rights recognized in the constitutions and laws of Member States, in the Convention for the Protection of Human Rights and Fundamental Freedoms and the European Social Charter, notably freedom, equality and social justice." The Common Provisions of the Treaty on European Union, signed in Maastricht in 1992,[23] lay down that the Union ". . . shall respect fundamental rights as guaranteed by the European Convention".

---

[23] Article F. The Convention is also referred to in Article K2.

In the meantime, the Luxembourg Court has been establishing a jurisprudence which refers constantly to the Convention and requires that Community law shall be applied consistently with the European Convention.[24]

Where an individual in a Community state feels that an act of the Community infringes his rights under the European Convention, he would seem to have two possible courses of action. He may pursue relief via the machinery set up by the Community, or he may apply to the European Commission of Human Rights. The latter process requires that he has exhausted local remedies, which in turn means that he must be able to produce a decision of the Luxembourg Court, to which his case has been referred by a national court or through direct access. It could happen, of course, that a Member State finds that to comply with a regulation of the Community would place it in breach of its treaty commitments under the European Convention on Human Rights. Similarly, one State Member of the Community wishing to avoid implementing a Community directive which it feels is contrary to the European Convention could bring an application before the European Commission of Human Rights against another Member State which has implemented the directive. In this way, the European Community might find itself involved in a case before the European Commission or Court of Human Rights with the disability of not being a party.

In a Memorandum issued in April 1979 the European Commission recommended that the European Communities should accede to the European Convention on Human Rights,[25] and after a long break this course of action was reaffirmed in 1990.[26] There have been objections to this as a solution, and there are also problems of a legal and technical nature in the accession. For example, the Convention is only open to states which are Members of the Council of Europe. Similarly, the number of judges in the Court of Human Rights is equal to the number of members of the Council of Europe, while no two judges may be of the same nationality. These, and others, are impediments which could be overcome by means of an amending

---

[24] See, for a brief and useful survey of this jurisprudence and the way it affects British law: Nicholas Grief, "The Domestic Impact of the European Convention on Human Rights as Mediated through Community Law" (1991) *Public Law* 555.

[25] *Bull E.C.* Supp. 2/79.

[26] *Bull E.C.* 1/90, para. 72.

treaty of accession which had gained the assent of all the present parties to the European Convention. The role of the Committee of Ministers of the Council of Europe would be cast uneasily in such an arrangement, since this might necessitate the Committee of Ministers of the Council of Europe sitting in judgment over the Commission and Council of the European Communities. It may be possible, however, to limit the judicial role which the Committee plays. The European Communities do not appear to fit well into the Convention scheme, but, on the other hand, if their membership of the Convention proves beneficial in the protection of fundamental human rights and has the effect of furthering the progress of European unification, there would seem to be no good reason why such an accession treaty, enabling the Communities to become party to the European Convention on Human Rights, should be resisted.

THE CONFERENCE ON SECURITY
AND CO-OPERATION IN EUROPE

The Helsinki Final Act, which was the culmination of the 1975 Conference on Security and Co-operation in Europe (CSCE), was signed by all European states (except Albania), and by the USSR, the United States and Canada. Within its broad scope were included human rights matters. The CSCE process, which has developed through a number of follow-up meetings, has remained political rather than legal but has set up a series of procedures and institutions which can be seen as furthering human rights law in Europe and which also have the participation of the United States and Canada. The breakup of the former Soviet Union and the return to democracy in most Central European states has served to highlight the human rights potential of the CSCE. Nevertheless its contribution to European human rights, rather than human rights in general, is likely to be marginal, particularly since some of the Central European states have now become parties to the European Convention.[27]

---

[27] For the human rights activities of the CSCE see D. McGoldrick, "Human Rights Developments in the Helsinki Process", (1990) 39 *ICLQ* 923 and, the same author, "Human Rights in the Helsinki Process" *Southampton Papers in International Policy*, No. 2 p. 17. Mountbatten Centre for International Studies, Southampton, 1992.

HUMAN RIGHTS IN THE UNITED NATIONS

It should be remembered that the Universal Declaration of Human Rights, which provided much of the inspiration for the provisions of the European Convention, also became the first part of the International Bill of Rights. In addition to the Declaration, this consists of the International Covenant on Economic, Social and Cultural Rights, and the International Covenant on Civil and Political Rights, with its Optional Protocols.[28] The Civil and Political Rights Covenant overlaps to a large extent with the European Convention, but some of the rights are treated more extensively and in many respects it reflects the views prevalent at the time of its conclusion. Nevertheless, comparison of its provisions with its European counterpart is often rewarding for purposes of interpretation.

The Economic, Social and Cultural Covenant is implemented by a system of regular reporting under the scrutiny of the Committee on Economic, Social and Cultural Rights. This Committee, set up by ECOSOC, is modelled on the Human Rights Committee provided for in the Civil and Political Rights Covenant. Made up of eighteen independent experts, the Human Rights Committee also receives reports from Contracting States on the progress made in implementing the listed rights and examines government representatives who present them. In addition to receiving reports, the Human Rights Committee, following a prior declaration from a Contracting State,[29] may deal with petitions from States Parties alleging violation of the Covenant. Under the Optional Protocol, this may be extended to individual petitioners.[30] Although in the latter case the Committee may express views as to whether there has been a violation of the Covenant there is no provision for an enforceable judicial decision. Admissibility conditions are similar to those in the European Convention and in most human rights treaties but, interestingly, the

---

[28] The Covenants were not concluded until 1966, and entered into force almost ten years later, in 1976. The First Optional Protocol to the Civil and Political Rights Covenant came into force during the same year. The Second Optional Protocol, aiming at the abolition of the death penalty, was signed in 1989 but is not yet in force.

[29] International Covenant on Civil and Political Rights, Article 41(1).

[30] See D. McGoldrick *The Human Rights Committee: Its Role in the Development of the International Covenant on Civil and Political Rights,* Oxford, Clarendon 1991.

Committee may receive petitions even if they have been rejected by other procedures, such as those of the European Commission.[31] There is a growing jurisprudence of the Human Rights Committee which, together with that of the Inter-American Court of Human Rights, is providing a useful basis of international human rights law. In addition to the International Covenants, the United Nations has concluded a series of other Conventions on human rights matters which are similarly implemented.[32]

[31] Article 5(2) of the Optional Protocol says that the Committee may not consider a communication unless it has ascertained that it is not being examined under another procedure of international investigation or settlement. Article 27 of the European Convention, on the other hand, precludes examination of petitions that have already been submitted to another international procedure.

[32] For the texts of such Conventions, see, *inter alia*, Brownlie, *Basic Documents in Human Rights*, 3rd edition, OUP, 1992 or *Human Rights in International Law: Basic Documents*, Council of Europe, 1992.

CHAPTER THREE

How the European Convention on Human Rights Works

The coming into force of the American Convention on Human Rights in July 1978, twenty-five years after the European Convention, brought into being the Inter-American Court of Human Rights. This was only the second body devoted to the judicial determination of human rights since the Universal Declaration in 1948 and indeed its work has consisted, in the main, of handing down advisory opinions. The European Convention, despite the hesitation of the states involved in its negotiation, and littered as it is with compromises and restrictions, is dedicated inevitably to adjudication. Even friendly settlement is, in principle, subject to agreement by one of the bodies involved in the complex mechanism of implementation which it sets up. Although, with the exception of the Inter-American Court, it has not been possible to institute bodies furnished with the full panoply of judicial procedure, the intriguing mixture of decision making and investigation revealed in the work of the European Commission and Court of Human Rights, not forgetting the Committee of Ministers of the Council of Europe, has had a tremendous influence, not only on the substantive interpretation of human rights but also as an indication of the inter-relation of states, their citizens and international organizations in the protection and promotion of human rights. It is to the machinery of implementation of the European Convention that we should now turn.

THE EUROPEAN COMMISSION OF HUMAN RIGHTS

Section III of the Convention lays down the composition and procedure of the European Commission. The Commission consists of an equal number of members to that of the High Contracting Parties.[1] This differs from the Court, which has a judge nominated by each of

---

[1] Article 20(1).

the members of the Council of Europe irrespective of whether all the states have signed or ratified the Convention.[2] At present there are twenty-six members of the Commission, and the same number of judges. Failure to recognize the Court's compulsory jurisdiction does not render a state ineligible to nominate a judge. The reason for this is that it was considered that the Court should represent all the European states in order to give a truer picture of public opinion and fulfil the function of a sort of conscience of Europe.

No two members of the Commission may be nationals of the same state[3] and they are deemed to serve as individuals and not as representatives of their own countries.[4] The pattern has been set, however, that there is a national of each state on the Commission. The election is by the Committee of Ministers following an absolute majority of votes for candidates from a list prepared in the Consultative Assembly where each state nominates three persons, at least two of whom must be its nationals.[5] The members of the Commission hold office for six years but may be re-elected. Membership of the Commission, unlike that of the Court, is not a full-time appointment and most of the members hold other posts in their own countries as university professors, legal advisers or judges.[6] There was a tendency on the part of some countries to nominate as members of the Commission well-trusted servants in need of reward. However, this trend was short-lived and it is now accepted that membership of the Commission is an arduous task not suitable for the semi-retired. Members are paid expenses but otherwise are offered no financial reward, whereas the judges of the Court receive payment for each day of duty.

---

[2] Article 38.

[3] Article 20(1).

[4] Article 23.

[5] The Convention failed to mention the qualifications required for candidature to the Commission. This has now been remedied by Protocol 8, Article 2 which adds a further paragraph to Article 21 of the Convention. The qualifications are basically the same as those required to be a Judge but add, as an alternative quality, recognized competence in *national* law.

[6] Article 3 of Protocol 8 added a new sentence to Article 23: "During their term of office they shall not hold any position which is incompatible with their independence and impartiality as members of the Commission or the demands of this office".

The Right to Petition the Commission

It is a feature of human rights treaties that they allow for scrutiny of events which would normally be within the domain of domestic jurisdiction and therefore protected from international interference. The European Convention was the first post-war human rights treaty and indeed goes further than any of those concluded since, in so far as its provisions allow one state to refer for adjudication, under specially set up procedures, allegations of violation of its terms. The later American Convention makes such procedures optional,[7] while the United Nations Covenant on Civil and Political Rights tends towards conciliation without final adjudication.

The European Convention's development owes much to the fact that under its provisions alleged violations may be brought before the European Commission of Human Rights which, while encouraging a friendly settlement in the first instance, nevertheless can bring the matter to such adjudication if necessary.

Article 24 of the Convention empowers any High Contracting Party to refer to the European Commission of Human Rights, through the Secretary-General of the Council of Europe, any alleged breach of the provisions of the Convention by another High Contracting Party. It should be noted that this Article allows petitions in regard to *any* of the Convention's terms and does not limit their subject matter to the substantive rights set forth in the Convention. More importantly, a Contracting State may complain about legislation or legal or administrative practices within a state which would amount to a violation of the Convention. There is no need to show that anyone is in fact being injured by such legislation or practices, nor is there any need for a link between the complaining state and the defendant state, other than that they are both Parties to the Convention. The "nationality of claims" doctrine does not apply in human rights law. As we have seen, inter-state applications are rare and are usually triggered by unfriendly motives or by previous debate and criticism within the Parliamentary Assembly.[8] Nevertheless, Article 24 does present the

---

[7] Article 45, American Convention on Human Rights.

[8] See, for example, *Resolution 346 (1967)* of the Consultative Assembly "On the Situation in Greece", 10 *YB* 94.

opportunity to raise a case *actio popularis* before the Convention organs.

Article 25 which provides for applications from individuals does, however, seem to preclude consideration *actio popularis*. The Article is subject to acceptance by a Respondent State and reads:

> (1) The Commission may receive petitions addressed to the Secretary-General of the Council of Europe from any person, non-governmental organization or group of individuals claiming to be the victim of a violation by one of the High Contracting Parties of the rights set forth in this Convention provided that the High Contracting Party against which the complaint has been lodged has declared that it recognizes the competence of the Commission to receive such petitions. Those of the High Contracting Parties who have made such a declaration undertake not to hinder in any way the effective exercise of this right.

The Commission must at all times be certain of its competence within the terms of the Convention as regards the parties. It must therefore satisfy itself that an applicant is a "victim" of a violation of one of the rights or freedoms guaranteed by the Convention.[9]

In Application 436/58, against the Federal Republic of Germany,[10] the applicant alleged violation of certain rights guaranteed in the Convention by virtue of a decision of the German courts. Madame Y, a cook, brought an action against her employer in the Federal Labour Courts for breach of a law of 1948, whereby all married women looking after a household are entitled to a certain number of days holiday with pay from regular employment. She was successful in this claim and on this result the applicant, who was in no way connected with the original action, asked the Commission to rule that the 1948 law was a violation of the Convention. The equality of women with men, he stated, should be maintained, unless discrimination is justified by the physiological and functional status of women, and as such the 1948 law should only apply to mothers. The applicant claimed that he was directly wronged by the decision, for all employers, including his own, would become bound by it and

---

[9] The United Nations Treaties, which provide for individual petition, require petitioners to be "victims", but this same requirement does not exist in Article 44 of the American Convention on Human Rights.

[10] 2 *YB* 386.

accord to all their female employees, without distinction, an advantage only justified in the case of mothers. The Commission decided that, since the applicant was not a party to the case he cited, he could not claim to be a victim of a violation.

The applicant must be affected by the matter alleged to be a breach of the Convention and in most cases he must be an aggrieved party. Where the applicant has earlier complained before a domestic body - and most will be required so to do in the process of exhausting local remedies - the decision of that tribunal or court will normally denote the applicant as a victim. Where an application was brought claiming the incompatibility of certain Irish Acts of Parliament with the Convention, the Commission stated:[11]

> it follows that the Commission can examine the compatibility of domestic legislation with the Convention only with respect to its application to a person, non-governmental organization or group of individuals and only in so far as its application is alleged to constitute a violation of the Convention in regard to the applicant person, organization or group in question.

In *Donnelly et al* v. *UK*[12] the applicants complained of inhuman treatment by the British authorities while in detention in Northern Ireland. Their allegation was that there was a widespread administrative practice in the province which allowed such mistreatment to be carried out not only on the applicants but on others and asked the Commission for an investigation into the matter. The Commission agreed that such an extra-legal practice might not be revealed in the process of exhaustion of local remedies and was prepared to forgo that requirement. It held that any person could complain to the Commission about such practices provided he or she could produce *prima facie* evidence of mistreatment. It might be taken from this that an individual can complain about legislation, therefore, only after it has been applied to him.

In two cases, *Dudgeon* v. *UK*[13] and *Norris* v. *Ireland*[14] in 1981 and 1988 respectively the Court was called upon to consider the plight of homosexual men in situations where homosexual activity was

---

[11] Application 290/57, 3 *YB* 214.
[12] 43 *CD* 122, 4 *D&R* 4, and 16 *YB* 212.
[13] (1981) Series A, No. 45, and 4 *EHRR* 149.
[14] (1988) Series A, No. 142, and 13 *EHRR* 186.

criminal. In each case, the applicants themselves had not been prose-
cuted for an offence, but pointed out that their lives were led in the
shadow of potential prosecution. In these and similar cases, the
Court's view has been that Article 25 of the Convention entitles individuals to contend that a law violates their rights by itself, in the
absence of an individual measure of implementation, if they run the
risk of being directly affected by it.[15]

Similarly in *Brüggemann and Scheuten* v. *Federal Republic of Germany*[16] two women complained that the restrictions on abortion
brought about by a decision of the Federal Constitutional Court
were contrary to their rights of private life under the Convention.[17]
They had not been denied an abortion under the new law nor were
they even pregnant. The Commission recognized, however, that they
were "victims" of the legislation. That part of the application
brought by a pressure-group organization and its male chairman
was rejected on the grounds that they were not "victims". The man
concerned in this case was the chairman of the organization, but
there would seem to be a good argument that a man who was alleging
similar interference with his private life may be a "victim".[18]

In the *Klass Case*,[19] the applicants were complaining about the interception of telephone calls. Since it is the essence of telephone
monitoring that it should be secret the victim in such cases is not
always able to verify that his 'phone has been tapped and therefore
has no decision of the domestic courts on which to rely. In that case
the Commission, later supported by the Court, was of the view that
the secret nature of the measures in question could not be used to
deny the applicants "victim" status without destroying the purpose
of the Convention's substantive provisions. This decision opens up
the question of how far the rights themselves may be claimed by
potential or future victims before their application is rejected as
abstract.

In a recent case against France, however, *Vijayanathan and Puspa-
rajah*,[20] where the applicants were complaining that deportation to

---

[15] *Supra*, note 13, para. 13.
[16] Application 6959/75, 5 *D&R* 103, 10 *D&R* 100 and 21 *YB* 638.
[17] See later discussion Chapter 4.
[18] See, for example, Application 8416/78, 19 *D&R* 244.
[19] Application 5029/71, 17 *YB* 178.
[20] (1992) Series A, No. 241-B.

Sri Lanka would amount to a violation of Article 3, the Court rejected the case on the grounds that the deportation had not been executed, that there was a strong possibility that it might not be, and that therefore the applicants were not victims.[21]

In other cases where the applicant would not be able to withstand the impact of legislation in the future, the Commission has accepted "victim" status. Paula Marckx complained that Belgian law deprived her illegitimate daughter of, *inter alia*, inheritance rights. The Court in her case, was of the opinion that

> Article 25 of the Convention entitles individuals to contend that a law violates their rights by itself, in the absence of an individual measure of implementation, if they run the risk of being directly affected by it.[22]

In line with this view, the Commission in *Kjeldsen, Busk Madsen* v. *Denmark* [23] admitted, without discussion, an application by parents complaining about legislation which would apply to their daughter when she reached primary school age.[24]

In all of these cases, the impact of legislation had, or would have had, serious consequences on the lives of the applicants or their children. In other instances where the Commission has felt that the detriment was likely to be less direct, or more remote, it has been less willing to grant "victim" status. So where, for example, the decision by the House of Lords that Harriet Harman had acted in contempt of court by showing confidential documents which had already been read out in court to a journalist led that journalist and two newspapers to bring an application alleging a violation of their right to receive information, the Commission was not prepared to grant "victim" status.[25] It may be that this decision can be criticized, particularly since the Commission also stated that the House of

---

[21] In view of the speed with which the French police and immigration authorities can operate, as evidenced in the *Bozano* case, (see *infra*, p. 142) this seems, perhaps, an unrealistic decision.

[22] (1979) Series A, No. 31 para. 27, also 2 *EHRR* 330 at 340.

[23] 44 *CD* 96 and 15 *YB*, p. 482.

[24] In Application 6853/74, *Forty Mothers* v. *Sweden*, 9 *D&R* 27 and 20 *YB* 214, the Commission, being able to admit the application on behalf of some of the mothers who were manifestly "victims", avoided consideration of the question of *future* "victims".

[25] Application 10039/82, *Leigh et al.* v. *UK* 38 *D&R* p. 74.

Lords' decision "affected every interested journalist in the United Kingdom".[26]

It seems an inescapable conclusion that the assignment of "victim" status seems to depend on the nature of the rights claimed – rights relating to the life-style and self-determination being more acceptable – and also to being able to point out a specific individual who is likely to be harmed.

In another sense, the Commission has intimated that the term "victim" must not be interpreted too strictly, and has allowed an applicant in some cases to be substituted. The *indirect victim* must, nevertheless, prove that he has a personal interest in the case and that the alleged violation has affected him in some way. In Application 113/55, the applicant was not allowed to bring an application on behalf of his three married sisters because he could not show that he was entitled to act in their names. Similarly, in Application 282/57 the applicant claimed she was the heir of the victim, but alas she had no means of proving this and the application was rejected. In other cases the Commission has heard petitions from close relatives of victims, and even from third parties, where they have shown that the victim himself cannot apply and that they themselves are harmed by the continued violation.

A Danish citizen sought the Commission's help with regard to the threatened repatriation of 199 Vietnamese children whom he had brought to Denmark. Although it was the children who were the proper applicants and alleged potential victims they were orphans in his care and the Commission recognized that he had a personal interest in their well-being which would enable him to bring an application on their behalf.[27]

In the application brought in 1974 by three applicants – *Times Newspapers Ltd., The Sunday Times* and Harold Evans – the Commission agreed with the Government of the United Kingdom that *The Sunday Times* had no personality under English law but thought that, inasmuch as it represented a group of journalists, it could be called a "victim" under the provisions of Article 25.[28] The Commission has also held that *majority* shareholders in a company may be considered

---

[26] It is so criticized by Van Dijk and van Hoof, p. 43.
[27] Application 7011/75, *Henning Becker* v. *Denmark*, 19 *YB* 416.
[28] Application 6538/74, 2 *D&R* 90 and 18 *YB* 203.

as direct "victims".[29] It is of course important that the applicant should remain a "victim" right up to the decision of the Commission.

In 1975 Dieter Preikhzas challenged the length of proceedings before the Federal German Labour Courts in a case brought by him in relation to the reduction of his pay and the dismissal from his post in the Social Insurance Office.[30] Before the final report of the Commission he reached a settlement with the Federal authorities which included retroactive payment of salary which had been withheld and, even though he was only thirty-seven years of age, the granting of a pension for life. In the circumstances the Commission, which had already admitted the case, held that he could no longer be termed a "victim" of the rights set forth in Article 6(1) and that it could therefore give no decision on a violation.

Similarly, where the applicant alleged violation of his right to examine witnesses under Article 6(3)(d) but yet had been acquitted, it was held he was not a victim. If, however, the alleged violation had been length of proceedings, a later acquittal would not have repaired the injury. Where the domestic authorities have acknowledged that the proceedings before the courts have been in violation of the Convention and have made appropriate reparations in the sentence or fine, then the legal interest of the individual applicant may have disappeared. Nevertheless, the Commission may examine the application to ensure that "victim" status has indeed been forfeited.[31]

The Procedure of the Commission

The provisions of the Convention were not intended to be sufficient to guide the Commission in its task, and the Commission was authorized by Article 36 to draw up its own rules of procedure. The first Rules of Procedure were drafted in 1955 and these have been amended from time to time.[32]

Any claims made under Articles 24 or 25 must be submitted in the form of an application in writing, signed by the applicant or his representative. Each application must mention the name, age,

---

[29] Application 9266/81 *Yarrow et al.* v. *UK*, 30 *D&R* 155, and 26 *YB* 66.

[30] Application 6504/74, 12 *D&R* 5.

[31] *Inze* v. *Austria*, (1988) Series A, No. 126 and 10 *EHRR* 394.

[32] The most recent revision of the Rules of Procedure of the Commission took place in January 1992.

occupation and address of the applicant and any representative, the name of the High Contracting Party against which the claim is made, and, as far as possible, the object of the claim and the provisions of the Convention alleged to have been violated. It must include a statement of the facts and arguments and make reference to any relevant documents.[33] The procedure of the Secretariat of the Commission is that following a preliminary letter of inquiry from an applicant an application form is sent to him which contains space for all the required details. An applicant's case is not, however, restricted to the application form, and other papers, documents and extra sheets may be attached.

Applicants should also provide information to show that all domestic remedies have been exhausted within the specified time limit, and indicate whether any other international procedure of investigation or settlement has been instituted. At the same time they must declare that they will respect the confidentiality of the Commission's proceedings and may say at this point whether they have any objection to their identity being made public. Although it is part of its rationale that the Commission should operate in private, it is obviously nonsense for this confidentiality to apply in those cases which have already received a great deal of publicity in the state concerned and where, for instance, the local hearings which have taken place have already rehearsed the main points of the dispute.

The official languages of the Council of Europe are English and French and the applicant may choose in the initial correspondence in which of these languages the Commission's decision should be. This restriction to the official languages could, of course, be distressful in itself and the Rules of Procedure provide for the President to authorize other languages to be used in any hearings and in any documents produced. The final Report, nevertheless, will be in one of the two official languages.

Some distinction should again be drawn between inter-state applications brought under Article 24, and petitions of individuals. Although the object of the Commission is often the same in both cases - to see that certain defined rights are guaranteed to individuals who are within the jurisdiction of one of the Contracting Parties - the procedure it adopts differs in the two instances. Doubt

---

[33] Rules 43 and 44.

was expressed by a great many delegates to the Consultative Assembly, especially those of the United Kingdom, about the wisdom of allowing individual petition. It was felt by these states that this would open the way for abuse of the Convention in the form of political propaganda. A compromise was reached, however, and individual applications were conditionally allowed. Because of this general agreement as to the competence of the Commission to receive inter-state applications the procedure concerning the progress of these through the Commission to the Court or Committee of Ministers was simplified when drawing up the Rules of Procedure. Rule 45 states that where, pursuant to Article 24 of the Convention, an application is brought before the Commission by a High Contracting Party, the President of the Commission shall give notice of such application to the High Contracting Party against which the claim is made, and shall invite it to submit to the Commission its observations in writing on the admissibility of such application.

In relation to individual applications, however, the procedure is different and the issue of admissibility is subjected to greater scrutiny. Under Rule 47 any application made to the Commission under Article 25 is referred to one of its members who, as *rapporteur*, examines the application and reports to the Commission on its admissibility and the procedure to be adopted. During this examination the *rapporteur* may seek further information from either party.

The *rapporteur* may if he wishes refer the application to a Committee. Under Article 20(3) of the Convention the Commission can appoint Committees of at least three from among its Members. The Committee's task is then to examine applications and to declare them inadmissible or strike them from the list where it considers that no detailed examination is called for and that the applications are manifestly inadmissible. This summary procedure was formally instituted to speed up the consideration of applications. It is a method which has been used informally in the past by the Commission and is to be found in the practice of the Supreme Courts of various Member States. It should be noted that an application will only be rejected following the unanimous decision of the Committee and, furthermore, that the plenary Commission, which has copies of the application, may determine that the decision should not be taken in Committee.

If the *rapporteur* decides not to submit the application to a Committee he or she will report to the full Commission. If it is felt that the application concerned can be dealt with on the basis of existing case law, or that it raises no serious questions affecting the interpretation or application of the Convention, then it will normally be referred to a Chamber of the Commission.

Protocol 8 amended Article 20 of the Convention to allow the Commission to set up Chambers of at least seven members, again with the objective of speeding up the procedure. Two Chambers have in fact been designated, each presided over by one of the two Vice-Presidents. The full Commission decides which Chamber shall deal with the matter and this is normally the one on which the *rapporteur*, or the member of the Commission elected in respect of the state against which the application has been brought, is sitting. The Chamber will deal with questions both of admissibility and of the merits, but it may refer the matter back to the plenary Commission at any time and would normally do so where difficult questions of interpretation or application arise.

It is interesting that the original version of the Convention, before amendment by Protocol 3, made provision for the Commission to elect a Sub-Commission for the later part of its procedure, including the negotiation of a possible friendly settlement. It was seen as advantageous for a smaller number of persons to be involved, particularly at a sensitive stage of the operation. Now that the number of Contracting Parties has grown, and is likely to increase further, there is a risk that the Commission could become an unwieldy body, so the move to Chambers is likely to prove welcome. The Sub-Commission proved to be unworkable, partly because of the relationship between the Sub-Commission and the full Commission, but this problem has been avoided by allotting the Chamber full control over all aspects of the case.

On receiving the report the full Commission or the Chamber may, on the basis of it, declare the application inadmissible or strike it off the list. It may request further information of either party or, if the Contracting State has not yet been notified of an application against it, invite that state to submit written observations on admissibility. It then falls to the Commission to carry out the first of its judicial functions, which is to decide whether an application fulfils the conditions laid down in Articles 26 and 27 of the Convention, namely that (i) all domestic remedies have been exhausted;[34] (ii) the application is not

---

[34] Article 26. See below Chapter 9.

anonymous; (iii) it is not substantially the same case as one previously examined; (iv) it is not manifestly ill-founded; or (v) it is not abusive of the right of petition.[35] If it deems it to be necessary it may invite the parties to make further explanations and hold an oral hearing for this purpose. This has frequently been done in cases which are not obviously inadmissible, but it has been found to be difficult to hold hearings purely on the question of admissibility without having regard to the merits of the case, partly because of the very nature of the substance, and partly by virtue of the fact that lawyers in the early years of the Convention were usually not well versed in the procedure of the European Commission, which is in so many ways a unique institution.

The trend during recent years has been for the Commission to adopt a more negative, and hence more liberal, attitude to the question of admissibility. If it seems that the question of admissibility is inextricably bound up with the merits of the application, or if it is not obviously inadmissible, or if it raises complex questions of law which are also of general interest, then the Commission will allow the application to proceed but may reject it later for inadmissibility should this appear to be the correct course. The reasoned decision of the Commission regarding admissibility is communicated to the applicant, and where the Government was asked for its observations it too is informed of the Commission's decision.

Having carried out the first and judicial part of its function the Commission must turn to the task of discovering what has in fact taken place. Article 28(1) reads:

In the event of the Commission accepting a petition referred to it:

(a) it shall, with a view to ascertaining the facts, undertake together with the representatives of the parties an examination of the petition and, if need be, an investigation, for the effective conduct of which the states concerned shall furnish all necessary facilities, after an exchange of views with the Commission;

(b) it shall at the same time place itself at the disposal of the parties concerned with a view to securing a friendly settlement of the matter on the basis of respect for human rights as defined in this Convention.

---

[35] Article 27. See below Chapter 9.

Originally, as we have noted, this task was carried out by means of a Sub-Commission, but this was found to be unmanageable and inconvenient since the Sub-Commission's work had in any case to be presented to the full Commission before any decision could be taken.[36]

The procedure after admissibility is also carried out by a *rapporteur* or *rapporteurs* appointed by the Commission. The *rapporteur* generally collects such information necessary for the Commission to do its task, and the practice has grown over the years, in cases where it would be inconvenient or uneconomic for the whole Commission to hear certain evidence or undertake a particular investigation, of appointing delegates from among members of the Commission to carry out the task and report back their findings. The Commission or any individual member has the right to put any questions to either of the parties with a view to clarifying the facts; it may also, at the request of a party or *proprio motu*, decide to hear, as a witness or expert or in any other capacity, any person whose evidence or statements seem likely to assist it in carrying out its task.

The role of the Commission here, then, is conciliatory; to ascertain the facts and bring about a friendly settlement. It is to be remembered that all the proceedings will so far have been *in camera* and the names of all applicants will have been kept secret except where the case has already achieved notoriety in its own country, or the applicant believes that the publicity might be good for his case. Even so the procedure before the Commission is always in secret. The part which the Commission plays at this point in the procedure was commented upon in 1958 by Sir Humphrey Waldock, its former President, when he said:

> The Convention was clearly right ... to make the Commission's task of conciliation the central feature of the remedies which it provides. Investigation of the shortcomings of a state in regard to human rights is a very delicate form of intervention in its internal affairs. The primary duty of the Commission is to conduct confidential negotiations with the parties and to try and set right unobtrusively any breach of human rights that may have occurred. It was not primarily established for the purpose of putting states in the dock and registering convictions against them.

---

[36] The Third Protocol to the Convention which came into force on 21 September 1970, replaced the Sub-Commission with the full Commission.

A body of trained lawyers which has the facilities either to hear witnesses or to visit the scene of the alleged violation itself, has an excellent opportunity not only of discovering whether a violation has taken place, but also of attaining a just and amicable solution between the parties, a solution which, in all probability, could not be reached in a court. Where a friendly settlement is reached the Commission submits a Report to the Contracting Party or Parties concerned, the Committee of Ministers, the Secretary-General of the Council of Europe, for publication, and to the applicant. The Report contains a brief statement of the facts and the terms of the settlement reached. If a solution is not achieved the Commission considers the conclusions of its *rapporteur* and draws up a Report in which it states its opinion as to whether the facts found disclose a breach by the state concerned of its obligations under the Convention. The Report, together with such proposals as the Commission deems appropriate, is sent to the Committee of Ministers and to the states concerned and may not be published at this stage. Under Rule 61 of the old Rules of Procedure, where the Commission referred a case to the Court it would, unless it decided otherwise, send a copy of the report to the applicant. This procedure was challenged unsuccessfully before the Court by the Irish Government in the *Lawless* case on the grounds that there was no way of ensuring secrecy. The current Rules of Procedure make no provision for transmitting the Report to the applicant but Rule 29(3) of the Rules of Court lays down that the Report shall be made public as soon as a case has been brought before the Court.

During the period of three months following the transmission of the report to the Committee of Ministers, the Commission must consider in plenary session whether or not to bring the case before the European Court of Human Rights.

THE ROLE OF THE COMMITTEE OF MINISTERS

The Committee of Ministers is the executive organ of the Council of Europe and is made up of the Foreign Ministers of each of the Member States. Most states, however, have appointed permanent representatives to the Council and these act as the Ministers' deputies in the majority of cases. In line with international law, no state may be brought before a Court without its consent. Therefore, where a state has not accepted the jurisdiction of the Court, the final decision in an application is made by the Committee of Ministers. At the present time all the Contracting Parties to the Convention have accepted the jurisdiction of the Court under Article 46, and it seems that this is now expected of all new Council of Europe members. Nevertheless, even where a state has recognized the jurisdiction of the Court, it is still possible for the Committee of Ministers to be seized of the case if, after three months following the report of the Commission, no move has been taken to bring the case before the Court. In addition to the Commission it is possible under Article 48 for states to bring the case to the Court; either the state whose national is alleged to be a victim, or the claimant state in inter-state applications, or, finally, the state against which the application has been made. It is to be noted that at present the individual himself cannot invoke the juris- diction of the Court, but this may soon change. On the 6 November 1990, forty years and two days after the signing of the Convention, Protocol 9 was opened for signature. This Protocol aims to grant to individuals, non-governmental organizations or groups, the right to bring a case before the Court.[37] The original view seems to have been that it was too dangerous to allow the individual to seize the Court, that such a concept was virtually unknown in international dispute settlement, and that the individual's interests could be safely left in the hands of the Commission. In a very short time, however, the role of the applicant and his lawyer in the proceedings before the Court became the object of contention.[38]

The new Protocol, which will come into force following the con- sent of ten Contracting States, will grant the right to refer cases to the Court to individuals, non-governmental organizations and groups, but builds in safeguards to avoid abuse. Any case referred by other than the Commission or a Contracting State Party will be subject to preliminary examination by a panel of three members of the Court.[39] If the panel is of the view that the case does not raise a serious question of interpretation or application of the Convention,

[37] This idea was not new. Having been rejected as unsuitable in the original discus- sions on the Convention, it was revived in 1972 but took until 1990 to be proposed, formally, in a Protocol.

[38] See for example the preliminary objections of the Irish Government in the *Lawless* case, 2 *YB* 308 and below in this chapter.

[39] Protocol 9, Article 5(2).

for instance where there is already established case law on the topic, or if for any other reason it feels that the Court should not consider the case, then it may, by unanimous decision, remove the case from the Court and refer it to the Committee of Ministers, in accordance with Article 32 of the Convention. Even where the applicant takes his case directly to the Court, however, the role of the Commission will not be altered and it will still participate in the proceedings before the Court.[40]

There is nothing in the Convention or the Rules of Procedure of the Commission which gives any guidance as to when a case should go before the Court and when it should be left to the Committee of Ministers. Of the 252 cases considered by the Court to the end of 1990 only five had been referred by states alone. Ten had been taken to the Court initially by a Respondent State and then referred also by the Commission, whilst in a further seventy cases the states followed the Commission in requesting the Court to exercise its jurisdiction. The majority of cases, however, 167 in number, were referred to the Court by the Commission alone. The *travaux préparatoires* show that the Committee's role was introduced for those states unwilling to accept a Court, and a possible implication is that the Commission has a duty to refer all cases to the Court. At the present time all the Contracting Parties accept the jurisdiction of the Court and the part to be played by the Committee of Ministers has a particular significance. According to the Convention[41] a decision by the Committee that there has been a violation must be taken by a two-thirds majority, whereas the Court gives its judgment on a simple majority; that is to say, by a minimum of five out of the nine judges sitting in a Chamber. It might be expected that states, naturally wishing to avoid an adverse decision, would prefer cases to go before the Committee. A recent proposed Protocol 10[42] would seek to replace the Committee of Ministers' two-thirds majority with a simple majority and so bring it in line with the other decision-making bodies. This proposal, if it is accepted, would serve to highlight the problem with which the Commission is faced. It has been suggested that a logical criterion as

---

[40] As laid down in: European Commission of Human Rights, Rules of Procedure, Title IV.

[41] Article 32(1).

[42] Opened for signature on 30 March 1992.

to the choice of Court or Committee would be whether the issue involved is predominantly legal or political. Although this is undoubtedly a factor in the decision, it is not always one which helps. The Commission, having failed to achieve a friendly settlement between the applicant and the state will, in all likelihood, be aware of the political problems facing the particular Government. In the *East African* cases against the United Kingdom[43] the social, political and demographic difficulties were known by the Commission, several concessions such as increasing the numbers of immigrants had been wrested from the Government, and it was doubtful whether a judgment by the Court would be useful or readily enforceable. That case was referred to the Committee of Ministers. By contrast, the *Belgian Linguistics* cases which had enormous political overtones were, nevertheless, sent to the Court. No doubt the nature of the problem involved and the amount of external concern on the international political scene were both factors to be included in the decision which the Commission is called upon to make. Characterization as "political" or "non-political" is, however, not an easy task. Wherever a complex matter of interpretation of the Convention is called for, the Commission, now that it has the choice in every case, should prefer the Court, but where such legal complexity does exist the state itself will, in many cases, welcome the judgment of the Court.

It is difficult to discern any consistent practice in the cases so far. Generally, where the Commission's members unanimously or by a large majority believe that there has been no violation, the Committee of Ministers will be chosen.[44] Sometimes, however, even though the Commission feels strongly that there has been no violation, if it thinks that an important or complex legal decision is involved it will refer the case to the Court.[45] Where the Commission is narrowly divided as to whether there is a violation the present trend is to send the case to the Court. In a number of cases, particularly where several applications with similar facts have been made against a state but have not been joined by the Commission, the Committee has been informed that although the Commission has found a violation this has been rectified by a change in the law which has met with the

---

[43] 13 *YB* 928, 1015, 36 *CD* 92.
[44] For example, *Nielsen* v. *Denmark*, 4 *YB* 490.
[45] For example, *Schmidt & Dahlström* v. *Sweden*, 19 *YB* 484, (1976) Series A, No. 21.

Commission's satisfaction. In such cases (e.g. the 14 cases against Austria following the pattern of *Pataki & Dunshirn* v. *Austria*[46]) the Committee has taken no further action. In a decision of 1974, in the case of *Inhabitants of Les Fourons* v. *Belgium*,[47] which concerned further applications in respect of linguistic problems in Belgium, the Committee noted legislation enacted by the Government and took no further action, even though the Commission's Report revealed a violation.

Article 32(1) of the Convention requires the Committee of Ministers to decide, when an application is left to it, by a majority of two-thirds of those entitled to vote whether there has been a violation of the Convention. What happens, however, if the Committee cannot obtain a two-thirds majority? In cases such as *Huber* v. *Austria*[48] and *Thirty-one East African Asians* v. *UK*[49] the Committee, unable to decide whether there was a violation by a two-thirds majority, resolved that no further action should be taken on the applications. It may be argued that since such a large majority is required by the Convention before a state is found to be in breach of its Treaty obligations, any lesser majority should be interpreted as giving the benefit of the doubt to the state. This interpretation is satisfactory unless one considers the context of the Treaty and its subject matter, whereby it is a state's obligations to individuals within its jurisdiction which is being tested, rather than its legal obligations to the other Contracting States. The Committee's decision in the *Huber* and *East African Asians* cases shows perhaps that it is ill-fitted for the judicial role required at this stage of proceedings in an alleged violation of human rights.

The Committee does not rehear a case or take fresh evidence from the state's representatives and the Commission's delegates, although there seem to be practical rather than legal impediments to such a course of action. In its Rules of Procedure, the Committee has stipulated that it will decide *ad hoc* the procedure to be followed or even whether to delegate the task to the Commission or to some other body should the need arise.

In those cases where the Committee of Ministers decides that there has been a violation of the Convention, it prescribes a period

---

[46] 6 *YB* 718 and 736. See also 7 *YB* 434.
[47] 17 *YB* 542.
[48] 18 *YB* 324.
[49] 20 *YB* 642.

of time during which the state must remedy the situation, and at the end of this time, if nothing has been done, then the Committee is required to decide what effect shall be given to its decision. In the application brought by Cyprus against Turkey in 1978[50] the Commission held that there had been a breach of the Convention and reported as such to the Committee of Ministers. The Ministers endorsed the Commission's view and asked that measures be taken to put an end to the violations, and consequently urged the parties to resume intercommunal talks. Some three months later the Committee learned that this request had not been taken up by the parties and resolved as follows:

> Convinced that the enduring protection of human rights in Cyprus can only be brought about through the re-establishment of peace and confidence between the two communities: and that intercommunal talks constitute the appropriate framework for reaching a solution of the dispute; decides strongly to urge the parties to resume intercommunal talks under the auspices of the Secretary-General of the United Nations in order to agree upon solutions on all aspects of the dispute. The Committee of Ministers views this decision as completing its consideration of the case of Cyprus versus Turkey.

There is, of course, a limit to what the Committee may do on finding a violation, or in enforcing a decision of the Court. It can bring pressure on the representatives of the state concerned in the meetings of the Committee; it may publish the Commission's report, as it does in most cases; or, as a last resort, it may suspend a state's membership of the Council of Europe. It is, in fact, the relative importance of the machinery, balanced against the prestige of the Convention, which must best guide the Commission in deciding which route an application should take.

THE EUROPEAN COURT OF HUMAN RIGHTS

Although Article 19 sets up the European Court of Human Rights, there were so many doubts and misgivings concerning its role in relation to municipal courts that it was not until five years after the coming into force of the Convention that the necessary eight

[50] Application 8007/77, 21 *YB* 100 and 22 *YB* 440.

declarations of recognition of compulsory jurisdiction were lodged which enabled it to come into operation. The United Kingdom recognized the jurisdiction of the Court only in 1966, fifteen years after it signed the original Convention.

The number of judges is equal to that of the members of the Council of Europe. They are elected by the Consultative Assembly from lists of persons nominated by Member States and each member is required to nominate three candidates, of whom at least two must be its nationals. The qualifications required of a judge are those necessary for a judge of the International Court, and paragraph 3 of Article 39 is textually similar to Article 2 of the Statute of the International Court. The Court, like the Commission, has drawn up its own Rules of Procedure.

Rule 4 of the Rules of Court forbids a judge from being a member of a Government or from otherwise holding a post or exercising a profession which is likely to affect confidence in his independence. Judges of the International Court and of the European Community Court are not allowed to hold any other posts during their terms of office as judges. This restriction obviously cannot apply in the case of the Human Rights Court which is not a Court in permanent session, and whose members are paid, as we have seen, at a daily rate. The newly added paragraph 7 to Article 40[51] reads:

> The members of the Court shall sit on the Court in their individual capacity. During their term of office they shall not hold any position which is incompatible with their independence and impartiality as members of the Court or the demands of this office.[52]

The Procedure of the Court

The actual form of the Court is stipulated by Article 43 of the Convention:

> For the consideration of each case brought before it the Court shall

---

[51] Amended by Protocol 8, Article 9.

[52] In 1977 the Parliamentary Assembly (Res. 809) urged Member States not to vote for nominees to the Court who were, by the nature of their functions, dependent on Government, unless an undertaking to resign had been given. They were similarly exhorted to refrain from electing candidates over the age of seventy-five.

consist of a Chamber composed of nine judges.[53] There shall sit as an *ex officio* member of the Chamber the judge who is a national of any state party concerned, or, if there is none, a person of its choice who shall sit in the capacity of judge; the names of the other judges shall be chosen by lot by the President before the opening of the case.

The two official languages of the Court, as with all Council of Europe institutions, are English and French, and all decisions of the Court are given in both languages, one of which is designated by the Court as authentic. If a party does not speak either of the official languages well enough to make himself understood, the Court may authorize him to use any other language, and in such a case the party concerned is responsible for providing translation into one of the official languages. The parties before the Court may be represented by agents who may be assisted by Counsel.

When the Commission, or one of the appropriate Contracting Parties, has decided to refer a case to the Court, an application is sent to the Registrar of the Court, who immediately forwards copies to the President, Vice-President and judges, to any Contracting Party involved, and to the President and members of the Commission. The Registrar also informs the Committee of Ministers through the Secretary-General.

If the President or Vice-President of the Court is one of the nine judges chosen by lot to sit in the Chamber he, or she, will act as President; otherwise the most senior judge will preside. The first stage of the procedure is generally written, and memorials and documents are lodged with the Registry. The oral stage will then follow, and the President will conduct the hearing and prescribe the order in which the Court will hear the agents, the delegates of the Commission and any other person whom it or the Commission desires to call. Meanwhile, at any time during the proceedings the Chamber may depute one or more of its members to carry out any form of investigation or on-the-spot inquiry which it thinks might help its deliberations; it may also entrust any body, office, commission or authority with the task of obtaining information, expressing an opinion, or making a report, upon any specific point. Witnesses called by the Court have

---

[53] Increased from the original 7 by Article 11 of Protocol 8.

their expenses borne by the Council of Europe; witnesses at the suggestion of a party have their expenses paid by that party.

Where a case raises a serious question affecting the interpretation of the Convention, the Chamber may at any time relinquish jurisdiction in favour of the plenary Court. Up to the end of 1991 it had done this on eighty-four occasions.

All oral hearings of the Court are held in public, while its deliberations are secret. The judgment, signed by the President and Registrar, is read by the President of the Court at a public hearing. It is then sent to the President of the Committee of Ministers which, under Article 54 of the Convention, administers its execution. An interpretation of the judgment may be requested at any time within a period of three years following its delivery.

On those occasions when the Court decides that there has been a violation of the Convention its decision is then conveyed to the Committee of Ministers, which is responsible for supervising its execution. Under Article 50, however, the Court is authorized to award "just satisfaction" of a pecuniary nature if the domestic law of the violating state does not provide for adequate reparation of the breach. This may represent compensation for damage as well as the reimbursement of costs and expenses.

The Relationship Between the Commission and the Court

As we have seen, an individual cannot appear as a party before the Court and his petition can be heard only after action taken by the Commission, or one of the Contracting Parties. With the exception of the *Ireland* v. *United Kingdom* case,[54] inter-state applications have not been referred to the Court. The application by the Scandinavian countries and the Netherlands against Greece ended in the Committee of Ministers because that respondent Government had not recognized the Court. Moreover, we have seen above that a decision of the political body of the Committee of Ministers will often be more welcome, especially in view of the larger number of votes required in that Committee for an adverse judgment. It is therefore to be expected that the bulk of the Court's work will be based on individual petitions, and that these must depend on the decision of the

---

[54] 21 *YB* 602, (1978) Series A, No. 25, and 2 *EHRR* 25.

Commission to refer the case to Court. The Commission, in practice, could relieve the Committee of Ministers in many cases of any decision in a human rights matter, and could pass every case to the Court if it believed that this body should be the one to have final judgment. This is but one example of how the Commission has had the power indirectly to supervise the development of the Convention and its organs. So much has depended and still depends on the character of the Commission and its attitude to its task.

An interesting point arises in connection with the Commission's right to bring cases before the Court. Some of the High Contracting Parties have accepted the Court's jurisdiction on condition of reciprocity. Does the condition apply on the occasions when the Commission wishes to refer a case against one of these states to the Court? The Committee of Legal Experts discussed the point in 1950. It was argued that no reciprocity existed in the case of the Commission, and that therefore the Court had no jurisdiction; on the other hand, the condition of reciprocity could be held to apply only to cases brought by other Contracting Parties and not to affect the ability of the Commission to bring a case. A decision on this point would rest with the Court itself under Article 49, but it is unlikely that reciprocity will be held to be required for any actions of the Commission.

Article 48 lays down in detail who may bring a case before the Court, whereas Article 44 has already announced that only the High Contracting Parties and the Commission shall have such a right. A likely explanation for repeating this provision is that the drafters wished to emphasize that no individuals could bring cases before the Court. In the *Lawless* case, the Irish Government pointed out that in the French text the Commission and the Contracting Parties were the only ones who *"... ont qualité pour se présenter devant la Cour,"* and, as such, the applicant should not be given a platform from which to criticize his Government. The Commission agreed that the French text appeared to be different in scope from the English, but maintained that in the interests of justice Article 44 could not be interpreted in this restrictive way.

What then is the position of the Commission before the Court? Does it appear as a party? Rule 29(1) of the Rules of Court states:

The Commission shall delegate one or more of its members to take part in the consideration of a case before the Court. The Delegates may be assisted by other persons.[55]

Rule 63 of the Commission's Rules of Procedure[56] begins similarly:

> The Commission shall assist the European Court of Human Rights in any case brought before the Court. When a case is referred to the Court the Commission shall appoint, at a plenary session, one or more delegates to take part in the consideration of the case before the Court. These delegates may be assisted by any person appointed by the Commission...

In the *Lawless* case Professor Waldock, one of three delegates to the Court, outlined the role which the Commission expected to play:

> The Commission, although not a party to the case, participates in the proceedings and stands in a position intermediate between the government and the individual. Moreover, if the Commission considers the rights of the individual to have been violated, it is the Commission's duty to say so in its report, and to present that opinion to the Court. The Commission, however, does not understand its function before the Court to be to defend the interests of the individual as such. The Commission's function is that stated in Article 19, namely to ensure the observance of the engagements undertaken by the Contracting Parties in the Convention ... The function of the Commission before the Court, as we understand it, is not litigious: it is ministerial. It is not our function to defend before the Court, either the case of the individual as such, or our opinion simply as such. Our function, we believe, is to place before you all the elements of the case relevant for the determination of the case by the Court.[57]

According to the Convention, then, the individual has neither the right to bring a case to the Court nor to appear before it as a party to the action. Also, the Commission has shown clearly that it does not consider that it should act as advocate for the individual applicant. If the Commission is not to act in this way, how can the point of view of the applicant be made known to the Court?

---

[55] Rules of Court, in force 20 April 1992.
[56] Rules of Procedure, 7 January 1992.
[57] *Lawless* v *Ireland*, Series B, 1960-1 at p. 261.

On 30 March 1960, at the same session in which it decided to refer the *Lawless* case to the Court, the Commission adopted a new Rule 76 of its Rules of Procedure:

When a case brought before the Commission in pursuance of Article 25 of the Convention is subsequently referred to the Court, the Secretary of the Commission shall immediately notify the Applicant. Unless the Commission shall otherwise decide, the Secretary shall also in due course communicate to him the Commission's Report, informing him that he may, within a time limit fixed by the President, submit to the Commission his written observations on the said Report. The Commission shall decide what action, if any, shall be taken in respect of these observations.

After it had referred the case to the Court, the Commission sent the report to Lawless and invited his observations. At the same time, the Commission pointed out that the report was to be kept secret and not to be published. The Government of Ireland complained on this point. Article 31 of the Convention says that the Commission's report shall be transmitted to the Committee of Ministers and the Governments concerned, which shall not be at liberty to publish. Therefore, maintained the Irish Government, the intention was that the report should be secret, and the absence of a provision authorising transmission to the individual was intentional. The Government continued to be bound by the obligation of secrecy even after the report had been referred to the Court. The Committee of Ministers had refused the Government's request to publish the Commission's conclusion that there had been no violation. In view also of the fact that the Commission had no way of compelling the applicant to keep the report secret, the Government's position was inferior to that of the applicant. The Irish Government therefore asked the Court to rule that the publication of the report by the Commission amounted to a violation of the Convention and that a correct interpretation of the Convention does not permit of action of the nature contemplated by the new Rule 76 of the Rules of the Commission. It was maintained by the Commission, on the other hand, that although Article 31 imposed secrecy, it related purely to publication in the press or to third parties, but not to a party to the proceedings:

Obvious considerations of equity militate in favour of a party to the proceedings before the Commission being informed of the Commission's conclusions concerning his own case.

Also, the obligation to secrecy applied only while the case was pending before the Committee of Ministers, in order to facilitate any final attempts at conciliation. That this was the intention of the drafters of the Convention, the President showed by quoting from the *travaux préparatoires;* the application before the Court took on a completely different character.

In its judgment, the Court was cautious as to competence, making it clear that the Commission and the Court were completely independent organs with their own functions. It was not within the competence of the Court to delete a Rule from the Commission's Rules. The judgment went on to consider the question of the communication to Lawless. The Court recognized the need for secrecy in the Commission's affairs, and that while it was necessary to distinguish these from the public hearings of the Court, it had to be kept in mind that only the oral proceedings and judgments were public, and not documents. It went on, however, to point out the differences between publication in general, and communication to a person directly concerned. In view of this decision the Commission's Rule still stood, for no other body was competent to declare it invalid.

Under Rule 76, the Commission not only sent the report to Lawless, but also invited his written observations thereon. The role of the individual in proceedings before the Court is not made clear in the Convention, nor was it developed to any greater extent than we are showing in the Rules of Procedure of the Commission or Court. As a result, the Commission requested the applicant's observations with the intention of transmitting them to the Court, since he had no *locus standi.* It asked the Court to give leave for the submission to the Court of the applicant's comments on the Commission's report, as one of the Commission's documents in the case, and, in general, to give directions as to the right of the Commission to communicate to the Court the comments of the applicant in regard to matters arising in the proceedings. The Government objected that the Commission was virtually bestowing on the individual the right to bring his own case, and that this was explicitly against the wishes of the High Contracting Parties. The Commission agreed that the Convention was silent as to the position of individuals before the Court, but found it

difficult to attribute to the authors of the Convention "... an intention to place an impenetrable curtain between the individual and the
organ specifically set up as a judicial tribunal to make judicial determination of his case." The Commission could not accept that Article
44 was intended to prevent an individual from having any contact
at all with the proceedings before the Court. The President cited the
opinion of the International Court, in the case of the *Administrative
Tribunal of the International Labour Organization*, in which it was held
that UNESCO could transmit in writing the observations of individuals, although they had no *locus standi* before the Court.

The Irish Government distinguished that case on the grounds that
the procedure then followed was adopted after discussion and by
agreement with the Organization, whereas in the present case the
Commission had acted without consulting the Government, and
contrary to its wishes. The Irish Attorney General argued that the
position of inequality of the individual was, "more fanciful than
real", and went on:

> The inequality, such as it is, is in my submission deliberate, not in the
> sense of states wishing to place individual citizens at a disadvantage, but
> because in agreeing to the limited, I concede, very limited, jurisdiction of
> the Court created by the Convention, states went as far as it appeared to
> them that they would be warranted in doing at present in recognising for
> individuals, a status of any kind in international law.

The Commission replied that Rule 29 of the Rules of Court allowed its delegates to have the assistance of any person of their
choice, and this seemed to authorize them to refer to the applicant.
The Court said in its judgment:

> It is in the interests of the proper administration of justice that the Court
> should have knowledge of and, if need be, take into consideration, the
> applicant's point of view.

This could be done from the Commission's report, from the statements of the Commission's delegates, or by hearing the applicant as
a witness. It reserved the right to answer on the general question
after hearing the merits of the case.

The final outcome of this debate can now be seen in Rule 33 of
the Rules of Court which provides that once the Court receives an

application from a Contracting Party or a request from the Commission to commence proceedings, a copy of the Report is to be sent *inter alia* to the individual applicant.

Another procedural point in this case, connected with the one just discussed, arose later during the period between the decisions on procedure and on the merits. Between November 1960 and April 1961, further written pleadings were exchanged by the Parties. First came the "statement" of the Commission commenting on the Counter-Memorial of the Irish Government, and then the "observations" of the Government in reply. In the "statement", the Commission considered it was entitled to submit to the Court the written observations of the applicant on its own earlier report; obviously in reliance on the Court's decision that the Commission was entitled, of its own accord, to make known the applicant's views to the Court. The "statement" thus incorporated nearly twenty pages of the applicant's comments, including, it must be noted, criticism of the Commission. The Government objected. The Court ruled that the passage reproducing the applicant's views was not, at that stage, to be considered as part of the proceedings of the case. However, it held that the Commission could "... take account of the applicant's views and implicitly make use of them in oral hearings. This seems a rather restrictive interpretation of its own earlier judgment, but perhaps the Court was stressing that the Commission should take an active role in the proceedings as the "conscience" of the Contracting States, and not merely act as a post-box for making known the views of the applicant. The Court may have had in mind here the Government's fear that Lawless would use the agency of the human rights procedures for political propaganda.

The position of the individual's relations to the Court came up again in the *De Becker* case.[58] It will be recalled that in that case a law promulgated by the Belgian Government in June 1961 considerably modified the Penal Code and particularly the section which, it was initially claimed, violated the Convention. The representative of the Belgian Government invited the Court to say that there was no longer a breach of the Convention and later the applicant, in a declaration to the Commission, made known his wish to withdraw from the case since his claims had been met by the new law. In its second

---

[58] 4 *YB* 436 and (1962) Series A, No. 4, and 1 *EHRR* 43.

sitting on the case the Court pointed out that De Becker's declaration had not come from a party represented before the Court, and could not possess legal character or take effect as a notice of discontinuance of the proceedings, as provided for in the then Rule 47 of the Rules of the Court:

> It is not binding on the Commission, which, as the defender of the public interest, had a duty to take the statement into account if it considered that it was a means of enlightening the Court on the points at issue...[59]

In view of the Commission's recognition that there was no need to proceed further, the Court, after due consideration of the facts, relinquished the case.

The Court has continued to use material prepared by the applicants' lawyers without complaints from the Governments. In the *Vagrancy* cases the applicant's lawyer, who was assisting the delegates of the Commission, addressed the Court which rejected Belgian Government objections.

After all these agonisingly legalistic debates the present Rule 30 of the Rules of Court reads:

> 1. The applicant shall be represented by an advocate authorized to practise in any of the Contracting States and resident in the territory of one of them, or by any other person approved by the President. The President may, however, give leave to the applicant to present his own case, subject, if need be, to his being assisted by an advocate or other person as aforesaid.

---

[59] *Supra*, note 57, *YB* at para. 23.

CHAPTER FOUR

The Individual's Personal Life

GENERAL

To be effective, a treaty guaranteeing human rights must necessarily be dynamic. In earlier chapters we have examined the European Convention in its political and institutional context. It has been suggested that the setting within which the Convention was drafted and signed was an important factor in determining its contents. A Convention drafted today would probably differ quite considerably in detail, and possibly in principle, from that conceived during the immediate post-war period. Not only might certain rights emphasized in the Convention appear in a more circumscribed form, but other rights which were ignored might well feature more prominently. An obvious example is that of privacy. Article 8 of the Convention guarantees respect for private and family life, home and correspondence. In view of the progress of modern electronic technology and the interest paid generally to the subject of privacy, it seems very likely that a treaty provision drafted today would define more carefully and precisely what is meant by "private life".[1]

The Commission and Court are frequently faced with the problem of what to do where the Convention's references to a right or freedom are minimal or where a right which would nowadays be taken for granted in Europe, is missing entirely from the Convention. Of course, if a right claimed is not to be found in the Convention, the Commission's normal procedure is to reject an application as incompatible with the Convention's terms, *ratione materiae,* under Article 27 (2). In recent years, however, the Commission has recognized that if a human rights treaty is to remain of use, it must stay in line with modern thought on individual rights and on sociological theory.

An international treaty is governed by the rules of international

---

[1] The Council of Europe has indeed not been idle in its work on privacy and data protection. See, for example, *The European Convention on the Protection of Individuals with regard to Automatic Processing of Personal Data, 1981,* Cmnd 8341.

law. It is an agreement between states, creating rights and obligations for the parties. A treaty is the only form of written agreement recognized by international law, and yet this document is used to regulate many different types of legal relationship. It may be argued that human rights treaties differ from most other international treaties because of the position of the individual. Although there are treaties which purport to grant rights to individuals, this is very often as a secondary means to fulfilling the legal obligations of the States Parties. Because human rights treaties have as their only aim the securing of individual rights, it is difficult to imagine these instruments laying down duties and obligations *vis-à-vis* states and not creating rights, and perhaps, by implication, duties, which may be claimed by the individual citizens within those states. If one state violates a human rights treaty to which it is party, it will be in breach of its legal obligations to the other States Parties. In practice, it is the individual who suffers damage rather than the other states; he or she is probably the person who has acted on the strength of the treaty promises and the person who, in the case of the European Convention, is seeking redress. The other States Parties are there because international law knows of no legally enforceable agreement between a state and individuals without the involvement of other states. In such circumstances, therefore, it would seem that the object and purpose of the treaty, namely the protection of the individual, should be highlighted.

If one can determine a definition of human rights outside the treaty, then it is fair to expect a treaty such as the European Convention to be interpreted in accordance with such a definition. For example, the Universal Declaration of Human Rights states in Article 3 that everyone has the right to life. The International Covenant on Civil and Political Rights expresses this as "the inherent right to life of every human being". The European Convention, however, takes as read the sacredness of life and declares directly in Article 2 ". . . everyone's right to life shall be protected by law." Article 6(1) provides that everyone is entitled to a fair and public hearing in determination of his civil rights and obligations. Read strictly, this does not appear to grant right of access to the courts, but merely the requirement that a matter *sub judice* will be dealt with fairly. In the *Golder* case,[2] the Court, by a majority decision, held that

---

[2] (1973) Series A, No. 18, and 1 *EHRR* 524.

Article 6 implied access to the courts and that a British prisoner who had not been allowed to consult a solicitor, with a view to bringing an action for defamation, was the victim of a violation of the Convention. If one talks of a like-mindedness among European states, of the same cultural traditions and spiritual values, then this is what it means in terms of interpretation of a human rights treaty.

This approach, however, has its dangers above and beyond the risk that an enthusiastic Commission and Court might go further than the intentions of the Contracting Parties. In some of the jurisprudence there has appeared at times a tendency to examine the law of a Respondent State in the light of the laws of the other States Parties – to find the existence of a European norm. This may be acceptable practice in the course of European unity, but its value would seem to be limited if the ultimate aim is the further realization of human rights in general.[3] Again, one finds instances where the European Commission, particularly in its early days, imposed upon the Convention inherent restrictions beyond those mentioned in the Treaty itself. For example, the Commission, in the *Huber* case,[4] held that while everyone has the right to freedom of thought, conscience, and religion, and the right of expression, there may be restrictions on a prisoner's right of correspondence and his right to vote in a national election because this is "an inherent feature of lawful imprisonment". Thus any tendency to be swept away by a wave of European like-mindedness, unjustified within the terms of the Convention, must always be resisted.[5]

Even though there are wide cultural and social differences to be seen within the Council of Europe – for instance, the lifestyle of rural Turkey is likely to bear little resemblance to that of the Scandinavian states – it must be admitted that there is a common denominator of values which may be termed "European", and which is consistent enough to aid the formulation of a jurisprudence for the European Commission and Court. Indeed, the rationale of regional protection of human rights relies heavily upon this. In such a context, the contribution of the new Central and Eastern European

---

[3] See for example the discussion on "Margin of appreciation" below, Chapter 9.

[4] Application 4517/70, 18 *YB* 324, and 38 *CD* 90.

[5] Happily, the concept of the inherent limitation on the rights of prisoners has, more recently, been discredited – see further discussion, *infra*, Chapter 8.

Republics, and the effects on them of decades of socialism, will be fascinating to monitor.

The Convention deals for a great part with the "normal" everyday life of the European citizen, with birth and death, growing up and going to school and university, marrying and raising a family, working for a living and entering fully, or not at all, according to one's wishes, into the life of the community. Another major part of the Convention's concern, which we will deal with in Chapter 6, is the protection of the individual when he finds himself tangled with the law or the authorities in prison or in the courts.

LIFE AND DEATH

We have already noted that the United Nations Civil and Political Rights Covenant states that every human being has the inherent right to life, whereas the terminology of the European Convention differs in that it provides that the right to life should be protected by law. Fawcett points out that it is the right to life, and not life itself, which is protected.[6] This is not, however, always easy to understand.

The Convention prohibits the intentional taking of life, save in the case of capital punishment, or following the use of force in quelling riots or insurrections, preventing escape of a lawfully-held prisoner, effecting a lawful arrest or in self-defence. Although the death penalty is specifically excluded from Article 2, it is to be prohibited in those states that have accepted Protocol Number 6.[7] Interestingly, in the *Soering* case,[8] where the United Kingdom proposed the extradition of a prisoner to the United States, where he was likely to be sentenced to death, there was some discussion as to whether, in view of the virtual disappearance in practice of such a penalty in Europe, his extradition might amount to inhuman treatment.[9] The American Convention on Human Rights states that the death penalty may

---

[6] J. E. S. Fawcett, *The Application of the European Convention on Human Rights*, Oxford, Clarendon Press, 2nd edition, 1987, p. 37.

[7] Protocol 6 was opened for signature in April 1983 and entered into force in March 1985. It has eighteen Contracting Parties, which do not include the United Kingdom.

[8] (1989) Series A, No. 161, 11 *EHRR* 439.

[9] See, for example, the separate opinion of Judge De Meyer, *ibid.*, Series A, at p. 51, *EHRR* at p. 483.

not be re-introduced for crimes to which it does not presently apply, nor may it be introduced for crimes in those states which have abolished it. That Treaty similarly says that capital punishment shall not be imposed upon persons who, when the crime was committed, were under eighteen years of age, over seventy, or who are pregnant.[10] Moreover, the American Convention urges, a state is required not to take away life arbitrarily without respect to the provisions such as the right to a fair trial or the prohibition on retroactive criminal law.

The Commission has on several occasions voiced the opinion that a state's obligations under Article 2 should not be viewed in a wholly negative light, but that they include positive aspects. In an application brought against the United Kingdom in 1975,[11] the Commission stated:

> ... the first sentence of Article 2 imposes a broader obligation on the state than that contained in the second sentence. The concept that "everyone's right to life shall be protected by law" enjoins the state not only to refrain from taking life "intentionally" but, further, to take appropriate steps to safeguard life.

This would presumably include the enactment of suitable laws to prevent the taking of life, and also the provision of the necessary means of enforcing these laws, such as, at minimum, a rudimentary police force. In Application 9348/81, Mrs W. against the United Kingdom,[12] the applicant alleged that the failure by the British authorities properly to control the Ireland/Northern Ireland border and to take sufficient action to prevent terrorists from crossing the border to murder her husband, was a violation of Article 2. Similarly, the Article was invoked, but again unsuccessfully, by Mrs Stewart, whose son had been killed by a plastic bullet discharged by a soldier in Northern Ireland.[13]

More extremely, perhaps, an applicant who feared that his life was in danger from an assassin, complained that failure by the authorities to continue the provision of a personal bodyguard also

[10] The UN Covenant on Civil and Political Rights has similar provisions regarding youth and pregnancy.

[11] Application No 7154/75, 14 *D&R* p. 31.

[12] 32 *D&R* p. 190.

[13] Application 10044/82, 39 *D&R* 162, and 27 *YB* 129.

constituted a violation of this Article.[14] The Commission's view has been that once it is satisfied that the state concerned is aware of the risks to life involved and is taking positive action, it is not for the Commission to enquire into the detailed sufficiency of that action: it is certainly not the case that the Article excludes possible violence. As we have seen, Paragraph 2 of the Article lays down that a state will not be in breach where it uses force: (a) in defence of any person from unlawful violence; (b) to effect a lawful arrest or prevent the escape of a person lawfully detained or; (c) in action lawfully taken to quell a riot or insurrection. The Convention requires that such use of force must be "*absolutely* necessary", that is to say, not only must it be proportionate to the interests of the peace it is trying to protect, but also that the dangers to life and limb inherent in the situation must be borne in mind. The Government should be aware that any loss of life resulting should be strictly accountable for under the Convention.

Once it is recognized that positive action may be necessary under Article 2, the question arises whether this should be limited to protecting public safety from perpetrators of evil, or whether, for example, it might include an obligation to control the excessive speed of motor vehicles which may indeed be a threat to life. Might the provision of life-saving medicine or surgery for one section of the population, but not another, be a discriminatory protection of the right to life? Progression along these lines, of course, raises the insoluble problem of the distinction between political and civil rights, and social and economic rights, and the Commission has chosen, quite rightly, not to venture in this direction, but to limit the provisions of Article 2 to the protection of the individual from violent crimes.

A starting point for any discussion of the right to life is the question of when does life begin. The American Convention on Human Rights lays down that the right to life shall commence, in general, from the moment of conception. The European Convention, however, gives no indication as to when life begins. Since, according to

---

[14] Application 6040/73, *X* v. *Ireland* 44, *CD* 121, and 16 *YB* 388. The Commission was of the view that Article 2 does not impose a positive obligation on states to give individuals personal protection of the kind sought by the applicant, and declared the application manifestly ill-founded.

the Convention, only "victims" may bring an application before the Commission, it would seem that the right to life, at its beginning, may be difficult to protect. An unrestricted interpretation of the right to life would have the effect of outlawing abortion. There is a variety of views on this throughout the European states, but there is, in the majority of countries, agreement that abortion should be lawful when to act otherwise would put at risk the life, or even the health, of the mother. Attempts by various "pro-life" associations, or by individuals, to represent the "unborn child" have been met with rejections by the Commission on the grounds that the applicant cannot be described as a victim under Article 25.[15] For the most part, therefore, abortion cases have consisted of complaints that restriction on abortion has limited the private rights of the applicant mother to self-determination in her sexual life,[16] or alternatively, in claims brought by fathers, that abortion violates the family life rights of the applicant father but not, in this latter case, that the father is acting on behalf of the unborn child.

Presumably compulsory sterilization, particularly if carried out for population control purposes, would be claimed, *prima facie*, to be contrary to the Convention on grounds of interference with private life, rather than on those of the protection of the right to life. A European government instituting a programme of compulsory sterilization for population control would possibly argue that it was justified for the economic well-being of the country, a claim which would raise fundamental questions for the Commission.

The right to dispose of one's own life is not included in any of the human rights instruments. Suicide and euthanasia, as examples of wishes to die, would not normally involve the Convention in any way. The duty on states under the Convention to legislate to protect life would not, it is presumed, authorize them, as such, to outlaw suicide. Mercy killing, where an incurably ill patient is deprived of the means of life, leaves a decision on the patient's life elsewhere and one can envisage that in a dispute between relatives whether to "switch off the machine", the state's duty might be put to the test. Similar

[15] See, for example, an early case against Norway in 1960, Application 867/60, 4 *YB* 270 and the inadmissible parts of Application 6959/75, *Brüggemann & Scheuten* v. *Federal Republic of Germany* 21 *YB* 638, and 5 *D&R* 103.

[16] *Brüggemann and Scheuten* v. *Federal Republic of Germany, supra,* note 15 and further discussion, *infra,* Chapter 5.

questions arise in relation to the cost of medical care. There have been examples where a hospital authority, unable to afford kidney machines for all patients, has put an arbitrary upper age limit on their provision. Will a law which allows a health authority to save the life of one person, but refuse to do so for someone a year older, pass scrutiny under Article 2 of the Convention?

THE CHILD

In 1948 the Universal Declaration of Human Rights recognized the entitlement of childhood to special care and assistance,[17] but despite the Declaration on the Rights of the Child some eleven years later, it was not until 1989 that the United Nations Convention on the Rights of the Child joined the family of United Nations human rights treaties. Undoubtedly, the positive input of states, which is necessary to provide the appropriate care and protection, is one reason why the Convention received a lower priority than it might have deserved. A further difficulty, however, arises because of the tension which may occur between the rights of the child and those of other individuals or units of society.

The provisions of the European Convention apply to all individuals, irrespective of age, but, just as old age may require dependency on other people, so the child is always subject to the domination of his or her parents or guardians. In fact, it is often where the views of the parents differ from those of the authorities that a child's rights may be in jeopardy. Where this dispute concerns the child's welfare or upbringing, the Convention's machinery can provide a useful point of reference.

Many of the cases concerning children which have come before the Strasbourg organs have involved questions of custody and access to children who, for one reason or another, have been separated from their parents. Article 8 says that rights of family life and home shall be respected, but the same Article also protects private life, and it is in allocating these rights according to the wishes and needs of the respective parents and children that the Commission and Court have had some of their hardest tasks. Paramount in the eyes of both organs has been the interest of the child, and this should replace any

---

[17] Article 25(2).

private interests of either parent or any convenience of the authorities. In the *Rasmussen* case,[18] for instance, which concerned paternity proceedings, Denmark successfully defended its practice of imposing different time limits in paternity proceedings on fathers from those on mothers or children, on the grounds that it was in the interests of the happiness of the child that a father's intervention should be restricted. A similar decision was reached where the Commission decided that restrictions on the adoption of a foreign child which, *inter alia*, required that he should be below school age, were justified in the interests of his integration into a new country.[19] In the Federal Republic of Germany, the care and custody of a child of an unmarried couple is normally entrusted to the mother. Where, in an application in 1982,[20] a father objected that this was in violation of his rights to family life, the Commission pointed out that, should the union split up, then there were, unlike in the case of divorce, no automatic procedures for dealing with the child's custody. In that application, the Commission did not hesitate to point out, the father could acquire joint custody by marrying the mother.

The Commission does not underestimate the subtlety of its task. In Application 10141/82, *L. v. Sweden*,[21] it said:

> It goes without saying that it is difficult to ascertain what precisely is in the best interests of a child, in particular when it is of a tender age. The Commission stresses that the issue in these cases is not only what is the best solution for the child. Under Article 8, an interference with the right of the parents to continue to take care of their child cannot be justified simply on the basis that it would be better for the child to be taken care of by certain foster parents. In order to justify such an interference it is necessary under the terms of Article 8 that the state demonstrates sufficient reasons for the decision to take a child into care. These reasons should be of such weight as to render the care decision "necessary in a democratic society".

---

[18] (1984) Series A, No. 87, and 7 *EHRR* 371.

[19] Application 8896/80, *X v. Netherlands*, 24 *D&R* 176.

[20] Application 9639/82, *B., R. & J. v. Federal Republic of Germany*, 36 *D&R* 130, and 27 *YB* 102.

[21] 40 *D&R* 140, at p. 51.

The Court has taken a similar approach on questions of access and custody.[22] The Court must be satisfied that the authorities have grounds to interfere on the basis of one of the interests laid down in Paragraph 2 of Article 8, and that the interference fulfils a pressing social need. In the case of *Margareta and Roger Andersson* v. *Sweden,*[23] a mother and her son who were prevented from contacting each other, even to the extent of restriction on telephone communication and letter, were successful in challenging the Swedish authorities whose actions the Court held were disproportionately severe.

The problem, nevertheless, arises of deciding, in the first place, if a right under Article 8 has been infringed, and of reconciling the competing rights of the family and the individual. Where, for example, a child does not want to see her father and this reluctance has been brought about by the influence of her mother,[24] the Court and the Commission have to decide between the private right of the father to see his child, his right to family life, or the private life right of the daughter not to be forced to meet her father. In the *Hendriks* case,[25] although a majority of the Commission felt the ensuing tensions in such a situation might be bad for the child, the dissenting Commissioners were of the view that the father's rights were important and should be denied only where there was evidence of serious threat to the child, such as a history of ill-treatment.

Two inadmissible cases illustrate the dilemma further; in the first, against Netherlands,[26] a fourteen-year-old girl, having run away with her boyfriend, was returned to her parents. In Application No. 6854/74, against Denmark,[27] another fourteen-year-old girl left home after a dispute with her parents to live with an organization called "Children's Power" in deserted barracks in Copenhagen. The authorities in this case, however, refused to fetch her back for her parents and even gave her financial assistance.[28]

---

[22] See, for example, *O., H., W., B. and R.* v. *UK,* 1987, Series A, Nos. 120 and 121, and 10 *EHRR* 82; *Olsson* v. *Sweden,* 1988, Series A, No. 130, and 11 *EHRR* 259; *Eriksson* v. *Sweden,* 1989, Series A, No. 156, and 12 *EHRR* 183.

[23] (1992) Series A, No. 226, and 14 *EHRR* 615.

[24] As was alleged in Application 9018/80, *K.* v. *Netherlands,* 33 *D&R* 9.

[25] Application 9427/78, 29 *D&R* 5.

[26] Application 6753/74, 2 *D&R* 118.

[27] 7 *D&R* 81.

[28] This final point, however, was not fully discussed because of a failure to exhaust local remedies.

The Commission and the Court have taken a broad definition of "family" and have in general required some evidence of a close community among its members and usually some blood relationship. In the *Berrehab* case,[29] the applicant remarried his former wife in order to regain his residence permit and thereby acquire access to his daughter. The couple did not co-habit, but there was evidence that Mr Berrehab was close to his daughter and the Court was of the opinion that his original expulsion, although in the economic interest which Netherlands had in the regulation of the labour market, was not "necessary in a democratic society", being disproportionate to the original aim.

The *Marckx* case, in 1979,[30] concerned the Belgian laws on illegitimacy. Paula Marckx, an unmarried mother, and her daughter Alexandra, complained that under Belgian law a child born out of wedlock had no legal bond with the mother. Recognition of the child, a voluntary act which could follow later, allowed the child to inherit in the event of the mother's death intestate but even then, as against legitimate children of the same mother, such rights were restricted. A further legal act, adoption, gave the child full rights in cases of intestacy but then the child could not claim any rights on intestacy in the estates of grandparents. Ms Marckx and her daughter alleged violations of Article 8, in that the law failed to respect private and family life, and that this was discriminatory between legitimate and illegitimate children and between married and unmarried mothers, contrary to Article 14. They also alleged violations of Article 3 (degrading treatment) and of Article 1 of the First Protocol (right to enjoyment of possessions) both alone and in conjunction with Article 14. The Court's judgment, with some dissent, held that the Belgian law was in conflict with the Convention, in that there were violations of Articles 8, 14 and Article 1 of the First Protocol. There was no "degrading treatment" within the terms of the interpretation which has been given to Article 3, neither did the court uphold Ms Marckx's submission that Article 12 had embodied within it the inherent right not to marry. Belgium has since reformed its legislation on this subject.[31] A similar decision in

---

[29] (1988) Series A, No. 138, and 11 *EHRR* 322.
[30] (1979) Series A, No. 31, and 2 *EHRR* 330.
[31] A Belgian Act of March 1987 amended "various legal provisions relating to affiliation", but see a judgment of the European Court of Human Rights in *Vermeire* v. *Belgium*, Nov. 1991, Series A, No. 214, which concerns the application of that law.

the *Johnston* case,[32] which found that the absence of any provisions for divorce under the Irish Constitution led to discrimination against children born to unmarried couples one or both of whom were already married, was catered for by the passage of the *Status of Children Act* in 1987.

The European Convention on the Legal Status of Children born out of Wedlock was drawn up for signing by the Council of Europe in August 1978. Eleven states have now ratified the Convention, including Ireland but not Belgium. It reiterates a principle which is, in fact, accepted by a large majority of European countries, that maternal affiliation of a child born out of wedlock shall be based solely on the fact of the birth of the child. Paternal affiliation, the Convention provides, shall be by voluntary recognition or judicial decision, while the obligation to maintain the child shall be no different from the case of legitimate offspring. Article 9 of the treaty refers specifically to the Marckx situation, in requiring that a child born out of wedlock shall have the same rights of succession in the estate of its parents or grandparents as if it had been born in wedlock.

The rights of children and their disagreement with their parents do not only concern the stability of the family, but may in other ways involve the physical, moral or mental integrity of the child. Numerous cases have arisen in the United Kingdom, and no doubt these are mirrored in other European states, where children aged sixteen or seventeen have been required to undergo medical or other treatment without their agreement, or have been unable to follow their own convictions because in the eyes of the law and the courts they are still children.[33]

Although mental maturity is invariably calculated by reference to age, and the accepted magic number seems to be eighteen, there appears lacking in domestic law any way of challenging that assumption, and it would seem unlikely that the European Court will find a solution, since it will always allow states a margin of discretion.

A series of problems can be envisaged in situations concerning the right to receive information, the freedom of association, or of thought, conscience and religion, where an almost adult child may

---

[32] (1987) Series A, No. 112, and 9 *EHRR* 203.
[33] A well-known example in Britain is *Gillick* v. *West Norfolk and Wisbech Area Health Authority*, [1985] 3 *All E.R.* 402.

experience unhappiness because of his parents' unorthodox views, and yet be unable, in practice, to receive help from either the state or the European Commission. Often these problems, though small in themselves, loom large for the individual concerned. In most states, where a parent's behaviour is deemed to be intolerable, the child may be awarded the protection of the Court, but in many instances the matter does not achieve such proportions, even though the mental or even physical suffering may be tremendous.

Similarly, the problem of child labour where, for example, the child is expected to work in a family business, has implications upon the mental and physical development of the child, but the matter is unlikely, except in severe cases, to reach the authorities, let alone the European Commission. Most children in family businesses are wholly dependent on their parents, and it is doubtful whether legislation or machinery for supervision will ever be totally effective. This area, like so many in the field of human rights, relies on long-term education and pattern-setting.

One aspect of the child's development in which the state does interfere is his education. Article 2 of the First Protocol says that no person shall be denied the right to education and that, in the exercise of any functions which it assumes in relation to education and teaching, the state shall respect the religious and philosophical convictions of the parents. The right of education does not, of course, only concern children, but it is in this context that it has mainly given rise to decisions in Strasbourg. In the *Linguistics* case against Belgium in 1968,[34] the Court considered the inter-relationship of the rights in the Convention with regard to education. It noted the negative formulation of the conception, but confirmed that the Article does guarantee a right to education, but not such a right as would require the Contracting Parties to establish at their own expense, or to subsidize, any particular type or level of education.[35]

All the States Parties to the Convention have an official educational system and Article 2 of the Protocol guarantees to persons under their jurisdiction the right, in principle, to avail themselves of the means of instruction existing at a given time. The right must also

[34] (1968) Series A, No. 8, and 1 *EHRR* 252.
[35] See also the Decisions of the Commission in Applications 6853/74, 9 *D&R* 27 and 7782/77, 14 *D&R* 179.

include official recognition of the results of education. A particular type of teaching or education may affect the home life of the child; for instance, in sparsely populated areas the child may have to leave home in order to attend school. States must be wary that such arrangements do not render them in breach of Article 8 of the Convention. Similarly, it is difficult for states to comply with the wishes of all parents. In the Belgian *Linguistics* case, French-speaking parents who resided in areas designated under Belgian linguistic laws as Dutch-speaking were prevented from sending their children to French speaking schools. This, they complained, disrupted their family life because the children spoke one language at school and another at home. It was also, they alleged, contrary to the second sentence of Article 2 of the Protocol, being out of conformity with the philosophical convictions of the parents. They failed to convince the Court that Article 2 included language, or that there was a severe enough interference with family life. The only point on which the Court held against Belgium, by eight votes to seven, was with respect to the complaint that French-speaking schools in a Brussels suburb were not permitted to accept pupils residing outside the area, whereas Dutch-speaking schools were. This was held to be unjustifiable on educational grounds and hence discriminatory, and a violation of Article 2 of the Protocol in conjunction with Article 14.

The wishes of parents arose again in the sex education cases, *Kjeldsen, Busk Madsen & Pedersen* v. *Denmark*.[36] The Danish Ministry of Education, in 1970, on the recommendation of a Committee of Experts set up by the Government, issued orders that sex education should be integrated into the teaching of compulsory subjects on the curriculum of state schools. The applicants, who were parents, objected that this was contrary to the second sentence of Article 2 of the Protocol, and also to Articles 8, 9 and 14.

The Court felt that the setting and planning of the curriculum fell within the competence of the state. It went on to say:

> This mainly involves questions of expediency on which it is not for the Court to rule and whose solution may legitimately vary according to the country and the era. In particular, the second sentence of Article 2 of the Protocol does not prevent states from imparting through teaching or

---

[36] (1976) Series A, No. 23, and 1 *EHRR* 711.

education, information or knowledge of a directly or indirectly religious or philosophical kind. It does not even permit parents to object to the integration of such teaching or education in the school curriculum, for otherwise all institutionalized teaching would run the risk of proving impracticable. In fact, it seems very difficult for many subjects taught at school not to have, to a greater or lesser extent, some philosophical complexion or implications...

The second sentence of Article 2 implies on the other hand that the state, in fulfilling the functions assumed by it in regard to education and teaching, must take care that information or knowledge included in the curriculum is conveyed in an objective, critical and pluralistic manner. The state is forbidden to pursue an aim of indoctrination that might be considered as not respecting parents' religious and philosophical convictions. That is the limit that must not be exceeded.

The Court found no violation of the Convention. Many states, including the United Kingdom, have seen fit to register reservations to Article 2 of the Protocol.

Corporal punishment of children was the subject matter of a case decided by the Court in 1982, brought to the Commission by two Scottish mothers in *Campbell and Cosans* v. *UK*.[37] Gordan Campbell and Jeffrey Cosans attended schools in Scotland where a leather strap (tawse) was used as a means of punishment. Mrs Campbell requested an assurance from her son's school that he would not be beaten in this way but her request was refused. In the case of Jeffrey Cosans, he was to have been punished for misbehaviour, but, on his father's advice, refused to accept the punishment. He was thereafter suspended from the school. The parents' allegation that such a punishment was inhuman or degrading was dismissed by the Court, mainly on the ground that neither of the boys had in fact been beaten. The Court did agree with the applicants, however, that the second Article of Protocol 1 had been violated. As we have seen, this Article requires not only that no person shall be denied the right to education but also that the state shall respect the right of parents to the extent that such education and treatment as is provided shall be in conformity with their own religious and philosophical convictions. The Court rejected the Government's assertion that internal school administration in such matters as discipline did not amount

---

[37] (1982) Series A, No. 48, and 4 *EHRR* 293.

to "philosophical convictions", but felt that corporal punishment was used as an integral part of the process "... whereby a school seeks to achieve the object for which it was established, including the development and moulding of the character and mental powers of its pupils". The Court went on to decide that not only was the use of corporal punishment by schools a violation of Article 2 of the Protocol, but that in the present case the suspension from school of Jeffrey Cosans was a violation of the right to education. *Campbell and Cosans* led to the eventual banning of corporal punishment in state schools in the United Kingdom. The cases of *Y* and *Costello-Roberts* have sought to extend the ban to private schools, but in its judgment in the latter case of March 1993 a narrow majority of the Court was of the view that the punishment inflicted on Jeremy Costello-Roberts was not severe enough to invoke a violation of Article 3.[38]

In the *Tyrer* case[39] the Court, with a dissenting judgment from Sir Gerald Fitzmaurice, held that three strokes of a birch administered to a fifteen-year-old schoolboy was degrading punishment. This has led to some comment that Article 3 is being trivialized, and it may be that the Court has decided that it must draw a line. Nevertheless, the problem of mistreatment of children, "baby-battering", and sexual, mental and physical abuse, are constantly cause for concern. The Swedish Code of Parenthood *(Föraldrabalken)*, as amended in 1979, reads in Section 3 of Chapter 6:

> A custodian shall exercise the necessary supervision over the child with due regard to the child's age and other circumstances.
>
> The child shall not be subjected to corporal punishment or any other form of humiliating treatment.

Various attempts to extend this approach to the United Kingdom and to other European countries may be observed.[40]

---

[38] The cases are also interesting with regard to the Government's legislative obligations under the Convention. In the case of *Y* a majority of the Commission was again of the opinion that there had been a violation, but the Court, in November 1992, approved a friendly settlement whereby, without admitting liability under the Convention, it made an *ex gratia* payment of £8,000 plus costs to the applicant.

[39] 1978, Series A, No. 26, and 2 *EHRR* 1.

[40] A notable recent example is the 1992 Report 135 on Family Law by the Scottish Law Commission, paras. 267-2105.

MARRIAGE AND FOUNDING A FAMILY

The Convention's provisions on the right to marry illustrate as clearly as those of any other Article the need for a background standard as an aid to interpretation. "Men and women of marriageable age", Article 12 reads, "have the right to marry and to found a family, according to the national laws governing the exercise of this right". The Convention contains no guide, however, as to the scope within which these national laws may operate. In the four preceding Articles, the Convention lists those circumstances in which the national authorities may interfere, but most of these would be inappropriate to the right to marry. The restrictions which may be imposed on marriage must obviously be such as not to strike at the essence of the right itself; for instance, a national law which prohibited marriage until after the normal age of child-bearing would make a nonsense of the Convention. There must therefore be an acceptable norm to which "marriageable age" will conform. An Application, which complained that marriage to a twelve-year-old girl was illegal under British law, whereas it was allowed under Muslim law, was easily rejected.[41]

The Universal Declaration is more detailed in its approach. Article 16 of that document states:

> (1) Men and women of full age,[42] without any limitation due to race, nationality or religion, have the right to marry and to found a family. They are entitled to equal rights as to marriage, during marriage and at its dissolution.
>
> (2) Marriages shall be entered into only with the free and full consent of the intending spouses.

Article 5 of Protocol 7 adds to the European Convention's protection of marriage, by providing:

> Spouses shall enjoy equality of rights and responsibilities of a private law character between them, and in their relations with their children, as to

---

[41] *Janis Khan* v. *UK*, Application 11579/85, 48 *D&R* 253.
[42] Article 23 of the Covenant reverts to "marriageable age".

marriage, during marriage and in the event of its dissolution. This article shall not prevent states from taking such measures as are necessary in the interests of the children.

Not all States Members have ratified this Protocol, however,[43] and Article 5 does not feature in the jurisprudence.

The Commission is therefore correct in holding that national laws regulating and recognising the act of marriage are to be complied with, and should not in themselves be characterized as limiting freedom to marry. An applicant who considered himself married if he read a particular verse of the Old Testament to his intended spouse, was required also to follow the formalities prescribed by German law.[44] Similarly, the Commission has held the view that such requisite formalities are not to be regarded as restricting one's freedom of expression.[45] The Commission has been reluctant to accept that laws or practices which discourage marriage or make it difficult should be characterized as a violation of Article 12. So where, for example, a German national deported from Switzerland alleged that this prevented his marriage to a Swiss girl the Commission rejected the Application, since it had been shown no evidence as to why she could not follow him to Germany.[46] Similarly, loss of a disability pension upon marriage does not in fact *prevent* marriage,[47] nor do tax liabilities which make it cheaper to live together unmarried.[48] Article 14 requires that the rights in the Convention shall be enjoyed without discrimination, but it would seem that rights and benefits which may accrue to married couples and which are not available to single persons, can be justified as encouraging marriage and the foundation of a family even though there is no obligation on states to take positive action to legislate in this manner.

National restrictions on the right of prisoners to marry have been troublesome. Initially, the Commission was of the view that inability to marry was an inherent limitation on prisoners but subsequently

---

[43] In 1992 only thirteen states had ratified Protocol 7, while seven other states had signed.

[44] Application 6167/73, *X* v. *Federal Republic of Germany,* 1 *D&R* 64.

[45] See Application 11579/85, note 41, *supra.*

[46] Application 7031/75, *X* v. *Switzerland,* 6 *D&R* 124.

[47] Application 10503/83, *Kleine Staarman* v. *Netherlands,* 42 *D&R* 162.

[48] Application 11089/84, *D. G. and D. W. Lindsay* v. *UK,* 49 *D&R* 181.

they were convinced that this was the wrong approach in two cases against the British Government, *Hamer*[49] and *Draper*.[50] One of the reasons behind the Commission's initial stance, reflected in its earlier decisions, was that prison life precluded cohabitation or the exercise of Article 12. In the *Hamer* case, however, it stated in its Report: "The essence of the right to marry . . . is the formation of a legally binding association between a man and a woman. It is for them to decide whether or not they wish to enter such an association in circumstances where they cannot cohabit." As regards the exercise of conjugal rights by prisoners, the Commission has expressed its sympathy for prisoners denied visits or leave for such, but has concluded that states must be entitled to prohibit them on the grounds of good order or security.[51] It is to be noted, however, that an increasing number of European countries are providing for conjugal visits.

In the *Marckx* case the Commission and the Court rejected the notion that Article 12 implied the right not to marry, and in *Johnston* v. *Ireland*,[52] the Court held that the right to marry did not impose an obligation on the Irish Government to allow divorce so as to enable Mr Johnston, with the consent of his wife, to marry the woman with whom he lived and who had borne his child.

The Commission and Court have needed to define what is meant by "marriage", and up to the present time have been unwilling to countenance marriage between persons of the same sex. Several applications have been received from transsexuals who, having undergone treatment and surgery to change sex, have then encountered a refusal by the authorities to recognize their new status. In the *Rees* case,[53] the Court's judgment, in considering Rees' complaint that this refusal had the effect of denying him the right to marry, stated that Article 12 refers to the traditional marriage between persons of the opposite biological sex, since the wording of the Article made it clear to the Court that marriage is to be protected as the basis of the family.

Although this may have been the intention of the Parties when the Convention was drafted, it may be worthwhile to question whether procreation is an essential purpose of marriage, since many

---

[49] Application 7114/75, 10 *D&R* 174 and 21 *YB* 302, and 24 *D&R* 5 and 24 *YB* 464.
[50] Application 8186/78, 24 *D&R* 72.
[51] Application 8166/78, *X and Y* v. *Switzerland*, 13 *D&R* 241.
[52] (1987) Series A, No. 112, and 9 *EHRR* 203.
[53] *Rees* v. *UK*, (1986) Series A, No. 106, and 9 *EHRR* 56.

married couples now take advantage of modern birth-control techniques to avoid having children. If the Convention is to be applied as a dynamic instrument, then the advances of modern medicine and changes in social patterns should be taken into account in its interpretation. It must also be noted that the Court in *Cossey*, another transsexual case against the United Kingdom[54] allowed itself room for manoeuvre on this point in the future. In 1992, the Court held that France was in violation of Article 8 of the Convention in refusing to recognize the reassigned gender of Miss B.,[55] but her allegations under Article 12 were not considered because of her failure to exhaust local remedies on this point.

The view generally taken by the Strasbourg organs is that the right to marry and found a family is *one* right, and not two. As we have seen above, this has led to complications over the interpretation of "marriage". With regard to the second part of the right in Article 12 - the founding of a family - the Commission has accepted that although adoption may in some cases have that effect,[56] it is only in fact the case where the adoption is sought by a couple. Adoption by a homosexual couple would be outside the provisions of the Article, as was an attempt by a man to adopt his nephew.[57] A one-parent family, once it has been established, would be protected, as we shall see below, by Article 8 of the Convention.

FAMILY LIFE

In post-war human rights treaties the rights of the individual with respect to his family relations have been singled out from social and economic rights and dealt with as civil and political rights. This is explained by the perceived importance of the family as a unit of society, as part of the institution of the modern state. The family varies, of course, from society to society and history demonstrates its changing role. Even within Europe one sees a spectrum ranging from the large multi-generation, extended family to the nuclear

---

[54] (1990) Series A, No. 184 and 13 *EHRR* 622.

[55] *B.* v. *France*, Series A, No. 232–C.

[56] For example, Application 8896/80, *X* v. *Netherlands*, 24 *D&R* 176.

[57] Application 7229/75, *X and Y* v. *UK*, 12 *D&R* 32. In this case, however, the adoptee was living with his family in India and there was an implication that the proposed adoption was to facilitate his immigration.

unit of the industrialized Western nations. The one-parent family, too, is recognized by most states, and by the European Court of Human Rights, as an important form of the family group. Article 16 of the Universal Declaration of Human Rights refers to the family as the "... natural and fundamental group unit of society ... entitled to protection by society and the state." We must remember, however, that we are concerned with the rights of individuals, and that sometimes the rights of the family and those of its members are in conflict. Not on every occasion can the state settle family discord, nor is it right for it to imagine that it should try. As in the case of the rights of children, we are seeking to determine those areas in which the state *should* interfere. Article 8 of the Convention includes respect for family life and the home, but what is important in this area is to highlight the exceptions to non-intervention. Paragraph 2 outlines what state interference may be justified, and it reads:

> There shall be no interference by a public authority with the exercise of this right except such as is in accordance with the law and is necessary in a democratic society in the interests of national security, public safety or the economic well-being of the country, for the prevention of disorder or crime, for the protection of health or morals, or for the protection of the rights and freedoms of others.

In practice, it is not difficult to find examples of state intervention which fit uneasily into the Paragraph 2 exceptions but which have been accepted by generations of individuals and are, therefore, resistant to question. In *Brüggeman and Scheuten*, the German abortion case, Professor Fawcett, in his dissenting opinion, argued[58] that where the Government wished to change the law, even if as in this case the effects were to liberalize the position of individuals, the Commission, if asked, should examine the new legislation in the light of Paragraph 2 of Article 8 and not in relation to already accepted norms. The family is an ever-changing concept, but since it is recognized as a unit of society, it must be assumed that it can look after itself. Any intervention should be for the purpose and effect of respect for family life, with the aim of the better working of that institution and should in all cases represent a pressing social need.

---

[58] Application 6959/75, 10 *D&R* 100, at p. 118, and 21 *YB* 638.

Family life may be threatened where the acts of one member of the family come into conflict with the state. Where an individual wishes to enter a country to join his family, or where he is deported against his wish, leaving his family behind, there is a threat to family life. Some national courts have given weight to Article 8 as restricting domestic law concerning expulsion. In 1959 the Bavarian Constitutional Court said that ". . . if the composition and unity of the family are imperilled, the interests of family protection must take precedence over other public interests." Taken to extremes, however, this policy could amount, in many cases, to an excessive limitation on expulsion and similarly, on a state's discretion as to which aliens it wishes to enter its country.

The Commission has asked the question whether or not the family unit could be established in the country to which the member of the family has been expelled, or whether the individual himself has not been responsible for breaking up the family by entering a foreign country. In Application 2535/65[59] the applicant, who was the wife of an Austrian citizen, complained that her husband's deportation from Germany on account of his numerous convictions, was in violation of Article 8. The Commission held that the applicant had the possibility to leave Germany with her husband and live with him in Austria and that, therefore, the application was ill-founded. There is no right, outside Protocol 4, which has been ratified by only seventeen states, to enter a country, and an individual cannot normally claim that, having entered a country of his own free will, the state is in violation of Article 8 in not allowing his family to join him. If there is doubt as to whether the family can be established elsewhere and the immigration was forced upon the individual against his will, then the Commission will explore the merits of the application closely. In the *East African Asian* cases,[60] the Commission was faced with hundreds of applications from persons who were holders of British passports, and who were either citizens of the United Kingdom and Colonies or British Protected Persons, and, not being citizens of Kenya or Uganda, sought entry into the United Kingdom. In three cases,[61] the applicants additionally alleged that they were not being

---

[59] *X v. Federal Republic of Germany,* 17 *D&R* 28.
[60] 36 *CD* 92 and 13 *YB* 928.
[61] 20 *YB* 642 at 644.

allowed to join their wives and children who were already in this country. In these cases the Commission held that there was a violation of Article 8, of itself, and also taken in conjunction with Article 14 (freedom from discrimination). The Commission's view seems to be that where parents already have their residence in one country, children should be allowed to join them, and it will not reject such an application on the grounds that the father could establish the family unit by leaving the country to join his child.

In the case of *Abdulaziz, Cabales and Balkandali* which concerned the United Kingdom,[62] three foreign wives, lawfully settled in Britain, complained because their husbands were not allowed to join them. The Court in its judgment followed the line always taken by the Commission and reiterated that respect for family life does not mean that couples have a right to set up home anywhere, irrespective of immigration laws. In this case, however, had the husbands been settled in Britain, then their wives would have been able to join them and the Court held that although there was not a violation of Article 8, the discriminatory treatment activated Article 14.

In the same case, the British Government had argued that Article 8 refers to respect for an already existing family life, and not to an obligation to allow such a relationship to develop. The Court rejected this view. Although the Article generally presupposed the existence of a family, "... this does not mean that all intended family life falls entirely outside its ambit. Whatever the word 'family' may mean", said the Court, "it must at any rate include the relationship that arises from a lawful and genuine marriage ..." Similarly, in the *Marckx* case, which we have discussed above, and the *Johnston* case, the Court interpreted Article 8 to mean more than merely non-interference by the Government, but as an obligation to take positive action. In these cases, this meant legislation to readjust the status of illegitimate children and thereby prevent distortion in family life.

The Strasbourg organs have taken a broad view of "family", by adopting an autonomous, *de facto* interpretation. Usually, it is necessary to show that some legal or blood relationship exists and that an element of dependency is clear. Nevertheless, on those occasions where there might be resistance, *prima facie*, to characterising a unit as a family, for example in the case of homosexual marriage, it is still

---

[62] (1985) Series A, No. 94, and 7 *EHRR* 471.

possible to apply the same Article on the basis that it demands respect for "private life".

The Commission will examine applications alleging disruption of family life to see whether there is already a close relationship between the members. Thus, for instance, where an uncle and niece could not show that they had lived in the same household, it was held that the relationship was not sufficiently close. Usually, breach in family life has been claimed by husband, wife and children and the Commission has viewed carefully, and usually unfavourably, claims on behalf of grandparents and parents-in-law. As we have noted, questions of migration from one country to another can raise complex economic and social problems for the states concerned. It would seem that, in respect to immigration at least, the right to family unity is not always easy to guarantee.

CHAPTER FIVE

The Individual in the Community

To many people the idea of human rights involves the right "to do their own thing", the right to be different and to lead their lives the way they would choose. To some, however, the important thing may be the need, despite some impediment, to be treated the same as others. Such choice, it may be maintained, is a necessary concomitant of the right to live and be free – what the framers of the American Declaration of Independence dubbed "the pursuit of happiness" and what Article 22 of the Universal Declaration means when it refers to the free development of personality.

The European Convention does not talk of the right of personality but particularly within Articles 8 to 11 are found the rights which go towards the fulfilment of personal hopes, aspirations and ideals. Article 8 of the Convention requires respect for private and family life, home and correspondence. Articles 9 and 10 guarantee the freedom of thought, conscience and religion and the freedom of expression, while Article 11 secures the right to meet with others and predicates the dissemination of these ideas and thoughts.

There are necessarily restrictions on these particularly personal rights, especially where the manifestation of individual wishes clashes with the rights of other persons. The state has a responsibility both to its citizens and to the international community to govern and to keep the peace. The democratic ideal upon which the European Convention professes to have been built means that the authorities need to pay attention to the wishes of the people and, in most cases the majority of the people, in legislating for and administering the country. Within each of those rights protected in Articles 8 to 11, therefore, the balance between the rights of the individual and those of the other members of the community must be struck. Into this equation must also be fed the perceived nature of the particular state and, furthermore, its integration into a unified, "like-minded" Europe.

As we have explored in the previous Chapter, the European Convention is nowadays seen as a dynamic instrument and especially as one which must reflect the ideas and morals of late-twentieth-century Europe. Although it may be remarked that a principle of treaty interpretation requires that the intention of the Parties upon signing is respected, recent decisions of both the Commission and the Court seem to be based on the assumption that the Contracting Parties signed in the full knowledge that ideas and morals would change and that the meaning of the Convention would keep pace. There were, at first, obvious dangers in this approach but now that the Convention and its machinery are part of the fabric of Europe it would be too limiting to apply the social and moral norms of the 1940s, and to do so would be to subject the Convention to contempt.

SEXUALITY

In the eyes of most individuals sexuality may be one of the major factors in determining personality, and it is notable that in this area the Commission and Court in their interpretation of the Convention reflect the development of European thinking and behaviour.

In a very early decision the Commission took the view that the punishment of male homosexual behaviour was in order, for the protection of health or morals.[1] Again, twenty years later but with much more careful scrutiny, it believed that such prohibition was justified in the case of persons below the age of twenty-one, for the protection of the rights and freedoms of others.[2] It rejected the claim that the difference in treatment between male and female homosexuals was a violation of Article 14. The social danger posed by male homosexuality was, it stated, greater than that of lesbianism. In 1982 the Commission also refused to admit a complaint that prohibition of homosexual activities among seventeen-year-olds damaged their personalities.[3] Nevertheless, the Commission and the Court had taken note that attitudes towards consenting male homosexuals over the age of twenty-one had changed and in 1981, in the *Dudgeon* case,[4] the Court upheld a complaint that the law in Northern Ireland which prohibited all male homosexual intercourse was a violation of

[1] Application 104/55, 1 *YB* 235.
[2] *X* v. *UK*, 7215/75, 11 *D&R* 36, 3 *EHRR* 63.
[3] Application 9721/82, 7 *EHRR* 145.
[4] (1981) Series A, No. 45, and 4 *EHRR* 149.

Article 8. This was reaffirmed in the *Norris* case which concerned the Republic of Ireland.[5] In that case the Court expressed the view that although, in general, states were allowed a wide margin of appreciation when it came to morals, the fact that the law against homosexuals was not enforced indicated that there was no pressing social need, which was a prerequisite for interference under Article 8(2).[6]

The cases on homosexuality demonstrate that the authorities are under an obligation to respect private life and may interfere only according to the conditions laid down in the Convention. In a series of cases concerning transsexuals the judgments of the Court confirm, however, that the responsibility of the state "to respect" under Article 8 stretches beyond mere non-interference. All the cases concerned an individual who had undergone gender reassignment surgery. In each of the countries involved - Belgium, the United Kingdom and France - it was shown that there was no restriction on such surgery and the respective Governments argued that, accordingly, Article 8 had not been violated. In the opinion of the Court and of the Commission before it, however, Article 8 also contains positive obligations, with the result that the state should not only not impede the sex-change operations but also must take steps to ensure that the new sex receives appropriate legal recognition. In the first case, *Rees*, which concerned the United Kingdom,[7] the applicant complained that under English law he was unable to change the particulars entered in his birth certificate and that that document was, in practice, required for a large number of transactions entailing identification. One such occasion was emphasized by the other case against the United Kingdom, the *Cossey* case.[8] Miss Cossey, who had undergone gender reassignment surgery, wished to marry and for this purpose reference to her birth certificate, on which she was registered male, was necessary. The European Court, nevertheless, accepted the United Kingdom's argument that as the birth certificate was a record of facts at the time of birth the authorities were under no obligation, under Article 8, to allow it to be amended. The Court recognized the inconsistencies involved, however, and stressed that

---

[5] (1988) Series A, No. 142, and 13 *EHRR* 186.

[6] Neither could the non-enforcement of the Statute be used to argue that homosexuals were not "victims".

[7] (1986) Series A, No. 106, and 9 *EHRR* 56.

[8] (1990) Series A, No. 184, and 13 *EHRR* 622.

the need for appropriate legal measures in this area should be kept under review.[9] An even more recent case against France, decided in 1992,[10] recognized that the situation in France should be distinguished from that in Britain in so far as it was almost impossible for Miss B. to change her first name of Norbert and that the National Identification Register was a current record of civil status which could be amended without too much difficulty. In this case, therefore, a violation of Article 8 was held to have occurred.

PRIVATE LIFE

In determining whether there has been a violation of respect for private life the Strasbourg organs have a difficult task. First of all, the private life and the wishes of the individual will necessarily encroach upon the life of the community as a whole. A Government, having decided that a particular activity warrants respect under Article 8(1), then has to determine how far it has a responsibility to interfere with this right in the interests of societal control.

In 1974 a resident of Reykjavik complained to the Commission of an Icelandic law which forbade the keeping of dogs. The Commission's view was that Article 8 did not stretch as far as protecting the right to keep a dog.[11]

A British applicant alleged that Article 8 had been violated when she was photographed by the police while demonstrating against apartheid at a rugby match. The Commission rejected her complaint, remarking that this was a public occasion which she visited voluntarily and was not therefore to be classified as private life.

Some ancient races believe that the camera, by taking a photograph, captures the soul. How far should their views be respected in modern society? How far indeed does Article 8 protect you from being spied upon, watched or harassed? Can it prevent attacks on your reputation, on your physical or mental integrity, or your moral or intellectual freedom? In short, how far does the Convention protect what is commonly referred to as privacy?

---

[9] Under English law, and in accordance with the European jurisprudence, Miss (Mr) Cossey could not marry another man nor was it the applicant's inclination to marry a woman.

[10] *B.* v. *France,* (1992) Series A, No. 232–C.

[11] Application 6825/74, 5 *D&R* 86, and 19 *YB* 342.

We have already mentioned the application of *Brüggemann and Scheuten* against Germany.[12] It will be recalled that the two women who brought that application, relating to the restrictions placed on the law of abortion in Germany, alleged that the right to an abortion was an aspect of their private life and their right to self-determination. Despite a persuasive dissenting opinion from Professor Fawcett, the majority of the Commission was of the view that not every termination of pregnancy was a matter *solely* of the private life of the mother, and that there was not, therefore, a violation of the Convention.

The difficulties of balancing the wishes of the individual and those of the community as a whole are not to be underestimated and may be seen to encapsulate the major decision-making complexity of human rights law. That complexity involves, for instance, the question of how far the state should interfere in morals. It must be assumed that the usual aim of legislators is for a quiet life for themselves, the administrators and the law-enforcement officers. They legislate, in a democracy, to allow maximum freedom consonant with the good of the community as a whole as they see it. A Dutch court rejected a plea that a law requiring the wearing of seat-belts in vehicles was contrary to Article 8. Jay-walking across a busy street may well be a danger to other road-users but how far is a refusal to wear a seat-belt in a car more a matter of personal choice? Does the risk of lung cancer caused by passive smoking justify the banning of smoking in public places? Indeed, many of the arguments raised in favour of the decriminalization of certain drugs feature the right of the individual to private life. Do the expense and trauma of picking up the pieces of ruined lives, in those few cases where no other persons are involved, justify intervention and the prohibition of activities which some individuals believe are imperative to the full development of their personalities? Given the recognition that a particular activity is part of private life there may still be occasions where interference is called for. The Commission and the Court have found such questions hard to answer and initially they referred constantly, by excessive use of the "margin of appreciation" doctrine, to national standards or, later, European norms. The approach now taken seems to be that much of the onus is on the state to show

---

[12] Application 6959/75, 5 *D&R* 103, 10 *D&R* 100 and 21 *YB* 638. See above, Chapter 4.

that the interference is proportionate to the mischief it purports to counter and that it is "... necessary in a democratic society".

Concern about mis-use of electronically-stored data has increased in proportion to the development of technology able to process the information. A mountain of unsolicited mail, carefully planned to match the recipient's interests, hobbies or bank balance, can soon raise the suspicions of the even most laid-back individual. Many of the individual's anxieties as to the use to which such information may be put are often instigated by private individuals and institutions and are not the direct responsibility of governments. One might speculate, however, as to what extent the Convention might be used to ensure that the release of such information is regulated, and how far governments are under a duty to legislate.

The cases that have come before the Commission and the Court involve use which has been made, or might be made, of official records. In the *Leander* case concerning Sweden[13] the applicant was dismissed from temporary employment as a museum technician at a naval museum, and prevented from taking up permanent employment on the basis that he was a security risk. Information to this effect had been supplied from a secret police register. The Court in this case, as in many others involving national security, allowed the Swedish authorities a wide margin of appreciation and held that Article 8 had not been violated.[14]

The *Gaskin* case, involving the United Kingdom, concerned the accumulated records of Mr Gaskin's childhood and youth in care. In that case the confidentiality claimed by the authorities was for the protection of the contributors of the information, many of whom were unwilling for their comments to be made public, and other participants who could not be found. The Commission considered that respect for private life "... requires that everyone should be able to establish details of their identity as individual human beings", but saw that there was a difficult balance here between the rights of the applicant and of those who had compiled the reports. The Court

---

[13] (1987) Series A, No. 116, and 9 *EHRR* 433.

[14] The *Leander* case also alleged violation of Article 10 (freedom of expression), but this was equally unsuccessful. Similar cases on Article 10, involving Communist party connections, include those of *Glasenapp* v. *Federal Republic of Germany*, (1986) Series A, No. 104, and 9 *EHRR* 25, and *Kosiek* v. *Federal Republic of Germany*, (1986) Series A, No. 105, and 9 *EHRR* 328.

decided that the failure of the state to develop procedures whereby the files could be available to the applicant constituted a violation of a positive obligation of the state under Article 8.

Applications involving surveillance, interception of mail and telecommunications have also featured in the jurisprudence of the Court.

The *Klass* case,[15] which was referred to the Court in 1978, concerned surveillance and interception of mail and telecommunications in Germany. The applicants, a group of lawyers, complained that legislation passed in 1968 restricted the right of secrecy of mail, post and telecommunications in that it authorized surveillance, in certain circumstances, without the need for informing the person concerned. The Court was in no doubt that such a procedure was contrary to Article 8, but the cardinal issue was whether the interference was justified under Paragraph 2. That Paragraph, emphasized the Court, must be narrowly interpreted. It was of the opinion that "Powers of secret surveillance of citizens, characterising as they do the police state, are tolerable under the Convention only in so far as strictly necessary for safeguarding the democratic institutions". The Court felt that, in view of the threat posed to democracy nowadays by highly sophisticated forms of espionage and by terrorism, some powers of secret surveillance were necessary. Whatever system is employed, however, there must exist adequate and effective guarantees against abuse. After examining the German legislation the Court came to the conclusion that no breach of Article 8 could be found.

In the *Malone* case,[16] however, a breach of Article 8 *was* found. Mr Malone was suspected of handling stolen goods and, in accordance with the procedures in force, his telephone was tapped by the police, and in addition all his calls were "metered". The Court was not satisfied that these procedures were satisfactory and was of the opinion that:

... the law of England and Wales does not indicate with reasonable clarity the scope and manner of exercise of the relevant discretion conferred on the public authorities. To that extent, the minimum degree of legal

[15] (1978) Series A, No. 28, and 1 *EHRR* 214.
[16] (1984) Series A, No. 82, and 7 *EHRR* 14.

protection to which citizens are entitled under the rule of law in a democratic society is lacking.[17]

Similar violations have been held against France in the cases of *Kruslin* and *Huvig*.[18]

The right to do as you please within the privacy of your own home and without encroaching upon others raises the matter of "home", also to be respected under Article 8, and the peaceful enjoyment of your possessions protected under Article 1 of the First Protocol.

In the few cases that have been brought under Article 8 regarding the right to a home, it can be seen that the restrictions listed in Article 8(2) loom large. For instance, interference "... for the prevention of disorder or crime" will, on most occasions, justify the searching of property. Mr Chappell, who ran a video exchange club in Frome, found his house being searched by seventeen persons. Some of them were policemen executing a search warrant and looking for pornographic videos, the rest were acting on behalf of film companies who had obtained an Anton Pillar Order to look for copyright infringements. The European Court, although it criticized some particulars of the search operation, such as the numbers involved, found that both the procedures were justified under the listed limitation.[19] Irregularities in carrying out searches and the like will often be discovered by the local courts, and it would seem that the right not to be trespassed upon in this way will only rarely be the subject of successful applications to Strasbourg. Mrs Arrondelle was disturbed by the noise of low-flying aircraft and of the M23 motorway, occasioned by the increased use of Gatwick Airport. In the application she brought to the Commission the British Government argued that it was necessary in modern democratic societies to maintain an adequate number of airports with road links in order to serve public needs. This also provided work for many people in the area and relatively few were inconvenienced by it. Nevertheless, the Government was unable to consider all those affected and, although it

---

[17] *Supra*, note 16, para. 79. The case led to the *Interception of Communications Act* 1985, (c. 56).

[18] (1990) Series A, No. 176–B, and 12 *EHRR* 528 and 547.

[19] *Chappell* v. *UK*, (1989) Series A, No. 152, and 12 *EHRR* 1.

denied that there had been a violation of the Convention agreed to pay Mrs Arrondelle some compensation in a friendly settlement.[20]

Mr and Mrs Gillow were deprived of their home altogether. They built a house on Guernsey in 1958. Two years later Mr Gillow took a job with the FAO and they spent the next eighteen years employed overseas, while renting their furnished house to tenants. On his retirement they proposed to move back to Guernsey but discovered that new legislation enacted during their absence deprived them of a licence to live on the island in their house. The Court was of the view that because Mr and Mrs Gillow had left their furniture in the house and had no other place to live it could be deemed their "home" for the purposes of Article 8. The Court thought, however, that the restriction on the granting of residence licences was a legitimate aim in the economic interests of the island. Nevertheless, in this case, although the legislation was acceptable to the Court, it was unhappy about the way in which it had been applied and held that there had been a violation of the Convention.[21]

POSSESSIONS

An important aspect of living your life as you would choose may be the right to enjoy and take full advantage of your possessions. The right to property has proved, however, particularly sensitive. In the case of the United Nations Covenants the right is omitted altogether even though the Universal Declaration states:[22] "Everyone has the right to own property alone as well as in association with others". We have commented earlier on the contentious nature of the debates in the Council of Europe concerning this right, and on the fact that agreement was not reached in time to include it in the Convention. Ultimately, the right appeared as Article 1 of the First Protocol in the form: "Every natural or legal person is entitled to the peaceful enjoyment of his possessions".

In the *Van der Mussele* case, which we consider in more detail later in this chapter, the applicant alleged that the failure of the authorities to pay him for his services in defending impecunious persons as

---

[20] Application 7889/77, 19 *D&R* 186, 26 *D&R* 5, and 23 *YB* 166.
[21] *Gillow* v. *UK*, (1986) Series A, No. 109, and 11 *EHRR* 335.
[22] Article 17.

part of the legal aid scheme deprived him of his property. The Court was not convinced by this since there had not even been an assessment of fees and it was difficult to treat such unknown sums as Mr Van Mussele's property. It showed more interest with respect to his out-of-pocket expenses but these were not sufficiently large to persuade the Court to hold that Article 1 of Protocol 1 was invoked. Ms Marckx and her daughter raised the same Article with regard to the impediments which Belgian law placed in the way of illegitimate children's right to inherit property. Although the mother could properly complain that she had been denied the right to dispose of her property by Will, her daughter had no such right to *acquire* property. In the same way, the Commission has tended to restrict rights in pensions to schemes involving distribution of a share of the profits of funds already contributed, and not to those based solely on community responsibility.[23]

In *Van Marle et al.* v. *Netherlands*[24] Dutch legislation to reform the accountancy profession deprived the applicants of the right to call themselves accountants. The Court held that the interference in this case was justified in the interests of regulating the profession but that the "goodwill" which had been built up over a number of years constituted a "possession" for the purposes of Article 1.

Similarly, the revocation of a licence to indulge in some economic activity may involve the deprivation of property if there was a legitimate expectation that the grant would be continued. In *Tre Traktörer Aktiebolag* v. *Sweden*[25] the applicant's restaurant was so reliant on the renewal of a licence to serve alcohol that the licence was deemed to be a "possession" and could only be revoked for failure to comply with its conditions.

Article 1 of Protocol 1 goes on to provide that you may be deprived of your possessions only in the public interest and subject to the conditions provided for by law and by the general principles of international law. It also, in Paragraph 2, states that none of this shall impair the right of states to control the use of property in accordance

[23] For example, Application 4130/69, 38 *CD* 9, and 14 *YB* 224, Application 5763/72, 45 *CD* 76, and 16 *YB* 274, Application 10094/82, 38 *D&R* 84, Application 7624/76, 19 *D&R* 100, Application 7995/77, 15 *D&R* 198, Application 9776/82, 34 *D&R* 153.

[24] (1986) Series A, No. 101, and 8 *EHRR* 483.

[25] (1989) Series A, No. 159, and 13 *EHRR* 309.

with the general interest or to secure the payment of taxes or other contributions or penalties. Very often the distinction between deprivation and control of use is hard to draw. In a case against Sweden – *Sporrong and Lönnroth* [26] – the applicants claimed that the wide powers of expropriation enjoyed by the city of Stockholm had blighted their property, and thus interfered with the enjoyment of their possessions. In this case the Court agreed. Similarly, in farm consolidation schemes introduced by the Austrian authorities and which provided for the provisional transfer of land, the Court felt that the inflexibility of the schemes and the uncertainty as to the final fate of the applicants' property violated Article 1. [27]

It will be seen that in this way it is not always easy to distinguish between deprivation and control, and indeed the Court has recognized that a wide discretion must be left to the authorities. The use of the terms "public interest" and "general interest" is obviously wider than "necessary in a democratic society" and, indeed, unless the interferences are discriminatory (contrary to Article 14) or imposed with ulterior motives (outlawed by Article 18), the margin of appreciation might seem unlimited. In the *James* case [28] the Court said:

> ... the notion of "public interest" is necessarily extensive ... the decision to enact laws expropriating property will commonly involve considerations of political, economic and social issues on which opinions within a democratic society may reasonably differ widely. The Court, finding it natural that the margin of appreciation available to the legislature in implementing social and economic policies should be a wide one, will respect the legislature's judgment as to what is "in the public interest" unless that judgment be manifestly without reasonable foundation.

In its judgments, however, the Court has introduced the concept of proportionality, stating that some notion of fair balance should be struck ". . . between the demands of the general interest of the community and the requirements of the individual's fundamental

---

[26] (1982) Series A, No. 52, and 5 *EHRR* 35.

[27] *Erkner and Hofauer* v. *Austria* and *Poiss* v. *Austria*, (1987) Series A, No. 117, and 9 *EHRR* 464, 10 *EHRR* 231 respectively.

[28] (1986) Series A, No. 98 and 8 *EHRR* 123, para 46.

rights".[29] It cannot find this balance if the person concerned has had to bear, "... an individual and excessive burden."

In *Lithgow et al* v. *UK*,[30] seven applicants, most of them companies registered and incorporated in Britain, alleged that the compensation awarded to them as a consequence of the nationalization of the aircraft and shipbuilding industries was inadequate and discriminatory. They were not successful in persuading the Court, even though the Government had expressed the view at a late stage that some of the terms of compensation were unfair to some companies. In this case it was also argued by the applicants that Paragraph 1 of Article 1 which subjects deprivation to "the general principles of international law" meant that the compensation should be "prompt, adequate and effective." The Court's response, however, was that this was limited to the nationalization of non-nationals' property and that the ensuing discrimination was justified by the non-national's inferior political position.

In *James et al* v. *UK*, James and other trustees of the second Duke of Westminster complained that the Leasehold Reform Act of 1967, which allowed long-leaseholders to buy the freehold of property at a low valuation and then to realize the true value, was a violation of their right to enjoy their possessions. Again the Court respected the Government's reform policies and stated that it was for Parliament to assess the advantages and disadvantages involved in the various legislative alternatives available. In answer to the question whether it was "in the public interest" to transfer property from one individual to another, the Court was of the view that

> The taking of property in pursuance of a policy calculated to enhance social justice within the community can properly be described as being "in the public interest".[31]

---

[29] See, for example, *Sporrong and Lönnroth* v. *Sweden*, (1982) Series A, No. 52, para. 69. *Lithgow et al* v. *UK*, (1986) Series A, No. 102, and 8 *EHRR* 329 at para 120.

[30] *Supra*, note 29.

[31] *James et al* v. *UK*, (1986) Series A, No. 98 para. 41, also para 45. In *AGOSI* v. *UK* (1986) Series A, No. 108, and 9 *EHRR* 1, the Court differed from the Commission on the question of proportionality.

WORK

An important ingredient in developing one's personality is the way in which one earns, or fails to earn, one's living.

The right to work is to be found at the heart of the dispute as to what are civil and political rights, and what are those that may be characterized as social and economic. It appeared prominently in the constitutions of socialist states but often not at all in those based on other ideologies. Article 23 of the Universal Declaration contains the right to work, and in the Covenants it appears as Article 6, the first substantive right, in Part III of the Economic, Social and Cultural Rights Covenant.[32] In Europe, too, it surfaces in the European Social Charter, together with other related rights, such as just conditions of work and the right to safe and healthy working conditions.[33] Since 1919 the International Labour Organization has striven towards the laying down of an international labour code by means of a multitude of Conventions and Recommendations.

The European Convention, however, does not include the right to work in its provisions. Article 4 of the Convention guarantees freedom from slavery or servitude and forced or compulsory labour, while Article 11 deals, under freedom of association, with the right to form and join trade unions.

Forced labour has been the subject of two ILO instruments, the 1930 Convention Number 29 on Forced Labour, and the Abolition of Forced Labour Convention of 1957. Article 4, Paragraph 1, provides that no one shall be held in slavery or servitude. This is an absolute right subject to no stated exceptions and unable to be derogated from in times of national emergency under Article 15. "Slavery" occurs when the victim is wholly under the control of another person and within his legal ownership. "Servitude" seems to be a severe form of compulsory labour, lacking the quality of being in the ownership of another but whereunder an individual has no means to change his conditions of work or to escape. Debt-bondage, where it

---

[32] Under this Covenant, States Parties are required to take steps to achieve progressively the full realization of the rights enumerated.

[33] The European Social Charter was signed in 1961 and came into force in 1965. Many of its provisions are devoted to the right to work and aspects of employment.

exists, could amount to servitude. In the case of *Van Droogenbroeck* against Belgium, in 1982,[34] the Court rejected a claim that a recidivist placed at the Government's disposal was being held in servitude.

In 1968 the Commission held that minimal remuneration given to prisoners did not mean that the work they were required to do could be termed forced or compulsory labour, bearing in mind that all Member States of the Council of Europe followed similar practice, and that one of the functions of such work was to offer professional training and readaptation. Similarly, in the *Vagrancy* cases,[35] the Court stated:

> the duty to work imposed on the three applicants has not exceeded the "ordinary" limits, within the meaning of Article 4(3)(a) of the Convention, because it aimed at their rehabilitation and was based on a general standard ... which finds its equivalent in several Member States of the Council of Europe.

Paragraph 2 of Article 4 outlaws forced or compulsory labour. There would seem to be little difference, according to the interpretation, between forced and compulsory labour. The 1930 ILO Convention says that for the purposes of that Convention forced and compulsory labour "... shall mean all work or service which is exacted from any person under the menace of a penalty and for which the said person has not offered himself voluntarily". The Commission has added that the requirement that the work or service is performed must appear unjust or oppressive, or that the work itself involves avoidable hardship. Forced or compulsory labour is interpreted in the third paragraph of the Article not to include work done in the ordinary course of detention as long as this meets the requirements of Article 5. Similarly, work done during conditional release from detention, or service of a military character, is not deemed to be forced or compulsory labour. The Convention gives no right of conscientious objection but, where such a right exists in any state, any service exacted instead of military service shall be immune from Article 4(2). Finally, service exacted in cases of emergency or calamity threatening the life or well-being of the community, or work or

---

[34] (1982) Series A, No. 50, and 4 *EHRR* 443.
[35] *De Wilde, Ooms and Versyp* v. *Belgium*, (1971) Series A, No. 12, para. 90. and 1 *EHRR* 373.

service which forms part of normal civic obligations, shall also be excluded. The Commission has been called upon to apply Article 4 on several occasions, and quite a few cases have been referred to the Court.

In one application a group of young sailors brought complaints before the Commission alleging that the United Kingdom was in breach of Article 4(1) of the Convention.[36] At the ages of fifteen or sixteen the boys, with the consent of their parents, had joined the Army or Navy for a period of nine years, which was to be calculated from their eighteenth birthday. Applications for discharge had been rejected by the authorities. The boys contended that their position amounted to servitude rather than forced labour and that, therefore, there was an absolute prohibition under the Convention since it was not covered by Article 4(3)(b). The Commission found, however, that the duties of a voluntary soldier could not be referred to as "servitude", and that the unusual procedure of enlisting boys at such an early age could not render it so, provided that parental consent had been obtained and that proper laws existed for the protection of minors. The Commission, therefore, rejected the application. New Navy Service Regulations came into force shortly afterwards which made provision for such recruits to be discharged upon request three years after attaining their eighteenth birthday.

The parents of the boy sailors knew the conditions before the service of which they complained began; so did a Norwegian dentist whose application was rejected by the Commission in 1963.[37] The Norwegian Government, wishing to make dental services available throughout the whole of the country, enacted legislation whereby dentists, after their training, could be compelled to take up posts for a period of two years where it could be shown that, although the post had been advertized, it still remained vacant. Mr Iversen, a dentist, had already spent his military service in the inhospitable north of the country but was allocated to a practice in the same area. After some months he left his post and was duly fined under the said legislation. He alleged that the scheme amounted to forced or compulsory labour. The Commission decided eventually, by a small majority, that his application was inadmissible. Where an individual

---

[36] Applications 3435-3438/67, *W.X.Y.Z.* v. *UK*, 28 *CD* 109 and 11 *YB* 562.
[37] Application 1468/62, *Iversen* v. *Norway*, 6 *YB* 278.

is fully aware of the conditions of the work before he decides to enter into a profession, it may be difficult to allege later that the terms of employment amount to forced labour. The Norwegian Government pointed out in *Iversen* that he was being paid fully for his services and that he was provided with a well-equipped surgery and accommodation. Certainly it would seem that periods of time spent gathering practical experience should be classified as training prior to qualification, always provided that it can be shown that the rationale is the training of the individual rather than the provision of cheap labour.

The Court considered a similar problem in the case of *Van der Mussele* against Belgium.[38] The applicant's complaint here was that as a pupil *avocat* at the Antwerp bar he had been required to defend impecunious defendants without remuneration or any reimbursement of expenses. Had he refused he would have run the risk of his name being struck from the roll of pupils. The Court stressed, however, that in embarking upon the career of an advocate he was in full knowledge that this service would be expected of him, and that in many ways it could be regarded as training for the profession. Nevertheless, this alone would not exempt it from being forced or compulsory labour if the work involved imposed an excessive or disproportionate burden, or was not connected in any way with the profession in question. Since in this case the services did not fall outside the ambit of the normal activities of an advocate and could be seen, in fact, as enhancing the profession by preserving the right of audience to the bar, the Court held that Article 4 had not been violated. A view taken by the Commission in other similar cases,[39] that such service might be covered by Article 4(3) (d), which exempts from forced labour work which forms part of "normal civic obligations", a not entirely convincing argument, was also alluded to by the Court in the present case.

Once an individual is in work, and even in a job of his own choosing, it is important that his interests should continue to be represented, and this task is often performed by a trade union. Article 11 of the Convention guarantees freedom of association with others,

---

[38] (1983) Series A, No. 70, and 6 *EHRR* 163.
[39] See, for example, Application 4897/71, *Gussenbauer v. Austria*, 42 *CD* 41, 15 *YB* 558.

"... including the right to form and to join trade unions for the protection of his interests".

Generally, an "association" has been interpreted as a voluntary organization for a common purpose. It must have some institutional aspect, so that it does not, for instance, include the right of prisoners to associate with their fellow inmates,[40] nor can a legal deportation be said to deprive one of the association of one's friends and colleagues.[41] On the other hand in *Le Compte, Van Leuven and De Meyere*,[42] an association was held not to include the *Ordre des Médecins*, a professional organization set up by the Government and governed by public law, and whose purpose was to protect public interests as well as those of its members. The essence of a trade union is that it should represent its members in a labour conflict situation.

A likely course of events might be, however, that a state would recognize a union, while in practice putting the union in a position where its views were not taken into account; for example, by refusing to negotiate with it. Article 11 cannot merely mean that a state must grant legal recognition to the right of an individual to join and form a trade union without interference. It must also embody an obligation on the Government to consult and negotiate with the union, although the extent and form of that negotiation cannot perhaps be dictated from outside. It was this which formed the main subject of debate in Applications brought against Belgium and Sweden.[43] In these cases, the Court decided that there had been no violation of Article 11. In both Applications, the union or its members complained either that it was not recognized for the purposes of representation on negotiating committees, or had been refused the opportunity to negotiate with the Collective Bargaining Office.

The Court in the *Belgian National Police Union* case said:

> The Convention safeguards freedom to protect the occupational interests of trade union members by trade union action, the conduct and

---

[40] For example, Application 8317/78, *McFeeley et al* v. *UK*, 20 *D&R* 44, 23 *YB* 256, and 27 *YB* 251.

[41] For example, Application 7729/76, *Agee* v. *UK*, 7 *D&R* 164.

[42] (1981) Series A, No. 43, and 4 *EHRR* 1.

[43] *National Union of Belgian Police* case, (1975) Series A, No. 19, and 1 *EHRR* 578 and *Swedish Engine Drivers' Union* case, (1976) Series A, No. 20, and 1 *EHRR* 617.

development of which states must both permit and make possible . . . it follows that the members of a trade union have a right, in order to protect their interests, that the trade union should be heard.

In this case, however, the Court was of the opinion that the Union could engage in various kinds of activity *vis-à-vis* the Belgian Government, and that therefore the state's policy of restricting the number of organizations to be consulted was not incompatible with trade union freedom. Complications too may arise in these cases from the double role of the state, but the Court has decided that Article 11 binds the state not only as the holder of public power but also as employer. Article 11 does not secure any particular treatment of trade unions or their members, such as the right that the state should conclude any collective agreement with them,[44] and the Court has held that the state should be allowed discretion as to how its industrial relations should be handled.[45] In *Cheall* v. *UK* [46] Mr Cheall, having resigned from his Union, the ACTSS, wished to join another, APEX. Under the rules of the TUC, his former Union should have been approached by APEX, this had failed to occur and the TUC Disputes Committee required APEX to exclude him. The Commission rejected the Application as not engaging the responsibility of the Government but, in doing so, it pointed out that while Trade Unions could draw up their own rules and administer their own affairs, if the right to join a Trade Union is to remain effective the state must be able to protect the individual against any abuse by a Union of a dominant position.

This is, of course, a highly volatile, political area of everyday life, and one can understand the Commission and the Court being reluctant to interfere in it. These bodies must, however, remain ever-vigilant in ensuring that the ultimate purposes of Article 11 are not being eroded.

Article 11 contains a second paragraph, similar in form to those of Articles 8, 9 and 10, which allows for limitations on the right guaranteed. These do not include the economic well-being of the country,

---

[44] *Swedish Engine Drivers' Union* case, *ibid.* This was reaffirmed by the Commission in Application 9792/82 *Union A.* v. *Federal Republic of Germany,* 34 *D&R* 173.

[45] *Schmidt and Dahlström* v. *Sweden,* (1976) Series A, No. 21, and 1 *EHRR* 637.

[46] Application 10550/83, 42 *D&R* 178, and 28 *YB* 105.

but interference may be allowed in the interests of national security. Paragraph 2 also contains a specific restriction, which reads:

> This Article shall not prevent the imposition of lawful restrictions on the exercise of these rights by members of the armed forces, of the police or of the administration of the state.

In *Council of Civil Service Unions* v. *UK* [47] the Commission was of the view that the staff at the Government Communications Headquarters (GCHQ) were part of the "administration of the state" and that an Order in Council preventing membership of their Trade Union, in the interests of national security, was a "lawful restriction", even though it had the effect of denying them the right altogether.

Both United Nations Covenants include the right to form and join trade unions. The Universal Declaration has a provision - Article 20 (2) - which is omitted from both Covenants and from the European Convention, and which reads: "No one may be compelled to belong to an association". There would seem, therefore, to be no protection against the "closed shop" in the European Convention. In applications against the United Kingdom by *Young, James and Webster*,[48] the applicants alleged that their dismissal by British Rail, because they had refused to join a trade union when it became a condition of employment, amounted to a breach of Articles 9, 10 and 11 (1) of the Convention. Following the Trade Union and Labour Relations Act of 1974 and amendments in 1976, British Rail reached an agreement with the three railway unions which constituted a "closed shop" arrangement. The right to associate, the applicants argued, is a coin with two sides and must necessarily incorporate the right not to associate. The Commission, in 1969, had expressed the view that the right to associate is a right and not an obligation. Unfortunately, there is evidence in the *travaux préparatoires* that the right not to join a trade union was omitted specifically from the Convention in order not to conflict with "closed shop" requirements already in place. Both the Commission and the Court, however, felt that the *travaux* were not decisive for determining in this case whether the "closed

---

[47] Application 11603/85, 50 *D&R* 228.
[48] (1981) Series A, No. 44, and 4 *EHRR* 38.

shop" was contrary to Article 11. The final result was a holding that Article 11 had been violated, but the Court avoided a general pronouncement on the validity under the Convention of the "closed shop" system. In its report the Commission laid emphasis on the fact that the "closed shop" agreement in this case post-dated the start of the employment, that this had the effect of limiting the men's right to decide which trade union they wished to join and, similarly, that their sacking amounted to a sanction of the use of that freedom. The Court too regarded the discharge as a form of coercion, defeating the object of the freedom guaranteed in Article 11. It also felt that the compulsion to join the Union fell foul of Article 11(2), in not being "... necessary in a democratic society".

THE RIGHT TO DO AS YOU PLEASE

The social and cultural conditions within a state play a large part in determining the quality of life of the individual. Many rights contained in the Universal Declaration, such as the right to leisure, the right to holidays with pay, even, as we have seen, the right to work, have not found their way into the civil and political rights instruments. Just as one can argue, however, that the right to life may be negligible without the right to seek work, similarly freedom to grow up and enter into the social life of the state may be pointless without the opportunity to turn one's life into something worthwhile or to get involved in "doing one's own thing".

Certain rights, as we have seen, appear in the European Convention in answer to the particular problems of the time or of the recent past. Other rights, such as the freedom of thought, conscience or religion and the right to expression, feature in most human rights instruments. The European Convention, in the context of the respect paid to democracy by the Council of Europe's Statute, could scarcely omit the right to elections and to take part in political life. Indeed, it is surprising that agreement on elections could not be achieved in time to include these rights in the Convention itself rather than the First Protocol.

The right to do as you please includes the right to talk and listen freely, to read and write, to meet with others, to exchange ideas, and all the modern versions of these rights which recent technology has made available.

The Convention's provisions cover the freedom of thought, conscience and religion. Most states are happy that you should think and believe according to your own wishes although, of course, they may, through education and legislation, encourage you to think in line with socially-accepted norms. As the song puts it "you can't go to jail for what you're thinking", and until the invention of something like George Orwell's "Thought Police" it is only where the individual wishes to expose his views to other people, or where the state requires some activity which runs counter to the individual's beliefs, that conflict may arise.

Religion usually involves public worship and, again, most people of strong belief are not satisfied until they can convince others of the need to believe thus. It is therefore the manifestation of religion or belief which may cause problems of social organization and it is this which, according to Paragraph 2 of Article 9, may be subject to restriction by the authorities. In many instances the manifestation of thoughts or beliefs will involve freedom of expression and may, indeed, be more easily dealt with under Article 10. The Commission has tended to restrict the application of Article 9 to those cases where the actual practice of belief has been directly prohibited rather than where it has been impeded. So that, for example, when Pat Arrowsmith was prevented by the British authorities from distributing pamphlets to servicemen in Northern Ireland the Commission was of the view that this was not a practice which was intimately involved with her pacifism and hence rejected her application.[49] The difficulty, of course, is that sometimes actions are deliberately the result of beliefs and convictions whereas some activities are differently motivated.

The Commission has similarly rejected those applicants who have refused to pay taxes because these are used to finance matters contrary to their convictions.[50] Clergymen in Scandinavia who have left their posts or been dismissed because they disapprove of new legislation on abortion, or because they wish to impose greater

---

[49] Application 7050/75, 19 *D&R* 5, and 20 *YB* 316, 22 *YB* 446.

[50] For example, Application 10358/83 v. *UK*, 37 *D&R* 142 where a Quaker and pacifist objected to paying a part of his income tax in proportion to the budget for weapons procurement and other non-peaceful activities.

responsibilities on the parents of those to be baptized, have in the same way been unable to invoke Article 9.[51]

Conscientious objection from military or substitute service has been the subject matter of several applications. Mr Grandrath, who was a Jehovah's Witness, complained that although he was a conscientious objector he was required by the Federal German authorities to do substitute service which was contrary to his religious beliefs.[52] The question arose, first of all, whether the Convention's terms included the right of conscientious objection. Article 4 of the Convention, in one of the exceptions to the rule forbidding forced or compulsory labour, says that service exacted instead of military service is acceptable for conscientious objectors "... in countries where they are recognized". There would seem to be, therefore, no automatic right to conscientious objection. Article 14 of the Convention says there shall be no discrimination of enjoyment of the Convention's rights on, *inter alia*, religious grounds, and Grandrath complained that ministers of religion in some churches in Germany were excused substitute service whereas he, as a Jehovah's Witness, was not allowed such exemption. The Commission was of the view, however, that the restriction in Germany was imposed to avoid widespread avoidance of military service, was based on function, and that, since Mr Grandrath's ministry was only in his spare time, there was no case of discrimination. In an Application in 1983,[53] however, the complaint was that Jehovah's Witnesses were allowed exemption from military and substitute service in Sweden, whereas the applicant, a pacifist, was not. The Commission's view here was that membership of such a religious sect as the Jehovah's Witnesses was an objective fact which created a high degree of probability that exemption was not granted to persons who simply wished to escape service.

In many cases the Commission has been prepared to hold that restrictions imposed by Governments are for the protection of others or for the protection of public order or morals. So an applicant who alleged that motor car insurance was contrary to his religious

---

[51] Application 11045/84, *Knudsen* v. *Norway*, 42 *D&R* 247 and 28 *YB* 141, and Application 7374/76 *X* v. *Denmark*, 5 *D&R* 157.

[52] Application 2299/64, *Grandrath* v. *Federal Republic of Germany*, 16 *CD* 41, and 10 *YB* 626.

[53] Application 10410/83, *N.* v. *Sweden*, 40 *D&R* 203.

beliefs was turned away on the grounds that this was justifiably imposed for the protection of others. A necessary restriction on the rights of individual belief or conscience might similarly be involved by the compulsory use of crash helmets or seat-belts,[54] and, in the same way, medical treatment for oneself or one's children might raise a multitude of problems of this kind. An applicant who complained that the wedding service by which he and his wife were married was not recognized as creating a valid marriage, was informed by the Commission that the right to marry ". . . according to the national laws governing this right" was secured by Article 12 and that, therefore, the right to marry could not be considered as a form of manifestation of thought, conscience or religion.[55]

As might be expected, a not insignificant number of applications have been brought by members of churches and religious sects who are unhappy about the way they are, or perceive themselves to be, treated.

The United Kingdom Government decided that the Church of Scientology was harmful and refused to allow its members to claim student status while studying in England. Similarly, work permits were withdrawn and permission to stay in this country to study Scientology was refused to foreigners. An application by individual members of that Church that Article 9 had been violated was rejected by the Commission, however, in a rather summary and perhaps unsatisfactory decision.[56] In the same application, the Commission refused to accept that the Church itself could complain in its own name under Article 25, but this view was revised in 1979 when the Commission said:

> When a Church body lodges an application under the Convention, it does so in reality, on behalf of its members. It should therefore be accepted that a church body is capable of possessing and exercising the rights contained in Article 9(1) in its own capacity as a representative of its members.[57]

---

[54] For example, Application 7992/77, *X* v. *UK*, 14 *D&R* 234.

[55] Application 6167/73, *X* v. *Federal Republic of Germany*, 1 *D&R* 64.

[56] Application 3798/68, *Church of X* v. *UK*, 29 *CD* 70, and 12 *YB* 306.

[57] Application 7805/77, *Pastor X and Church of Scientology* v. *Sweden*, 16 *D&R* 68 at p. 70, and 22 *YB* 244 at p. 246.

Even so, a "church" cannot invoke Article 9 to cover statements of religious belief which appear in advertisements of a purely commercial nature merely to boost sales. The Commission thus rejected the complaint of the Church of Scientology in Sweden, whose advertisement for an "E-Meter" had been banned by the authorities in the interests of consumers.[58]

A particular creed or confession cannot exact from the concept of freedom of religion the right to be free from criticism. Only where the authorities can be shown to tolerate such a level of criticism and agitation as might prevent freedom of a particular religion altogether will their responsibility under the Convention be engaged.[59]

Where an individual is in prison the state must, if reasonable, permit him to worship according to his religious beliefs. The Commission noted, in an application against the United Kingdom, that the prison authorities had attempted to find a Buddhist minister for a prisoner and, failing to do so, had allowed the prisoner the extra privilege of writing to members of the same faith.[60] In another application an Orthodox Jew's allegations that Article 9 had been violated were rejected when it was shown that he had been offered a *Kosher* diet and had contacts with a lay Jewish visitor, assisted by the prison chaplain.[61] Another prisoner was unsuccessful when he complained of being deprived of a book which, he claimed, was religious and philosophical in character;[62] it was revealed that it also contained a chapter on the martial arts. Mr Guzzardi, who was kept under special surveillance by the Italian Government on a small island off Sardinia, complained, *inter alia,* that his right to religious worship had been interfered with. The Government, in that case, was able to point out, to the Commission's satisfaction, that there was a chapel and a priest on the island and that even though, in fact, there had been no services, the applicant and those detained with him had never requested that one should be held.[63]

The need to share one's views with others through the manifestation of beliefs and convictions amounts to an exercise of one type of

---

[58] *Supra,* note 57 at pp. 74 and 254 respectively.
[59] Application 8282/78, *Church of Scientology* v. *Sweden,* 21 *D&R* 109.
[60] Application 5442/72, *X* v. *UK,* 1 *D&R* 41.
[61] Application 5947/72, *X* v. *UK,* 5 *D&R* 8.
[62] Application 6886/75, *X* v. *UK,* 5 *D&R* 100.
[63] Application 7367/76, 8 *D&R* 185 and 20 *YB* 462.

freedom of expression. This right, secured by Article 10 of the Convention, remains as one of the most precious attributes of democracy.

The first case to come to the Court was *De Becker* v. *Belgium* in 1960.[64] The Belgian Penal Code included provisions whereby anyone found guilty of a serious offence in time of war could be prohibited from taking part in the administration, editing, printing or distribution of a newspaper or other publication. De Becker, who had collaborated with the enemy, was a journalist. He argued that these provisions of the Belgian Code deprived him not only of his livelihood but also of his right of expression. The life-long ban was not restricted to political writing and the Commission was convinced that it constituted a violation of Article 10. The Court was seized of the matter but before the hearing began the law was amended and the case was eventually withdrawn. Had the limitation on De Becker's expression been confined to political writing the claim that it was "necessary in a democratic society" would have had stronger consideration.[65]

Freedom of expression is, nevertheless, easily open to abuse and, as the Convention states, ". . . carries with it duties and responsibilities". It contains within it not only the right to express your thoughts and opinions and to give information, but also the right to receive information. The United Nations Covenant includes the right to seek information but the absence of this additional right in the Convention relieves the European states from the obligation to make all information available at all times. The right to seek information may be seen, however, as an important element by those campaigning for open government.

The *means* of expression would not seem to be material, but the Commission has limited the concept to the expression of information and ideas, and has rejected wider interpretations; so the physical expression of love was not accepted as an exercise of the freedom,[66] nor was the right to vote,[67] nor, as we have seen, the right to marry in your own style. Modes of expression have been accepted to include

---

[64] (1962) Series A, No. 4, and 1 *EHRR* 43.
[65] The De Becker affair still rolls on. See Application 9777/82, 34 *D&R* 158.
[66] Application 7215/75, 19 *D&R* 66, and 21 *YB* 354.
[67] Application 6573/74, 1 *D&R* 87.

painting[68] and music in addition to writing.[69] Furthermore in the case of *Autronic AG*[70] the Court said:

> Article 10 applies not only to the content of information but also to the means of transmission or reception since any restriction imposed on the means necessarily interferes with the right to receive and impart information.

The freedom which an individual has to express his or her views is matched by the right of the public generally to receive information and opinions which will help them to participate in public debate, which is the very core of democratic society.

Equally important, of course, is the right of weaker members of the society to be protected from the expression of harmful ideas, and it is for this reason that laws on defamation, those for the protection of health and morals and for the protection of national security exist.

Mr Lingens, the editor of the Austrian magazine *Profil*, published two articles criticising Bruno Kreisky, the Chancellor of Austria, for his support of former SS officers and his attacks on Nazi-hunter Simon Wiesenthal. Following a private prosecution for defamation by the Chancellor, at the end of which he was fined, Mr Lingens lodged a case in Strasbourg alleging violation of Article 10.[71] There was no doubt that his freedom of expression had been interfered with but to what extent could this be justified for the protection of the reputation of others? Freedom of the press, the Court reiterated, afforded the public one of the best means of discovering and forming opinions about the ideas and attitudes of political leaders. It continued:

> The limits of acceptable criticism are accordingly wider as regards a politician as such than as regards a private individual. Unlike the latter, the

---

[68] *Müller* v. *Switzerland*, (1988) Series A, No. 133, and 13 *EHRR* 212. Also Application 9870/82, 34 *D&R* 208.

[69] In Application 10317/83, 34 *D&R* 218 the Commission questioned whether street musicians, since they were operating for gain, fell within the scope of the Article but did apply Paragraph 2 of the Article in justifying interference with the right, rather than rejecting the Application as incompatible, under Article 27(2).

[70] A case concerning Switzerland, (1990) Series A, No. 178, para. 47, and 12 *EHRR* 485.

[71] *Lingens* v. *Austria*, (1986) Series A, No. 103, and 8 *EHRR* 407.

former inevitably and knowingly lays himself open to close scrutiny of his every word and deed by both journalists and the public at large, and he must consequently display a greater degree of tolerance.

The lack of a defence of something like "fair comment" under Austrian law meant that the interference with the freedom of expression went too far and the Court held unanimously that there had been a violation of Article 10.[72]

Mr Castells, who was found by the Spanish courts to have insulted the Government in associating it with the lack of success in pursuing right-wing extremists, was similarly successful before the Court of Human Rights on the grounds that the national courts did not allow him to establish the truth of his allegations nor to plead good faith.[73]

At the other end of Europe Thorgeir Thorgeirson wrote two newspaper articles criticising alleged police brutality, and described the Icelandic police in one of them as "wild beasts in uniform". Such strong language and the generally unspecific nature of his allegations led to his conviction and fine under Icelandic law. However, the Strasbourg Court felt that, having regard to the purpose of the articles and the impact which they were designed to have, the language used was not excessive and that, therefore, his freedom of expression had been violated.[74]

We have seen earlier in this chapter that Pat Arrowsmith's attempt to dissuade soldiers from going to Northern Ireland fared badly before the Commission. So did Application 6084/73[75] where a British national, having had in his possession for distribution two documents - "A letter from a soldier of the I.R.A. to the soldiers of the Royal Green Jackets" and "A letter from a Ballymurphy mother" - the latter inviting soldiers to turn their guns on their officers - also found no support from the Commission for his allegation that his conviction under the Incitement to Disaffection Act was a violation of his freedom of expression.

[72] Similar more recent cases concerning Austria which also held a violation of Article 10 are *Oberschlick*, (1991) Series A, No. 204, and *Schwabe* (1992) Series A, No. 242-B.

[73] *Castells* v. *Spain*, (1992) Series A, No. 236, and 14 *EHRR* 445.

[74] *Thorgeir Thorgeirson* v. *Iceland*, (1992) Series A, No. 239, and 14 *EHRR* 843.

[75] 3 *D&R* 62.

When it comes to the administration of justice the Court has taken the strong line that the public has a right to know and that this will often take preference over the sensitivities of the judicial process.

The Sunday Times published an article headed "Our Thalidomide Children: A cause for National Shame". It announced its intention to publish a long article tracing the history of the tragedy and the manufacture of the drug. It was prevented from doing so by an injunction imposed by the High Court, following an application by the Attorney-General. This injunction was eventually confirmed by the House of Lords which found that the proposed article sought to interfere with pending court proceedings, including settlement negotiations, and thus constituted contempt of court. *The Sunday Times,* its owners and its Editor applied to the Commission. The application was admitted and in 1977 the Commission referred the case to the Court.[76] The Court's first task was to determine whether the law of contempt was, as the applicants argued, so vague and uncertain as to deprive the restraint of the requirement of being "prescribed by law". A particular problem arises here, of course, in relation to the Common Law but the Court felt that the English law on contempt satisfied the requirement in as far as the legal rules applicable were adequately indicated in the circumstances, and the consequences of any action were reasonably foreseeable. The problem with which the Court was then faced was one of balancing the right of freedom of expression with the fair administration of justice, which the law of contempt had as its general aim. The Court, after a long discussion of the exercise of the discretion embodied in Paragraph 2, stressed the importance of the principle of freedom of expression, which is as important in the administration of justice as in other fields. It concluded by eleven votes to nine that:

> ... the interference complained of did not correspond to a social need sufficiently pressing to outweigh the public interest in freedom of expression within the meaning of the Convention. The Court therefore finds the reasons for the restraint imposed on the applicants not to be sufficient under Article 10 (2). That restraint proves not to be proportionate to the legitimate aim pursued; it was not necessary in a democratic society for maintaining the authority of the judiciary.[77]

[76] *Sunday Times* v. *UK,* Series A, No. 30, and 2 *EHRR* 245.
[77] *Supra,* note 76, para. 67.

Accordingly, there had been a violation of Article 10.

Similarly, in 1991 the Court decided that the interlocutory injunctions restraining the publication of details from, and excerpts of, Peter Wright's book *Spycatcher* were, at least after its publication in the United States, a breach of the right of expression of English newspapers.[78]

In other cases, however, the scales have tipped in the opposite direction. In *G. Hodgson, D. Woolf Productions Ltd., N.U.J., Channel Four Television Co. Ltd.* v. *UK*,[79] the producers of the Channel Four programme *Court Report* proposed that on each evening of the trial of Clive Ponting, for an Official Secrets offence, actors in the studio would read edited transcripts of the day's proceedings. The trial judge, McCowan J., ordered that the presentation, in this format, should not take place. The Commission's view in rejecting the allegations of a violation of Article 10 was that the trial judge's on-the-spot evaluation of what was likely to prejudice a fair trial was, on the whole, reasonable in the circumstances and certainly within the margin of appreciation left to a state.

The *Barfod* case,[80] too, involved questions of the maintenance of the authority and impartiality of the judiciary. The applicant here wrote an article for *Grønland Dansk* criticising the High Court of Greenland and particularly two lay judges who happened to be Government employees. He questioned their impartiality but went further to suggest, sarcastically, that they had "done their duty" when the Court held for the Government in the case which concerned a tax dispute. In its judgment the Court of Human Rights held that although Mr Barfod might have properly objected to the composition of the Greenland Court, his personal attack on the two lay judges justified his prosecution for defamation.[81]

In these cases we see direct attempts, by use of the national law, to

---

[78] *The Observer and The Guardian* v. *UK*, (1991) Series A, No. 216, and 14 *EHRR* 153, and *The Sunday Times* (No. 2), 1991 Series A, No. 217, and 14 *EHRR* 229.

[79] Applications 11553/85 and 11658/85, 51 *D&R* 136.

[80] *Barfod* v. *Denmark*, (1989) Series A, No. 149, and 13 *EHRR* 493.

[81] An interesting observation is that the Court was unanimous in its opinion, whereas the Commission had previously reached the opposite conclusion by a vote of fourteen to one. The Commission had commented: "For the citizen to keep a critical control on the exercise of public power it is essential that particularly strict limits be imposed on interferences with the publication of opinions which refer to activities of public authorities, including the judiciary".

muzzle individuals and the Press. In another trend of cases it can be seen that the exercise of the freedom of expression by an individual may prove to be disadvantageous to him in the future. In the cases of *Glasenapp*[82] and *Kosiek*[83] the applicants were schoolteachers. In Germany schoolteachers are civil servants and are required to sign a declaration of loyalty to the Constitution. In each of these cases the applicants had previous associations with political parties which the Government thought were undemocratic; in Mrs Glasenapp's case, the German Communist Party (KPD), and in Mr Kosiek's, the extreme right-wing NPD. There had been, of course, no repression of their freedom of expression but because of it they were dismissed from their posts. The Court's approach in both these cases, however, was to argue that the Convention does not grant a right to employment in the civil service, and that if the Government was of the view that only persons without previous extremist taint were qualified to hold such posts, it was entitled to impose such conditions. A similar result befell Mr Leander[84] whose application for the post of museum technician at the Naval Museum at Karlskrona was frustrated when security vetting proved positive. Mr Leander was not allowed access to his files and declared himself to be unaware of the information filed against him.[85]

We have commented that freedom of expression carries with it responsibilities to others, and it is this balance which is particularly difficult to maintain. In some examples, such as the cases on the freedom of the press, the Court has indicated that the right to receive information should be paramount. Problems arise, however, with the application of the doctrine of "margin of appreciation", when the authorities decide that certain information should not be imparted because it is immoral or unconstitutional.

Two recent cases against Ireland highlight these factors: *Open Door Counselling Ltd* and *Dublin Well Woman Centre Ltd. et al.*[86] Both cases concerned companies engaged in non-directive counselling of pregnant women in Ireland, including, if requested, advice on

[82] (1986) Series A, No. 104, and 9 *EHRR* 25.
[83] (1986) Series A. No. 105, and 9 *EHRR* 328.
[84] *Leander* v. *Sweden*, (1987) Series A, No. 116, and 9 *EHRR* 433.
[85] This case was discussed earlier in relation to private life together with the case of *Gaskin* v. *UK*, see p. 100.
[86] (1992) Series A, No. 246.

obtaining abortions in clinics in the United Kingdom. The Supreme Court of Ireland found that such advice assisted in the destruction of the life of the unborn, contrary to the Irish Constitution, and granted an injunction. A majority of the European Court of Human Rights was of the view, however, that this was a violation of Article 10.

In the *Handyside* case[87] the Court was of the opinion that the restriction for the "protection of morals" varied from time to time and from place to place.

That case, against the United Kingdom, concerned the seizure of *The Little Red Schoolbook* and Mr Handyside's subsequent conviction under the Obscene Publications Act. He alleged, *inter alia,* that this amounted to a violation of his freedom of expression. The Court examined the case under paragraph 2 of Article 10 and came to the conclusion that the interference with his freedom was justified. It thought that, in principle, state authorities were in a better position than the international judge to give an opinion on the necessity of a restriction. Article 10 (2) left to the Contracting State, therefore, a "margin of appreciation" which was "... given both to the domestic legislator and to the bodies, judicial amongst others, that are called upon to interpret and apply the laws in force". This discretion was, however, subject to review and supervision by the organs of the Convention. The Court concluded that:

> ... despite the variety and constant evolution in the United Kingdom of views on ethics and education, the competent English judges were entitled, in the exercise of their discretion, to think at the relevant time that the *Schoolbook* would have pernicious effects on the morals of many of the children and adolescents who would read it.[88]

Nevertheless, the Court has reiterated on many occasions that, subject to Paragraph 2, Article 10 is applicable "... not only to 'information' or 'ideas' that are favourably received or regarded as inoffensive or as a matter of indifference, but also to those that offend, shock or disturb the state or any section of the population".[89]

[87] (1976) Series A, No. 24, and 1 *EHRR* 737.
[88] *Supra*, note 87, para. 52.
[89] See, for example, the Judgment in *Müller* v. *Switzerland*, Series A, No. 133, para. 33, and 13 *EHRR* 212 at 228.

It must be recalled, of course, that Mr Handyside's book was for sale and that its publication might have been primarily motivated by the profit which could be expected. Commercial factors must perforce play a part in the interpretation of Article 10.

Mr Barthold, a Hamburg vet, featured in a newspaper article describing how he had treated a cat outside normal working hours. His opinion that a system of regular night clinics was required was quoted and the article included his name and photograph. The *Frankfurt-am-Main Central Agency for Combatting Unfair Competition* brought a successful action against him in the civil court, alleging that the article amounted to advertising and was contrary to the rules of professional conduct and to relevant legislation. In that part of its judgment concerned with the alleged violation of Article 10, the European Court of Human Rights held that the article was intended to inform the public about a genuine problem of current interest and that "A criterion as strict as this in approaching the matter of advertising and publicity in the liberal professions is not consonant with freedom of expression. Its application risks discouraging members of the liberal professions from contributing to public debate ..."[90]

In *Markt intern Verlag GmbH and Beerman v. Germany*,[91] the Court decided, by the casting vote of its President, that no violation of Article 10 had occurred. Markt intern, whose aim was to protect the interests of small retail businesses against competition from large scale distribution, published bulletins to its members. In one bulletin it criticized a cosmetics firm for not refunding money on faulty goods and canvassed any further information about the firm from its members. The Court was of the opinion that despite its limited circulation and the fact that it conveyed information of a commercial nature, the bulletin should not, as such, be excluded from the scope of Article 10.

POLITICAL LIFE

The right to hold opinions and to express them, taken with the right of assembly guaranteed in Article 11 of the Convention, secures for

---

[90] *Barthold* v. *Federal Republic of Germany*, (1985) Series A, No. 90, and 7 *EHRR* 383, para. 58.

[91] (1989) Series A, No. 164, and 12 *EHRR* 161.

the individual the opportunity to take part, should he or she wish, in the political life of the state. Article 14 lays down that there shall be no discrimination in the enjoyment of the Convention's rights and freedoms on political grounds, although Article 16 permits the Contracting Parties to impose restrictions on the political activity of aliens. The Universal Declaration states that everyone has the right to take part in the government of his country, directly or through freely chosen representatives, and the right of equal access to public service. The Covenant repeats that such rights and opportunities shall be available to "every citizen". The right to take part in government in a democracy means, at the very least, the right to vote in a secret ballot at an election. The European Convention is, however, less explicit than the United Nations instruments with regard to political life. Article 3 of the First Protocol is not couched in the usual form of rights guaranteed in the Convention, whereby an individual is given a specific right, or such a right is not to be denied him. It reads:

> The High Contracting Parties undertake to hold free elections at reasonable intervals by secret ballot, under conditions which will ensure the free expression of the opinion of the people in the choice of the legislature.

After some early doubts the Commission has decided that this includes the right of the individual to vote and to stand for election and that universal suffrage is implied.[92] It does not follow from this that the right is absolute and that there can be no disqualification, as long as this is not arbitrary. For example, the Commission has held that a Dutch national, disqualified from voting for uncitizen-like conduct, could properly be prevented from misusing his political rights in future.[93] States may therefore attach limitations and conditions upon the right to vote and to stand, as long as these are not arbitrary and do not infringe the expression of the opinion of the people. A requirement that a political party should obtain 500 certified signatures before it would be eligible to take part in an election was, on these grounds, held to be acceptable within Article 3.[94] The

---

[92] Applications 6745/74 & 6746/74 v. *Belgium*, 2 *D&R* 110.
[93] Application 6573/74 v. Netherlands, 1 *D&R* 87.
[94] Application 6850/74 *Association X, Y and Z.* v. *Federal Republic of Germany*, 5 *D&R* 90.

state, by means of its Constitution, shall determine the institutions which make up its legislature.[95] Article 3 does not apply to local elections, nor did it provide the basis for complaint by a British prisoner that he was not allowed to vote in the EEC referendum,[96] nor by a Sudeten German that he was not consulted before an international treaty was signed by the Federal Republic of Germany and Czechoslovakia.[97] The Commission has held that the phrase "free expression of the opinion of the people" signifies ". . . that the election cannot be made under any form of pressure in the choice of one or more candidates, and that in this choice the elector not be unduly induced to vote for one party or another". This means that the Convention does not guarantee a particular type of voting such as proportional representation.[98]

---

[95] For example, Applications 6745/74 & 6746 /74 v. *Belgium,* 2 *D&R* 110 and 11391/85, *E. Booth-Clibborn v. UK,* 43 *D&R* 236. In *Mathieu-Mohin and Clerfayt* v. *Belgium,* (1987) Series A, No. 113, and 10 *EHRR* 1, the Court held that "legislature" may not necessarily mean only the national parliament but must be interpreted in the light of the Constitution as a whole.

[96] Application 7096/75 v. *UK,* 3 *D&R* 165.

[97] Application 6742/74 v. *Federal Republic of Germany,* 3 *D&R* 98.

[98] For example, Applications 7140/75 v. *UK,* 7 *D&R* 95. 8364/78; *Lindsay et al* v. *UK,* 15 *D&R* 247. 8765/79; *The Liberal Party et al* v. *UK,* 21 *D&R* 211.

CHAPTER SIX

The Individual and the Law

Quite often an individual finds himself at variance with the law and sometimes this may result in arrest and detention followed by some kind of judicial hearing.

On occasions a person may be unlawfully arrested or improperly accused of a crime of which he is innocent, and it is at times like this that to most people the concept of human rights and of civil liberties really begins to mean something. It is no accident that a large part of the jurisprudence of the European Commission and Court is taken up with cases dealing with detention, treatment during imprisonment, or events occurring before or during a trial in a court of law.

LIBERTY

The right to liberty and security is recognized as a major right to be guaranteed to each individual and is secured in Article 5 of the Convention, which lays down that everyone has a basic right to liberty and security of person.

Some queries have been raised as to the exact meaning of "security of person". Kenyan Asians, fleeing to Britain via India, discovered that they were unable to gain admittance to this country and unable also to remove their savings from India. They alleged before the Commission that their personal and economic security had been infringed because of the political uncertainty of their situation coupled with the effects of the Indian Foreign Exchange Regulations; the feelings of fear and terror engendered by the penal provisions of immigration control were matters which spelled great peril and personal insecurity. The position of a person made stateless under immigration legislation was akin, they suggested, to that of a person in perpetual fear of arrest - "the knock at the door at three o'clock in the morning". Such a person has no security even though he is not actually deprived of his liberty. The Commission was not prepared, however, to interpret security with such width.[1] It considered that the term "security of person" in Article 5 of the Convention was to be interpreted in its context, that is to say, in the context of liberty:

> . . . In the Commission's view, the protection of "security" is here concerned with *arbitrary* interference by a public authority with an individual's liberty. In other words, any decision concerning the individual's right to "security of person" must conform to the procedural as well as to the substantive requirements laid down by an already existing law.[2]

Similarly, the Commission decided in another case that the retention by the police of photographs that they had taken of demonstrators could not affect the applicant's physical security.[3]

In Application 8334/78[4] the applicant complained that the threat of six weeks' compulsory committal to a mental institution unless he submitted to a psychiatric examination was a violation of Article 5. Again, the Commission was of the view that since he had not actually been deprived of his liberty his right to security of person could only be infringed if he had been threatened with arbitrary or unjustified detention.

The term "liberty" itself also needs some explanation. It is possible to put a broad interpretation on the word and so encapsulate the whole spirit of human rights. Needless to say, such an approach is unhelpful in implementing the Convention. It must, therefore, be limited to aspects of the freedom to move about unrestrained. It might be envisaged as including liberty of movement: to move about your own country and choose where you would like to live. It could include the freedom to leave any country, the right to enter the country of which you are a national, or to enter the European Community. It is clear that Article 5 does not extend to cover these rights, however, because they are each expressed as separate rights in Articles in later Protocols to the Convention, particularly Article 2 of Protocol 4.[5]

---

[1] Application 5302/71 v. *UK*, 4 *CD* 29.
[2] *Supra*, note 1 at p. 46.
[3] Application 5877/72, 16 *YB* 328.
[4] Application 8334/78, 24 *D&R* 103.
[5] An unfortunate consequence is that some states may choose not to ratify these Protocols. The United Kingdom, for instance, has not accepted Protocol 4 and this in turn has put strain on the interpretation of, or the claims made under, Article 5. Applications such as the one from African Asians discussed above, note 1 *supra*, have ensued.

The Court in the case of *Engel and others*[6] in 1976 said:

> In proclaiming the "right to liberty", paragraph 1 of Article 5 is contemplating individual liberty in its classic sense, that is to say the physical liberty of the person. Its aim is to ensure that no one should be dispossessed of this liberty in an arbitrary fashion. As pointed out by the Government and the Commission, it does not concern mere restrictions upon liberty of movement ... This is clear both from the use of the terms "deprived of his liberty" "arrest" and "detention", which appear also in paragraphs 2 to 5, and from a comparison between Article 5 and the other normative provisions of the Convention and its Protocols.

Even deprivation of liberty is not always easy to determine. Mr Guzzardi was arrested in 1973 on suspicion of kidnapping and, indeed, in 1979 was convicted and sentenced to eighteen years imprisonment. Under Italian law he could not be detained on remand prior to his trial for longer than two years but he was considered a dangerous man with Mafia connections. He was therefore removed, with his wife and immediate family, to a small island off Sardinia. His movements throughout the island were restricted, he was subject to a night-time curfew and he was able to leave the island only under surveillance. The question before the Court was whether Article 5 applied at all.[7] Was this a case of detention or restriction of movement? It decided that the difference between "deprivation of and restriction upon liberty" was "one of degree or intensity" rather than nature or substance, and that in this case Article 5 was relevant.

Along the same line in *Engel et al v. Netherlands*,[8] the Court decided that being "confined to barracks" was one of the exigencies of being a soldier, and did not qualify as deprivation of liberty.[9]

Liberty and security of person refers, then, only to arrest and detention. There are some occasions, however, when imprisonment is obviously called for, and Article 5 goes on to list, exhaustively, six instances when deprivation of liberty is acceptable. In each case, however, the deprivation of liberty must be allowed for in the law of

---

[6] 15 *YB* 508, (1976) Series A, No. 22 para. 58, and 1 *EHRR* 647.
[7] *Guzzardi* v. *Italy*, (1980) Series A, No. 39, and 3 *EHRR* 333.
[8] *Supra*, note 6, para. 61.
[9] See discussion, *infra* Chapter 8, on "inherent" limitations.

the state concerned, and must always be carried out in accordance with the procedure prescribed by that law.

We have seen[10] that in *The Sunday Times* case the Court was of the opinion that two requirements flow from the expression "prescribed by law".

> First, the law must be adequately accessible: the citizen must be able to have an indication that is adequate in the circumstances of the legal rules applicable to a given case. Secondly, a norm cannot be regarded as "law" unless it is formulated with sufficient precision to enable the citizen to regulate his conduct: he must be able - if need be with appropriate advice - to foresee to a degree that is reasonable in the circumstances, the consequences which a given action may entail.[11]

In addition, the Court has said on several occasions:[12]

> Whilst it is not normally the Court's task to review the observance of domestic law by the national authorities, it is otherwise in relation to matters where, as here, the Convention refers directly back to that law; for, in such matters, disregard of the domestic law entails breach of the Convention, with the consequence that the Court can and should exercise a certain power of review.

The Court's view has been, therefore, that it is not enough to show that the procedural and substantive rules of domestic law have been applied, where these have resulted in arbitrary deprivation of liberty.[13]

It is generally accepted that a person's arrest and detention is justified when it follows a conviction for an offence, or where failure to meet some legal obligation can best be compensated for by imprisonment. The first two Paragraphs of Article 5(1) provide for these incidents. Article 5(1)(a) allows for the detention of a person after conviction by a competent court. This obviously must entail an activity characterized as illegal by the law and, under the provisions of Article 7 of the Convention, must have been so designated at the

---

[10] Chapter 5, *supra.*

[11] *Sunday Times* v. *UK*, (1979) Series A, No. 30, at para. 49, and 2 *EHRR* 245.

[12] For example, in *Winterwerp* v. *Netherlands*, (1980) Series A, No. 33, and 2 *EHRR* 387 at para. 46.

[13] See, for example, *Bouamar* v. *Belgium*, (1988) Series A, No. 129, para 47, and 11 *EHRR* 1.

time of its commission. "Conviction" appears to cover not only conviction for a criminal offence, but also detention characterized as "disciplinary" by the national law.[14]

Sometimes a court makes an order providing for the preventive detention of recidivists in the interests of public safety, or declares that a prisoner shall be placed "at the Government's disposal". The word "after" in Article 5(1)(a) does not simply mean that the detention shall follow the conviction in point of time, but that it should be a result of, or a consequence of, such conviction. It would seem that where there is a sufficient link between the conviction and the order of preventive detention then the Article has been complied with. On the other hand, decisions on rehabilitation, conditional release or recall are usually not taken by the courts themselves but by administrative authorities, and the question has been raised on several occasions as to the responsibilities of such decision-makers under the Convention. In *Van Droogenbroeck* v. *Belgium*[15] the applicant, on being sentenced to imprisonment for theft, was ordered to be "placed at the Government's disposal" for a period of ten years. Under Belgian law this was regarded as a penalty and not a security measure for recidivists. After some years he was released into "semi-custody", but disappeared. He was later arrested on a further charge of attempted theft but, although acquitted, he was detained in a block reserved for recidivists. In considering his application to Strasbourg, the Court decided that the Minister of Justice's decision was properly taken since the order to be placed at the Government's disposal was a part of the original sentence. In *Weeks* v. *UK*[16] the applicant, having been sentenced to life imprisonment "in the interests of public safety", was released on licence after ten years. His failure to stay out of trouble led to the Home Secretary's revoking the licence some fifteen months later. However, the Court was of the view that the trial judge, in passing an indeterminate sentence, must have been aware that Mr Weeks' liberty would be at the discretion of the Minister and that a sufficient

---

[14] *Engel et al* v. *Netherlands,* (1976) *supra,* note 5. See also Application 7341/76 *Eggs* v. *Switzerland,* 15 *D&R* 35, and 20 *YB* 448, 22 *YB* 454.

[15] (1982) Series A, No. 50, and 4 *EHRR* 443.

[16] (1987) Series A, No. 114, and 10 *EHRR* 293.

causal connection could be perceived. Nevertheless the Court conceded that this link might be broken:

> if a position were reached in which a decision not to release or to re-detain was based on grounds that were inconsistent with the objectives of the sentencing court. In those circumstances, a detention that was lawful at the outset would be transformed into a deprivation of liberty that was arbitrary and, hence, incompatible with Article 5.[17]

Article 5(1)(a) also requires that the conviction shall have been determined by a "competent court". This is a concept which appears from time to time in the Convention and requires consistent interpretation. The Court has said that this denotes bodies which exhibit "common fundamental features, of which the most important is independence of the executive and of the parties to the case", and also "the guarantee of judicial process." This implies, presumably, that the conviction must follow a fair trial within the conditions laid down by Article 6. There are instances where the Commission has supported the execution of foreign judgments even though the original trial was carried out outside the jurisdiction of the Convention.

The second sub-Paragraph of Article 5(1) provides for the lawful arrest or detention of a person for non-compliance with the lawful order of a court, or in order to secure the fulfilment of an obligation prescribed by law. There are many instances of a non-criminal nature where arrest or deprivation of liberty are acceptable; for example, when requiring the attendance at court of unwilling witnesses, or detaining a person in order to carry out a blood or urine test. The majority of these are statutory in nature. In the cases of *Lawless* and *Engel*, the Court held that detention to secure fulfilment of an obligation prescribed by law, refers to a "specific and concrete obligation" and not merely to a general, unspecified duty to obey law. In the *Guzzardi* case which we referred to above, the Italian Act of 1956, under which Mr Guzzardi was detained, imposed such general obligations as not "notoriously and habitually to indulge in illegal activities", or not "to indulge in other activities contrary to public morality". These were obligations binding on everyone and not covered by Article 5(1)(b). Similarly, in the *Ciulla* case[18] the applicant's

---

[17] *Supra*, note 16 at para. 49.
[18] *Ciulla* v. *Italy*, (1989) Series A, No. 148, and 13 *EHRR* 346.

failure "to change his behaviour", as required by the same Act, was also not specific enough to warrant deprivation of his liberty. Sympathetic though one may be towards government efforts to combat terrorism and mafia-type activities, it is important that general powers which may encourage abuse should be limited and their application strictly scrutinized.[19]

The general purport of the sub-paragraph is to allow for civil detention. It is to be noted, however, that Article 1 of the Fourth Protocol provides that no one shall be deprived of his liberty merely on the ground of inability to fulfil a contractual obligation.

Most legal systems, quite rightly, provide for the arrest of persons reasonably suspected of having committed or of being about to commit offences, or for the detention of such persons when they are likely to flee. Sub-paragraph (c) of Article 5(1) permits: "... the lawful arrest or detention of a person effected for the purpose of bringing him before the competent legal authority on reasonable suspicion of having committed an offence or when it is reasonably considered necessary to prevent his committing an offence or fleeing after having done so". This applies where there is reasonable suspicion that an offence has been committed, notwithstanding that it has in fact not taken place. Similarly, where an arrest takes place at a moment when the crime has not actually been committed but is imminent and is in the process of being, or about to be, attempted, then it would seem justifiable. By contrast, arrest on the basis that, if remaining at liberty, the accused is likely to commit a crime, is harder to deal with.

In the *Lawless* case[20] the Irish Government tried to justify the detention of Lawless on the ground that this was necessary to prevent his committing an offence. However, the Commission and Court pointed out that the phrase "when it is reasonably considered necessary to prevent his committing an offence" cannot be interpreted independently of the earlier phrase, "for the purpose of bringing him before the competent legal authority". Article 5(1)(c) proscribes

---

[19] In Application 8022/77, 8025/77 and 8027/77, *Mc Veigh, O'Neill and Evans* v. *UK*, 25 *D&R* 15, and 23 *YB* 222, the Commission was of the view that an obligation under the 1976 Prevention of Terrorism (Temporary Provisions) Act to submit to examination by an Examining Officer on arriving in Britain, and to furnish information, were specific and concrete obligations falling under Article 5(1)(b), but that detention to secure their fulfilment might only be used when justified by the circumstances.

[20] (1960) Series A, No. 1, and 1 *EHRR* 1.

internment without trial, and in those cases where this has been the subject matter of complaint, such as the *Lawless* case and the *Irish* case, it has been necessary to show that the application of this part of Article 5 is the subject of a valid derogation under Article 15.

In the *Brogan* case[21] the question was raised whether the arrest of the applicants in Northern Ireland under the *Prevention of Terrorism (Temporary Provisions) Act* of 1984 was compatible with Article 5(1)(c). Section 12 of that Act allows for the arrest without warrant of anyone reasonably suspected of being concerned in the commission, preparation or instigation of acts of terrorism. The applicants complained that their arrest was based on a suspicion of their being involved in unspecified acts of terrorism rather than for specific criminal offences. The Court, referring to its previous discussion in the *Ireland v. UK* case, felt that the concept of terrorism was "well in keeping with the idea of an offence". It also noted that within a very short time of his arrest each applicant was indeed questioned about a specific offence of which he was suspected. The case may well be contrasted with that of *Ciulla v. Italy* which we discussed above, where the Court was of the opinion that preventive detention based on a record of involvement in serious, mafia-like offences was not compatible with Article 5(1)(c), which allowed deprivation of liberty only in connection with specific criminal proceedings.

To satisfy Paragraph (c) the arrest or detention must be based on "reasonable suspicion". In another case emanating from Northern Ireland – *Fox, Campbell and Hartley* v. *UK* [22] – the applicants pointed out that Section 11 of the *Northern Ireland (Emergency Provisions) Act* of 1978 provided that a constable might arrest without a warrant any person whom he suspected of being a terrorist, and that the House of Lords in *McKee* v. *Chief Constable for Northern Ireland* [23] had held that such suspicion need not be reasonable as long as it was honestly held. This, it was alleged, rendered the applicants' arrest outside the terms of the Convention. The Court agreed and said at Para. 32:

> The "reasonableness" of the suspicion on which an arrest must be based forms an essential part of the safeguard against arbitrary arrest and detention which is laid down in Article 5(1)(c) . . . having a "reasonable

---

[21] (1988) Series A, No. 145-B, and 11 *EHRR* 117.
[22] (1990) Series A, No. 182, and 13 *EHRR* 157.
[23] [1985] 1 *All E.R.* 1.

suspicion" presupposes the existence of facts or information which would satisfy an objective observer that the person concerned may have committed the offence.

It went on to add that what may be regarded as "reasonable" will, however, depend upon all the circumstances, and that terrorist crime may fall into a special category because of the attendant risk of loss of life and of human suffering. Nevertheless, it concluded that

... the exigencies of dealing with terrorist crime cannot justify stretching the notion of "reasonableness" to the point where the essence of the safeguard secured by Article 5(1)(c) is impaired.

A violation of Article 5(1) was found.

Paragraph (3) of Article 5 says that everyone arrested or detained in accordance with Paragraph 5 (1) (c) "... shall be brought promptly before a judge or other officer authorized by law to exercise judicial power and shall be entitled to trial within a reasonable time or to release pending trial".

A person arrested on suspicion of having committed a crime must be able to test judicially the action taken by the authorities, and he must similarly be able to demand his release if continued detention is unjustified. Assertions by the state that the prisoner is likely to abscond or to commit further crimes, or that collusion or suppression of evidence may take place, must be shown to be real risks. For example, it may be possible to prevent the accused from fleeing by placing him on bail, or requiring other such guarantees. In the *Neumeister* case[24] the Court said,

It is for the national judicial authorities to seek all the facts arguing for or against the existence of a genuine requirement of public interest justifying a departure from the rule of respect for individual liberty.

The phrases "competent legal authority" in Article 5(1)(c), and "judge or other officer authorized by law to exercise judicial power" in Article 5(3), which are obviously related, were considered by the Court in the *Schiesser* case.[25] Friedrich Schiesser, a Swiss citizen, was

[24] (1968) Series A, No. 8, and 1 *EHRR* 91 at para. 5.
[25] (1979) Series A, No. 34, and 2 *EHRR* 417.

detained on remand by the order of the District Attorney on suspicion of having committed several serious offences. He alleged that the District Attorney, being a prosecuting authority, was unqualified to fulfil the terms of Article 5(3). The Court accepted that that "officer" was not identical with "judge", but that he must nevertheless satisfy conditions which constitute a guarantee for the person arrested. In particular, he should appear independent of the executive and of the parties; he should personally hear the individual brought before him; have power, by reference to legal criteria, to review the circumstances requiring detention; and be able to order release where he deems detention unjustified. In this particular case the Court held that the District Attorney offered "... the guarantees of independence and the procedural and substantive guarantees inherent in the notion of officer authorized by law to exercise judicial power". In *De Jong, Baljet and van den Brink* v. *Netherlands*[26] the Court reiterated:

> ... formal visible requirements stated in the "law" are especially important for the identification of the judicial authority empowered to decide on the liberty of the individual in view of the confidence which that authority must inspire in the public in a democratic society.

In that case the fact that the advice on release or otherwise given by the *auditeur militair* was invariably followed was not sufficient since it had no binding effect.

Where it is considered that continued detention on remand is justified at all, attention must then turn to deciding what is a "reasonable" time. The period of detention on remand is normally reckoned to end at the point of conviction by the court of first instance, although differences in European legal systems have caused the Commission to raise doubts as to whether this should not extend to time spent in prison pending appeal.

It is clear that a "reasonable time" to be detained prior to your trial is not to be calculated in the same way as the "reasonable time" which is contemplated by Article 6(1) for preparation of a fair trial. The circumstances of detention, in themselves, raise a serious departure from the rules of respect for individual liberty.

[26] (1983) Series A, No. 77, and 8 *EHRR* 20 at para. 48.

On several occasions, the Court has been called upon to determine what is a "reasonable time" for detention on remand. A series of cases against Austria and Germany in the late 1960s demonstrates that the length of time is not the only criterion for determining whether there has been a breach of Article 5(3). In the *Wemhoff* application[27] the Commission listed seven factors which it thought necessary to take into account in assessing reasonableness:

(1) the actual length of detention;

(2) the relation of the length of detention to the penalty on conviction;

(3) the material, moral or other effects on the detainee;

(4) the conduct of the accused during the investigation;

(5) the difficulties of the investigation;

(6) the manner in which the investigation was carried out;

(7) the conduct of the judicial authorities.

The Court, on the other hand, rejected this procedure.[28] Any applicant, it pointed out, must have exhausted domestic remedies prior to coming before the Commission, so there are, in every case, reasoned decisions by national authorities on the reasonableness of the time spent in detention on remand. The Court was therefore to judge whether these reasons were both relevant and sufficient to show that detention was not unreasonably prolonged, contrary to Article 5(3) of the Convention. The factors laid down by the Commission must, however, operate as a check-list, both for the national authorities and for the Commission and Court, in determining what is reasonable. The reasonableness of the time spent by an accused person in detention up to his trial must be assessed, so the Court declared in the *Neumeister* case, in relation to the very fact of his detention. A member of the Baader-Meinhoff group was detained on remand for over three and a half years, and yet the Commission held that in view of the circumstances and complexity of the case there had been no violation of Article 5(3). In 1969 the Court, in the *Stögmüller* case[29]

---

[27] Application 2122/64, *Wemhoff* v. *Federal Republic of Germany*, 7 *YB* 280 and 11 *YB* 796.

[28] (1968) Series A, No. 6, and 1 *EHRR* 55 at para. 17 *et seq.*

[29] (1969) Series A, No. 9, and 1 *EHRR* 155.

decided that there had been a violation of that Article, notwithstanding that the detention was for a lesser period of twenty-four months.

Release of an individual detained on suspicion may be conditioned by guarantees to appear for trial, but, as the Court pointed out in the *Neumeister* case, such a guarantee must be designed to ensure the presence of the accused at the hearing and not the reparation of any loss. The Court also went on to say that the provision

> ... cannot be understood as giving the judicial authorities a choice between either bringing the accused to trial within a reasonable time or granting him provisional release even subject to guarantees.

The purpose of Article 5(3) is essentially to require provisional release once continuing detention ceases to be reasonable.

Sub-paragraph (d) of Article 5(1) provides for the detention of minors for the purpose of educational supervision or for bringing them before the competent legal authority. The Court has shown, in the case of *Bouamar* v. *Belgium*,[30] a strict approach to the interpretation of this sub-paragraph. Naïm Bouamar was an adolescent with a disturbed personality. The Belgian authorities, however, seemed unable to find any institution or family which would take him and, as a result, he was shuttled back and forth between home and a remand prison. Even though the maximum time he was allowed to stay in prison at any one stretch was fifteen days, during the period of 291 days from January to November of 1980 he spent 119 so detained. The Court held that Belgium was under an obligation to provide appropriate educational facilities, and that

> The detention of a young man in a remand prison in conditions of virtual isolation and without the assistance of staff with educational training cannot be regarded as furthering any educational aim.

Sub-paragraph (e) of Article 5(1) allows for the detention of persons who, if allowed to remain free, might constitute a danger to the public at large; namely, those with infectious diseases or of unsound mind, alcoholics, drug addicts or vagrants. While restrictions of this kind must necessarily exist they do, at the same time, raise spectres of nightmarish proportions for the human rights lawyer.

---

[30] Note 13 *supra*, at para. 37.

Discussions of the use of compulsory detention as a means of containing AIDS, which were common at the early stage of the epidemic, give a foretaste of such horrors. The detention of dissidents in mental institutions, not unknown in the past in Eastern Europe and elsewhere, provides a further example where the right of liberty has been violated.

There are two major problems which arise in relation to the detention of persons for psychiatric reasons: how do you determine what "unsound mind" means, and who - doctor, judge or other administrative authority - should be permitted to make the "lawful" detention order?

In the *Winterwerp* case[31] the Court was asked to pronounce upon the reasonableness of the detention of the applicant in a Dutch mental hospital, and it held:

> In any event, sub-paragraph (e) of Article 5(1) obviously cannot be taken as permitting the detention of a person simply because his views or behaviour deviate from the norms prevailing in a particular society. To hold otherwise would not be reconcilable with the text of Article 5(1), which sets out an exhaustive list of exceptions calling for a narrow interpretation.

In this case, as in the *Vagrancy* cases[32] which concerned the definition of vagrancy, the Court scrutinized the national law to discover whether it appeared to be in any way incompatible with the definitions developed in the context of the Convention. In the *Guzzardi* case[33] the Italian Government, which was alleging that Mr Guzzardi should be subjected to "special supervision" on account of his previous anti-social activities, put forward as justification that he was a vagrant. The term, it argued, should be defined by reference to the concepts of the domestic law of the state concerned, as laid down by the Court in the *Vagrancy* cases. The Commission challenged the Government's interpretation of the Court's judgment:

> In fact, after finding that the Convention did not define the term "vagrant", the Court cited the definition in Article 347 of the Belgian

---

[31] *Supra,* note 12 at para. 37.
[32] *De Wilde, Ooms and Versyp* v. *Belgium,* (1971) Series A, No. 12, and 1 *EHRR* 373.
[33] Application 7367/76, 8 *D&R* 185 and 20 *YB* 462.

Criminal Code and went on to say that this "does not appear in any way irreconcilable with the usual meaning of the term 'vagrant'". The form of words used clearly shows that the Court found there was a coincidence of meaning and that it did not intend a reference to the domestic law.

Article 5(1)(e) places no limit on the duration of the detention of vagrants or persons of unsound mind, and Article 5(4), which allows the lawfulness of the detention to be challenged, may be of little use if the definition of such categories by the law lies within the area of "coincidence of meaning". The Court has recognized, however, that this is unsatisfactory where the detention ordered is of indefinite duration, and that the detained person does have the right to claim release if he can show that his condition no longer warrants incarceration.[34]

Indeed, of the cases listed in Article 5(1)(e) each one, with the exception of vagrancy, is now accepted as a medical condition for which there may be a cure. The result is that careful examination of such applications, especially those alleging "a cure" as "new information" under Article 27(1)(b), should enable the Commission and Court to guarantee individual liberty. Nevertheless the Convention does not guarantee appropriate treatment leading to early release.[35]

The final exception to liberty contained in Article 5(1)(f) authorizes the lawful detention of a person to prevent his effecting an unauthorized entry into the country, or of a person against whom action is being taken with a view to deportation or extradition. Problems may occur here where the individual is detained and then deported with such speed that it renders him unable to challenge his detention.

Lorenzo Bozano, wanted on charges of kidnapping and murder in Italy, fled to France. He was nevertheless tried *in absentia* by the Italian courts, convicted and sentenced to life imprisonment. Almost four years later he was arrested and detained by the French authorities with a view to extradition. The French courts, however, refused to order his extradition on the grounds that trial *in absentia* was contrary to French public policy, and he was released. At the same time a deportation order was issued. A month later Mr Bozano was seized

[34] See the *Winterwerp* case, *supra*, note 12.
[35] See *Winterwerp*, note 12, *supra*, and also *Ashingdane* v. *UK*, (1985) Series A, No. 93, and 7 *EHRR* 528.

by plain-clothes policemen at 8.30 one evening and taken to the Swiss border, where he was handed over to the Swiss police. It appeared that at the time when he was arrested the nearest border was in fact that of Spain, but an important feature seems to have been that Switzerland has an extradition treaty with Italy and so Mr Bozano was returned to Italy to serve his prison sentence. The European Court found that the irregular behaviour of the French authorities indicated a breach of Article 5(1)(f).[36] The deportation order had been issued and executed in such a way that it could not be effectively challenged and, furthermore, the sudden and secret deportation to Switzerland, when Spain was not only the choice of the prisoner but more convenient, all indicated a lack of good faith on the part of those carrying out the order.

Applications from persons likely to be deported or extradited need expeditious consideration by the European Commission.[37]

Although Paragraph (1) of Article 5 allows an individual to be imprisoned, not only must such detention be carried out lawfully and unarbitrarily but it must also be in accordance with certain minimum requirements laid down in paragraphs 2-5 of that Article.

Everyone who is arrested must be told the reasons for his arrest and the details of any charge against him. This must be done promptly in a language he understands and presumably in a manner which takes into account the circumstances and the mental capacity of the detainee.[38] As is the case in English law, the arrest does not have to be accompanied by a statement of the charges in any special form. The right to be informed of charges also appears in Article 6 as one of the rights appertaining to a fair trial. In this latter case, presumably, the information must be more detailed and formal since it is given in order to enable the preparation of a defence.

If you are deprived of your liberty you are entitled to take proceedings before a court to challenge the lawfulness of your detention and, if successful, you must be released - that is to say, the

---

[36] *Bozano* v. *France*, (1986) Series A, No. 111, and 9 *EHRR* 297.

[37] In the case of *Cruz Varas* v. *Sweden*, Series A, No. 201, the Swedish authorities chose to disregard an interim measure indicated by the Commission, and made under Rule 36 of its Rules of Procedure, to delay the applicant's deportation pending the Commission's consideration of his case.

[38] See, for example, *Van der Leer* v. *Netherlands*, (1990) Series A, No. 170, and 12 *EHRR* 567.

European equivalent of *habeas corpus*. However, where the original detention is ordered by a court at the end of the judicial proceedings, such as are laid down in Article 5(1)(a), then the right under Article 5(4) would seem to be satisfied. In the *Vagrancy* cases which came before the Court in 1971[39] the applicants were detained by order of a magistrate as vagrants, where the magistrate was acting in an administrative capacity. The Court agreed with the applicants that under Article 5(4) the Government was bound to make available the right of recourse to a court to test the administrative decision. It went on to say that

> there is nothing to indicate that the same applies when the decision is made by a court at the close of judicial proceedings.

This limitation placed on Article 5(4) by the Court would seem to render its protection somewhat narrower than the writ of *habeas corpus* which may be used even to test a conviction by a court. Indeed, the subsequent case law of the Strasbourg organs has recognized that Paragraph 4 will apply on a broader basis, so that where an individual is found to be mentally defective and ordered to be detained for an indefinite period, then Article 5(4) ought to give the detainee the right to have the legality of his deprivation of liberty verified by a tribunal at a later stage, irrespective of whether it was ordered by a judicial or administrative authority. In the case of *X* v. *UK*[40] the Court held that:

> ... a person of unsound mind compulsorily confined in a psychiatric institution for an indefinite or lengthy period is in principle entitled, at any rate where there is no automatic periodic review of a judicial character, to take proceedings at reasonable intervals before a court to put in issue the "lawfulness" ... of his detention, whether that detention was ordered by a civil or criminal court or by some other authority.[41]

In a similar way, even though Article 5(3) requires that a prisoner on remand should be entitled to a trial within a reasonable time, it does not, as such, entitle proceedings to be initiated to question the

---

[39] *De Wilde, Ooms and Versyp* v. *Belgium.* See note 32, *supra*, at para. 46.
[40] (1982) Series A, No. 46, and 4 *EHRR* 188 at para. 52.
[41] See also *Weeks* v. *UK, supra,* note 16.

lawfulness of the detention. Paragraph 4 would seem to be relevant at this stage.[42]

The Court has expressed the view that although proceedings under Article 5(4) are not governed by the procedural guarantees laid down in Article 6 for a fair trial, they should, nonetheless, be seen to be fair.[43]

Finally, Article 5(5) lays down that everyone who has been a victim of arrest or detention in contravention of the provisions of Article 5 should have an enforceable right to compensation. In the *Wemhoff* case[44] the Commission was of the opinion that before Article 5(5) could become the subject matter of an application the Court or Committee of Ministers must have given an opinion that Article 5(3) had been violated, and the subsequent claim for compensation must have been made at national level, in order to comply with the rule necessitating exhaustion of domestic remedies. It must be said that Article 5(5) would apply to all the paragraphs of the Article, not only to Paragraph (3). If the Court or Committee of Ministers finds a violation of Article 5(1)-(4) then the applicant would seem to qualify in any case, so that if paragraph (5) is not to prove superfluous it must mean that compensation should be available at national level without recourse to the machinery of the Convention. Indeed, in the *Huber* application against Austria[45] the Commission revised its jurisprudence on this point, when it stated:

> ... where a breach of paragraphs (1)-(4) has been established by a national court - either directly if the said provisions form part of the domestic law concerned or in substance - the applicant who has been denied compensation can bring before the Commission a breach of Article 5 paragraph (5), after exhaustion of domestic remedies in this respect.

In order to obtain information on the working of this Paragraph in national legal systems, in 1972 the Secretary-General of the Council of Europe, acting under powers bestowed by Article 57 of the

---

[42] See *Bezicheri* v. *Italy,* (1989) Series A, No. 164, and 12 *EHRR* 210.

[43] See, for example, *Sanchez-Reisse* v. *Switzerland* (1986) Series A, No. 107, and 9 *EHRR* 71, and *Lamy* v. *Belgium,* (1989) Series A, No. 151, and 11 *EHRR* 529.

[44] See *supra,* note 27.

[45] Application 6821/74, 6 *D&R* 65, at para. 3.

Convention, requested the Contracting Parties to furnish him with information concerning the implementation of Article 5(5).

TREATMENT OF DETAINEES

Having established that an individual is lawfully detained in a prison or other institution, we should next turn to consideration of the treatment he receives while he is there. First of all, we should not be unaware of the difficulties which prisoners may face when trying to reveal the conditions under which they may be held

We have seen that Article 8 of the Convention respects the right of correspondence.[46] The censoring and reading of prisoners' mail has been the subject of several important applications. The view now taken by the Strasbourg organs is that the censoring of such letters should be subject only to the grounds for interference listed in Article 8 paragraph 2, and that correspondence should not be censored or withheld unless it involves violent threats or plans further crimes.[47] Personal letters should be allowed[48] and correspondence with lawyers should not be inhibited.[49]

Under Article 25 of the Convention, which makes provision for individual petition to the Commission, the Contracting Parties undertake not to hinder in any way the effective exercise of this right. It is, of course, most important that any person who feels that his rights have been violated should be free to communicate with the Commission, and this is especially so in the case of prisoners.

The European Agreement relating to persons participating in Proceedings of the European Commission and Court of Human Rights was signed in 1969,[50] and has now been ratified by twenty states. The Contracting Parties agree that individuals should correspond freely with the Commission when exercising their rights under Article 25 of the Convention. In relation to applicants who are prisoners the Agreement recognizes that the authorities may examine all correspondence, but

[46] *Supra,* Chapter 5.

[47] *Silver et al* v. *UK,* (1983) Series A, No. 61, and 5 *EHRR* 347. There has been some modification of rules on prisoners' correspondence in the UK since this case.

[48] See, for example, *Boyle and Rice* v. *UK,* (1988) Series A, No. 131, and 10 *EHRR* 425.

[49] *Golder* v. *UK,* (1975) Series A, No. 18, and 1 *EHRR* 524. *Schönenberger and Durmaz* v. *Switzerland,* (1988) Series A, No. 137, and 11 *EHRR* 202.

[50] 788 *UNTS* 2 44; *UKTS* 44 (1971), Cmnd 4699.

provides that there shall be no delay in its dispatch and no alteration of the contents. It further requires that no disciplinary measures should be taken arising out of any communication.

Article 3 of the Convention, a short provision containing no exceptions and from which there can be no derogation under the terms of Article 15, declares that no one shall be subjected to torture or to inhuman or degrading treatment or punishment. In many cases, instances of ill-treatment in prisons are isolated affairs brought about by the attitude of the prisoner himself or of prison officers. The Convention imposes a duty on States Parties to secure to individuals within their jurisdiction the rights it contains, and a state must be able to justify to the Commission the treatment that a detainee has received. Where a prison officer has taken matters into his own hands and ill treatment has occurred, the prisoner must be able to gain redress through local remedies made available at national level. If local remedies are not to be found, then the state must bear responsibility, and if the acts in question amount to inhuman or degrading treatment or punishment, then a state will be liable for a breach of Convention.

Often, of course, harsh treatment meted out to prisoners may be a practice which has developed with or without the knowledge of the Government, but where such practices come to light the Government will bear responsibility, since it must be deemed to know what is happening within its prisons and institutions. Félix Tomasi was an active member of a Corsican political party. He was arrested on suspicion of being involved in murders resulting from commando-style bomb attacks. His detention for over five and a half years amounted to a breach of Articles 5(3) and 6(1).[51] He alleged that, during interrogations at the start of his detention, he was beaten up for a period of forty hours. The French Government conceded that they could not explain the cause of his injuries. The Court, in finding a violation of Article 3, said:

> The requirements of the investigation and the undeniable difficulties inherent in the fight against crime, particularly with regard to terrorism, cannot result in limits being placed on the protection to be afforded in respect of the physical integrity of individuals.

[51] *Tomasi* v. *France*, (1992) Series A, No. 241-A.

In *McFeeley et al* v. *UK*,[52] a group of prisoners in the Maze prison in Northern Ireland, protesting their denial of special status, refused to wear prison uniform and to wash or use toilet facilities. The Commission rejected the complaints of inhuman and degrading treatment but pointed out that even though much of the prisoners' humiliation had been brought about by their own behaviour, this did not absolve the Government of its responsibilities under Article 3:

> ... the Convention requires that the prison authorities, with due regard to the ordinary and reasonable requirements of imprisonment, exercise their custodial authority to safeguard the health and well-being of all prisoners including those engaged in protest insofar as that may be possible in the circumstances.

In the *Greek* case[53] the Commission considered allegations of ill-treatment and torture in Greek prisons which seemed, in many instances, to be carried out as a matter of routine. In such circumstances, the Commission felt, it was likely that the prescribed remedies for such brutality had been sidestepped or rendered inadequate. It stated in its report:

> Thus, if there was an administrative practice of torture or ill-treatment, judicial remedies prescribed would tend to be rendered ineffective by the difficulty of securing probative evidence, and administrative enquiries would either not be instituted, or, if they were, would be likely to be half-hearted and incomplete.

As a result, the Applicant States in that case were excused from exhausting domestic remedies. In a case brought by the Republic of Ireland against the United Kingdom[54] a similar "administrative practice" was discovered in the shape of the "five techniques" of interrogation used by the British authorities in Northern Ireland. The Court, holding that there had been inhuman and degrading treatment, stated:

> A practice incompatible with the Convention consists of an accumulation of identical or analogous breaches which are sufficiently numerous and

---

[52] Application 8317/78, 20 *D&R* 44, and 23 *YB* 256 at para. 46.
[53] 12 *YB* (special volume), 186 *et seq.*
[54] *Ireland* v. *UK*, (1978) Series A, No. 25, and 2 *EHRR* 25.

inter-connected to amount not merely to isolated incidents or exceptions but to a pattern or system; a practice does not of itself constitute a violation separate from such breaches.

It is inconceivable that the higher authorities of a state should be, or at least should be entitled to be, unaware of the existence of such practice. Furthermore, under the Convention those authorities are strictly liable for the conduct of their subordinates; they are under a duty to impose their will on subordinates and cannot shelter behind their inability to ensure that it is respected.[55]

In the application *Gerard Donnelly and others* v. *United Kingdom*[56] - which also concerned the treatment of prisoners in Northern Ireland - the Commission considered, by similar reasoning, that where an applicant under Article 25, that is to say an individual petitioner, submits evidence substantiating the existence of an administrative practice of ill-treatment contrary to Article 3, and claims that he has been a victim of it, then he too will be released of the requirement of exhausting domestic remedies in relation to that part of his application.

"Inhuman treatment" was defined by the Commission in the *Greek* case as "... such treatment as deliberately causes severe suffering, mental or physical, which, in the particular situation, is unjustifiable."

The term "torture" it went on to define as an aggravated form of inhuman treatment, while treatment or punishment was to be seen as degrading if it grossly humiliates the individual before others, or drives him to act against his will or conscience. In the *Ireland* v. *UK* case, the Court added that degrading treatment might also be "... ill-treatment designed to arouse in victims feelings of fear, anguish and inferiority capable of humiliating and debasing them and possibly breaking their physical or moral resistance". The word "unjustifiable", in the Commission's *Greek* case definition, does not mean that the motive for ill-treatment may be considered, but that treatment or punishment which may be suitable on one occasion may be inhuman and degrading on another, after taking into account the circumstances and the identity of the victim. Punishment which may

---

[55] *Supra*, note 54, para. 159.
[56] Applications 5577-5583/72 (joined), 43 *CD* 122, and 19 *YB* 84.

be suitable for a man may be wholly unjustifiable if used against a child.

In the *Bonnechaux* case[57] the Commission stated that it could not rule out the possibility that the detention for thirty six months of a prisoner aged seventy-four, suffering from diabetes and cardio-vascular disorders, might, in certain circumstances, raise problems in regard to Article 3 of the Convention. In the application of *Char- tier* against Italy[58] the prisoner suffered from extreme obesity, which needed specialist treatment. The Commission examined his application carefully and, while it commented on the fact that Italian law was already sensitive in its approach, urged the authorities to keep his condition of health under review and to hospitalize him if necessary. The Commission has also not been unaware, in some cases, that the un-cooperative attitude of the prisoner may have contributed to his ill-health and suffering.[59] In an application in 1979, concerning the questioning of a ten year old girl,[60] it stated in similar vein:

> It is necessary that interrogations of children be carried out in a manner respecting their age and susceptibility.

When determining the severity of punishment or treatment which is to be allowed, we come particularly upon the problem of inherent limitations. No matter what the major reason for locking up prison-ers, one desired consequence is restriction of liberty. How far that liberty should be restricted is, however, a matter of much debate. We have seen that in the early days of the Commission there was a great tendency to cling to "European" norms, without assessing them by reference to the Convention and its jurisprudence. More recently the Commission has shown a far more open mind in this area. Nevertheless, it is no easy problem to decide whether certain conse-quences which flow from imprisoning men together, away from so-ciety, should be accepted as conditions of imprisonment, or whether the Government has a duty to alleviate those which may be termed cruel, inhuman or degrading.

---

[57] *Bonnechaux* v. *Switzerland,* Application 8224/78, 18 *D&R* 149, and 23 *YB* 496.
[58] Application 9044/80, 33 *D&R* 41.
[59] See, for example, Application 9559/81, *de Varga-Hirsch* v. *France,* 33 *D&R* 158.
[60] Application 8819/79, *X* v. *Federal Republic of Germany,* 24 *D&R* 158.

Solitary confinement is not necessarily inhuman, but the Commission has put forward the view that prolonged solitary confinement, especially of prisoners on remand, is undesirable, and has said on many occasions:

> Complete sensory isolation coupled with complete social isolation can no doubt ultimately destroy the personality.

Nevertheless, it has to be recognized that there may well be reasons for keeping a prisoner separate from others; for instance, there may be a risk that information that a prisoner holds and which may lead to his or others escaping justice could be spread or, again, it may be necessary for the physical safety of the other inmates or the prisoner himself that he should be kept apart. The Commission will have regard to such factors as the conditions of detention, the stringency of the measures, their duration and objective, and the effects on the prisoner concerned, in concluding whether solitary confinement violates Article 3. Needless to say, the personality of the prisoner and the nature and seriousness of the crime are important elements, and the discretion of the authorities has to be respected.

The application of *Ensslin, Baader and Raspe* against Germany[61] involved such a consideration. The applicants were notorious members of a West German terrorist gang and were kept apart from other prisoners. All of the applicants committed suicide and, necessarily, the question of how much their isolation was a contributory factor achieved prominence. After careful consideration the Commission reached the view that:

> ... having regard to the overall circumstances of the case, and in particular the continuous review of the detention arrangements by the authorities of the Federal Republic of Germany and the behaviour of the applicants themselves, particularly their rejection of certain opportunities for contact open to them, the applicants cannot be deemed to have been deliberately subjected to a range of physical or mental suffering designed to punish them, to destroy their personality or to break down their resistance ... The special arrangements imposed upon them were therefore not in the nature of inhuman or degrading treatment.

---

[61] Applications 7572/76, 7586/76 and 7587/76 (joined), 14 *D&R* 64, and 21 *YB* 418, at para. 10.

In the application of *Kröcher and Möller*,[62] concerning the secure and isolated conditions in which terrorists were held in a Swiss gaol, the Commission's opinion that Article 3 had not been breached was reached by a majority of only eight to five votes.

The prisoner who brought Application 10263/83[63] was detained in solitary confinement for five months while on remand on a charge of being an accomplice in the murder of a suspected drug trafficker. It was pointed out that he was allowed periods of exercise, had access to books, television and radio, and contacts with the prison staff and doctors. The Commission felt that, although the period was undesirably long, the need to keep him out of circulation while the investigation proceeded had been established and that the treatment was not, therefore, severe enough to warrant a finding of a violation of Article 3.

The same view prevailed in a case against the United Kingdom,[64] where the prisoner complained that he was detained in the notorious "cage" at Wakefield gaol. This involved strict security, exercise of only one hour per day and no contact with other prisoners. Furthermore, the prisoner was accompanied by five prison officers whenever he left his cell, even to bath. It was pointed out, however, that he had killed persons on three occasions, the last two being fellow prisoners whom he appeared to murder for no apparent reason. In the case of *Reed* v. *UK*,[65] which ended with a friendly settlement, the rough treatment and assaults on a prisoner involved in a riot in Hull Prison in 1976 were deemed to constitute inhuman treatment, while strict and severe treatment meted out when he was transferred to Winchester and Leeds Prisons were justified by the nature of his participation in the riot.

The additional penalty imposed in Austrian gaols of *hartes Lager* (sleeping hard) has been deemed by the Commission to be acceptable.

In the well-known *Tyrer* case[66] the Court held that the punishment of birching practised in the Isle of Man was contrary to Article 3 of the Convention. In the related field of corporal punishment of

---

[62] Application 8463/78, 34 *D&R* 24.
[63] 41 *D&R* 149.
[64] Application 9907/82, 353 *D&R* 130.
[65] Application 7630/76, 19 *D&R* 113, and 23 *YB* 110, 24 *YB* 394. The friendly settlement involved paying the applicant £2,000 compensation, and revision of the rules concerning the ventilation of complaints by prisoners.
[66] (1978) Series A, No. 26, and 2 *EHRR* 1.

juveniles in schools in the United Kingdom, the Commission was of the view in a 1981 application[67] that the beating of a sixteen year old girl by a male teacher in front of another man was sufficiently humiliating to involve Article 3. We have seen that the threatened use of the *tawse* on two schoolboys was not enough, in itself, to be inhuman or degrading.[68] Nevertheless, the result of these cases has been the abolition of the use of the cane in British state schools.[69] Two further cases went before the Court in 1992 concerning corporal punishment in private schools in the United Kingdom. In its judgment of 25 March 1993 in the case of *Costello-Roberts*[70] a majority of the Court was of the opinion that the punishment of "slippering" with a rubber-soled gym shoe did not reach the level of severity to amount to a violation of Article 3 of the Convention. The Court had some misgivings about the automatic nature of the punishment ascribed by the school rules and also about the three-day wait before its imposition. The minority of four of the nine judges, on the other hand, felt that the ritualised punishment of a lonely seven-year-old merely a month after he had started at boarding school was degrading and should amount to a violation of Article 3. Interestingly, in the other case of *Y* v. *UK* a friendly settlement was reached before the Court's judgment whereby the British Government, without admitting liability, agreed to pay the applicant £8,000 in addition to his costs.

Jacob Kamma[71] alleged that he was told by the police that "it was about time [he] confessed and that they would then take care that the penalty would not be so heavy, adding that in any case [he] would be convicted and that [he] would not leave the headquarters until they knew everything". The Commission held that this could not be described as undue pressure amounting to inhuman or degrading treatment. Another prisoner was told by the Commission that deprivation of conjugal rights could not be counted as a violation of Article 3. In the *Zeidler Kornmann* Application[72] the prisoner complained of

[67] Application 9471/81, *Warwick* v. *UK*, 36 *D&R* 49, and 60 *D&R* 5.

[68] *Campbell and Cosans* v. *UK*, (1982) Series A, No. 60. and 13 *EHRR* 441. See *supra*, Chapter 4.

[69] Education (No. 2) Act 1986.

[70] See *The Independent Law Report*, 26 March 1993. See also Chapter 4, note 38.

[71] Application 4771/71, *Kamma* v. *Netherlands*, 42 *CD* 14 and 18 *YB* 300.

[72] Application 2686/65, *Zeidler Kornmann* v. *Federal Republic of Germany*, 22 *CD* 1, and 11 *YB* 1020.

the rough treatment he had received at the hands of prison officers, which had culminated in his being put in a strait-jacket. After careful consideration the Commission rejected his claim that this was inhuman, taking into account all the circumstances and especially the prisoner's violent behaviour. It is of the essence of interpretation of Article 3 that the condition, health and age of the victim should be given especial consideration. A prisoner who claimed he should have been detained in a psychiatric hospital, rather than an ordinary prison, was receiving suitable medical care and was not considered a victim of inhuman punishment. On the other hand, Mr Simon-Herold,[73] partially paralysed from poliomyelitis, was detained in a closed ward of a psychiatric hospital, together with several violent lunatics. His case was admitted by the Commission, but a friendly settlement was achieved and the Austrian authorities issued directives concerning the accommodation of such prisoners. There is no doubt that harsh punishments for trivial crimes would amount to a violation of Article 3.

In 1973 the Committee of Ministers of the Council of Europe adopted by Resolution 73(5), Minimum Rules for the Treatment of Prisoners. As a result, Mr Eggs, as part of his complaint against Switzerland,[74] argued that any treatment below the standard laid down in these rules should be characterized as inhuman. The Commission was unconvinced, however, and indeed, in a case registered in the same year,[75] held that even where the treatment has been improved in line with the Minimum Rules this does not mean that the standard prevailing before was necessarily inhuman.

Generally, the Convention does not provide any right to call into question the length of sentences imposed by a competent court,[76] although it may be submitted that if these were cruelly excessive there might be a question under Article 3. Mr Hogben complained that a change in the British Government's policy on parole, dashing his expectation of early release, was inhuman, but he failed to convince the Commission.[77] Similarly, in an application against

---

[73] Application 4340/69, *Simon-Herold* v. *Austria*, 38 *CD* 18 and 14 *YB* 352.

[74] Application 7341/76, 6 *D&R* 170.

[75] Application 7408/76, 10 *D&R* 221.

[76] See, for example, Application 5871/72, 1 *D&R* 54 and Application 7057/75, 6 *D&R* 127.

[77] Application 11653/85, 46 *D&R* 231.

Luxembourg no violation of Article 3 was found where the prosecuting authorities had commenced executing a judgment but subsequently entered an appeal against the judgment.[78]

In *McQuiston* v. *UK* [79] the British authorities' policy of integrating
loyalist and republican prisoners in Northern Ireland prisons was
examined under the provisions of Article 3. The Commission scrutinized the conditions and the resulting incidents but was not prepared to hold a violation.

The death sentence itself is specifically allowed by Article 2 of the
Convention, but the circumstances in which, and conditions upon
which, it is imposed may still be subject to the tests of Article 3.

The *Soering* case[80] concerned the attempted extradition of the applicant by the United Kingdom to the United States. Jens Soering, an
eighteen year old German national, was wanted for the brutal and
horrific killing of his girlfriend's parents. His extradition was requested by the Federal authorities so that he could stand trial in Vir-
ginia. The British Government, on the basis of his youth, his mental
state and the likely consequences under Virginian law should he be
found guilty, sought assurances that the death penalty would not be
carried out. Although the Federal authorities were willing to comply
they could not, of course, commit the Virginian judge. Nevertheless,
the United Kingdom Secretary of State signed the warrant of surrender. The application to the Commission alleged a violation of
Article 3, not because of the likelihood of the death penalty – which
is, in any case, provided for in the exceptions to Article 2 of the Convention[81] – but because of the "death-row phenomenon", namely
that there was a substantial risk that the applicant would be condemned to death and spend a lengthy period (on average six to eight
years) awaiting a series of appeals and the like, with the ever-present
and mounting anguish of the impending execution of the death
penalty.

A major factor in the United Kingdom's arguments was that a
refusal to extradite involved an adjudication on the internal affairs

---

[78] Application 10142/82, 42 *D&R* 86.

[79] Application 11208/84, 46 *D&R* 182.

[80] (1989) Series A, No. 161, and 11 *EHRR* 439.

[81] Amnesty International submitted arguments in this case that within the European region the death penalty had, in effect, been abolished and that Article 3 might
apply to it. This attracted some support in the Commission.

of a foreign state which was not even a party to the Convention, and that this entailed grave difficulties of evaluation and proof, by requiring an examination of alien systems of law and conditions in foreign states. It also pointed out that refusal to extradite, and the consequent release, would leave dangerous criminals untried, unpunished and at leave to re-offend.[82] The Court, nevertheless, was of the view that a decision by a Contracting State to extradite a fugitive could give rise to an issue under Article 3 of the Convention, where substantial grounds were shown for believing that the person concerned, if extradited, faced a real risk of being subjected to inhuman treatment or punishment in the requesting country.

The Respondent State in the *Soering* case had pointed out that only a *prima facie* case had been made in the United Kingdom, that in all likelihood a verdict of insanity would be found and, furthermore, the recommendation that the death penalty should not be carried out could well be accepted. However, the Court felt there was a "real risk" that the threshold set by Article 3 would be breached.

In an earlier application against the United Kingdom by *Kirkwood*,[83] the Commission had rejected as inadmissible a similar complaint. In that case the prisoner's extradition to California was requested on a charge of murder and attempted murder, and the "death row phenomenon" was also considered. Youth and unstable mental condition, however, were not factors in this case and the application was rejected.

The Convention guarantees neither the right to political asylum nor the right not to be expelled, and the Strasbourg organs have been careful to ensure that claims under Article 3 are not used as a means of undermining these deliberate omissions. As a result an applicant must produce clear evidence both that he is likely to be persecuted and also that the treatment he is likely to receive is severe enough to cross the threshold required by Article 3.

In the *Cruz Varas* case against Sweden[84] the applicant had been refused political asylum and deported to his country of origin, Chile.

---

[82] In the present case, Mr Soering could have been extradited to Germany where he could have been tried and where there is no death penalty. Nonetheless, the United States would seem to have had a prior claim.

[83] Application 10479/83, 37 *D&R* 158, and 27 *YB* 170.

[84] (1991) Series A, No. 201, and 14 *EHRR* 1.

Although there was some evidence that the applicant had been tortured in the past, there had been some improvement in conditions in that country and the Court agreed with the Government that substantial grounds for believing that the applicant's expulsion would expose him to a real risk of being subjected to further inhuman treatment on his return had not been established.

A similar decision was taken in the case of *Vilvarajah et al* v. *UK*,[85] which concerned the fate of five young Tamils returned to Sri Lanka under British Immigration procedures. Even though there was evidence that they were badly treated, and in some cases tortured, the Court expressed its view as follows:

> The evidence before the Court concerning the background of the applicants, as well as the general situation, does not establish that their personal position was any worse than the generality of other members of the Tamil community or other young male Tamils who were returning to their country ... A mere possibility of ill treatment, however, in such circumstances, is not in itself sufficient to give rise to a breach of Article 3.

The Court also alluded to the importance it attached to the knowledge and experience that the UK authorities had in dealing with large numbers of asylum-seekers from Sri Lanka, many of whom were granted leave to stay.

Similarly the Commission has said that

> The mere fact that an offence is punished more severely in one country than in another does not suffice to establish that the punishment is inhuman or degrading.[86]

Philip Agee, a former member of the CIA, had written books and articles about the activities of the CIA which had provoked a political storm in the United States of America. He was informed by the British Home Office that his leave to enter the United Kingdom could not be further extended, and that his departure "... would be conducive to the public good as being in the interests of national security". He complained to the Commission, *inter alia*, that his deportation constituted degrading treatment in that it amounted to an arbitrary,

---

[85] (1991) Series A, No. 215, and 14 *EHRR* 248 at para. 111.
[86] Application 11017/84, *C.* v. *Federal Republic of Germany*, 46 *D&R* 176.

unjustified or disproportionate penalty.[87] The Commission rejected his application; there was no question of Mr Agee being inhumanly treated if he were returned to the United States of America, although he might face prosecution there. The deportation of an alien on grounds of state security cannot, in normal circumstances, be looked upon as a penalty. The Commission continued, at Paragraph 10,

> ... it has not been shown in the present case that the authorities' intention was to punish the applicant, as he has suggested, rather than to protect national security. Such deportation cannot be considered as contrary to Article 3 in itself.

---

[87] Application 7729/76, *Agee* v. *UK*, 7 *D&R* 164.

CHAPTER SEVEN

The Individual before the Courts

A FAIR HEARING

The existence of courts in a legal system, and the need to take care to
ensure the independence of those called upon to operate within
those courts, is fundamental to modern society and the rule of law. It
is not surprising that the European Commission and Court are called
upon frequently to decide cases involving interpretation of Article
6 of the Convention, the Article which guarantees a fair hearing. "In
the determination of his civil rights and obligations or of any criminal charge against him," reads Article 6(1), "everyone is entitled to a
fair and public hearing within a reasonable time by an independent
and impartial tribunal established by law".

The Article is about the settlement of disputes and claims which
may be made under domestic law, but there are problems in interpreting the phrase "civil rights and obligations". One obvious point
is that it should not be taken in the Anglo-American sense of "civil
liberties". The implication in the text, which receives some support
from the *travaux préparatoires*, is that "civil rights" refers to private
law rights as opposed to public law.

It is certain that all disputes of a private law nature between individuals and settled by judicial procedure, are covered by the terms
of the Article. The Strasbourg organs have rightly pointed out, however, that the characterization within the domestic law should not be
the criterion on which application of Article 6 is based. States may
draw differently the line between private rights and public rights,
whereas the procedural guarantees bestowed by the Convention
should be available wherever a dispute occurs in which the rights of
the individual arise for determination. In the *Ringeisen* application[1]
the Commission felt that the Austrian authorities were applying

---

[1] Application 2614/65, 27 *CD* 29 and 11 *YB* 268.

rules of administrative law. The Court did not agree with the Commission's final decision:[2]

> The character of the legislation which governs how the matter is to be determined (civil, commercial, administrative law, etc.) and that of the authority which is invested with jurisdiction in the matter (ordinary court, administrative body, etc.) are of little consequence.

Ringeisen had introduced proceedings before a Regional Land Commission in Austria, an administrative tribunal, requesting authorization to transfer farmland which he wished to develop as a building site. He alleged that those proceedings had been in violation of Article 6(1) of the Convention. The Court thought that the provisions of Article 6(1) were applicable:

> In the present case, when Ringeisen purchased property from the Roth couple, he had a right to have the contract of sale which they made with him approved if he fulfilled, as he claimed to do, the conditions laid down in the Act. Although it was applying rules of administrative law, the Regional Commission's decision was to be decisive for the relations in civil law (*"de caractère civil"*) between Ringeisen and the Roth couple. This is enough to make it necessary for the Court to decide whether or not the proceedings in this case complied with the requirements of Article 6(1) of the Convention.

Although decisions of public authorities are *prima facie* outside the protection afforded by Article 6(1), if the effect of such decisions is to interfere with existing relations under civil law between private individuals, Article 6(1) will become relevant. The Court confirmed this view in the *König* case when it decided that proceedings introduced by Dr König, challenging the withdrawal of authorization to run his private clinic and to practise as a doctor, involved rights of a private character. These were unaffected by the imposition of supervision by the authorities in the interests of public health and which were, as a result, subject to the provisions of Article 6(1). Thus "civil rights" will be determined as an autonomous concept. The Court has consistently avoided giving an abstract definition of "civil rights and obligations", but will examine each case to see if public or

---

[2] (1971) Series A, No. 13, and 1 *EHRR* 455 at para. 94.

private characteristics are predominant,[3] and to ensure that the outcome of the dispute is decisive for the applicant's civil rights. The Court has also held that the dispute[4] should not be construed too technically and should be given a substantive rather than a technical meaning and that the rights involved should have more than a mere tenuous connection with the decision-making process.[5] An extensive jurisprudence shows Article 6 applied to a large range of disputes, from decisions of an administrative nature affecting property rights,[6] to cases concerning the right to carry on a profession or other economic activity,[7] and to decisions of public authorities in social matters.[8]

It should be remembered that Article 6 is about the working of machinery for determining disputes within the domestic law and not strictly about the content of that law. As a result, the Commission and Court have frequently held that the domestic law does not provide a "right" which can be tested before the courts or other procedures,[9] or that the applicant's right to the determination of a "civil right" has been properly restricted.[10]

Where the "civil right or obligation" is dependent upon the exercise of the discretion of the decision-making authority, it could be argued that, provided the decision was lawfully made and was *intra vires*, Article 6 should not apply. Thus, in the case of *Kaplan* v. *UK*,[11] the Commission held that the restrictions placed on the applicant's

---

[3] See, for example, *Feldbrugge* v. *Netherlands*, (1986) Series A, No. 99, and 8 *EHRR* 425. *Deumeland* v. *Federal Republic of Germany*, (1986) Series A, No. 100, and 8 *EHRR* 448. *H.* v. *Belgium*, (1987) Series A, No. 127, and 10 *EHRR* 339.

[4] The English text refers only to the "determination" of civil rights and obligations whereas the French version makes reference to a *"contestation"* and, as a result, it is necessary to show some kind of serious disagreement concerning "civil rights and obligations".

[5] *Le Compte, Van Leuven and De Meyere* v. *Belgium*, (1981) Series A, No. 43, and 4 *EHRR* 1.

[6] For example, *Skärby* v. *Sweden*, (1990) Series A, No. 180-B, and 13 *EHRR* 90.

[7] For example, *Benthem* v. *Netherlands*, (1985) Series A, No. 97, and 8 *EHRR* 1.

[8] For example, a number of cases against the United Kingdom concerning access of parents to children, (1987) Series A, Nos. 120 and 121, and 10 *EHRR* 82 and 95.

[9] *James et al* v. *UK*, (1986) Series A, No. 98, and 6 *EHRR* 123; *Powell and Rayner* v. *UK*, (1990) Series A, No. 172, and 12 *EHRR* 355.

[10] For example in the case of a mental patient, *Ashingdane* v. *UK*, (1985) Series A, No. 93, and 7 *EHRR* 528; or servicemen *Dyer* v. *UK* Application 10475/83, 39 *D&R* 246, and 27 *YB* 170. *Wallace-Jones* v. *UK*, 47 *D&R* 157. The distinction is not always easy to make, however.

[11] Application 7598/76, 21 *D&R* 5, and 22 *YB* 190.

insurance business by a decision of the Minister were not subject to Article 6(1) because the applicant did not challenge their lawfulness. The Court, however, has taken a different view, and in such cases as *Le Compte, Van Leuven and De Meyere*[12] and *Benthem*,[13] has indicated that the dispute may be as to the existence of the right, its scope or the manner of its exercise, and this may involve questions both of law and fact, and therefore be governed by Article 6. Even if the decision is not taken by a tribunal the Court will require that it is at some stage subject to judicial review, and that this review includes an examination of the merits. In the case of *Van Marle* v. *Netherlands*,[14] which concerned the registration of accountants who satisfied conditions as to experience and competence, the Court drew a distinction and said:

> An assessment of this kind, evaluating knowledge and experience for carrying on a profession under a particular title, is akin to a school or university examination and is so far removed from the exercise of the normal judicial function that the safeguards in Article 6 cannot be taken as covering resultant disagreements.

While we can observe that Article 6 is not applicable to matters which are of a prominently public law character, such as taxation, it is not always easy to determine whether a dispute in such fields as planning and licensing, for instance, contains a sufficient element of individual rights so as to invoke the application of Article 6. The Court has adopted a fairly casuistic approach and it is difficult to say when, or even if, a set of satisfactory principles will be distilled from the jurisprudence. Judge Matscher has been consistently critical of the Court's approach under Article 6, as exemplified by his dissenting judgment in *Le Compte, Van Leuven and De Meyere* in 1981:

> The present judgment ... is, of course, based on the worthy intention of affording to the individual protection against interferences by public, professional or social authorities in an especially important area like the exercise of a profession. The fact that the Convention is defective in this respect is a point that I myself have emphasized on numerous occasions. But, according to my view of the judicial role, it is no part of the functions

---

[12] See *supra*, note 5, at para. 1.
[13] See *supra*, note 7.
[14] (1986) Series A, No. 101, and 8 *EHRR* 483 at para. 36.

of an international court to give recognition to rights which the authors of the Convention did not intend to include therein. This unsatisfactory situation cannot therefore be validly rectified by means of judicial interpretation, and this is all the more so because such an interpretation threatens to upset the Convention system in one of its most sensitive sectors.

In the same way that the Convention organs are not limited by domestic law in deciding when Article 6 applies to "the determination of civil rights and obligations", their approach to determining what is a "criminal charge" has been that this, too, must be autonomous, and that the decisive factor must be substance rather than form. A "charge" has been defined as

> The official notification given to an individual by the competent authority of an allegation that he has committed a criminal offence.[15]

Sometimes, the Court has said, it may take the form of other measures which carry the implication of such an allegation, and which substantially affect the suspect's situation.[16] It may be important to know the precise moment of the "charge" when the complaint concerns the length of proceedings.

Generally, a state will be free to choose what behaviour it wishes to characterize as criminal, and as long as this does not in itself go beyond the bounds of the Convention, the Commission and Court will accept that definition and apply Article 6. Problems can arise, however, where the state decides that certain behaviour will be subject to a different classification. For instance, what may be seen in other states or in other circumstances as a criminal offence may be treated by the authorities as an administrative or a disciplinary offence. This is often the case with respect to military law or prison regulations. Such a situation arose in *Engel et al* v. *Netherlands*,[17] a case which concerned military discipline. The Commission felt that it was important that the state should not, in the light of Article 14 of the Convention, substitute disciplinary proceedings for the purpose of

[15] *Eckle* v. *Federal Republic of Germany*, (1982) Series A, No. 51, and 5 *EHRR* 1 at para. 73.

[16] *Foti* v. *Italy*, (1982) Series A, No. 56, and 5 *EHRR* 313. See also *De Weer* v. *Belgium*, (1980) Series A, No. 35, and 2 *EHRR* 439, and *Adolf* v. *Austria*, (1982) Series A, No. 49, 4 *EHRR* 313.

[17] 15 *YB* 508, (1976) Series A, No. 22 and 1 *EHRR* 647.

depriving the individual offender of the protection of Article 6. The Court, in its turn, stated that the question of whether the offence was characterized as criminal or disciplinary, or both, was only a starting point to the enquiry. More important were the nature of the offence, to the extent of asking whether it should be generally binding or applicable only to a specific group, and the nature and severity of the penalty. For Mr Engel himself the sentence of two days "strict arrest" was not sufficient to overstep the threshold from disciplinary to criminal, whereas in the case of his fellow-applicants, De Wit, Dona and Schul, the threat of detention for several months was enough. In the case of *Campbell and Fell* v. *UK*,[18] loss of remission as a penalty for a breach of prison discipline was considered sufficient to invoke Article 6.

Where no punitive element is involved, even if the proceedings concern suspected criminal conduct, the Court has held that there has been no determination of a criminal charge.[19] In *Öztürk* v. *Federal Republic of Germany*,[20] however, proceedings concerning minor traffic offences were deemed by the Court to attract Article 6, despite the fact that the latter had been "decriminalized", on the grounds that they were criminal offences in the majority of Contracting States.

Application for a re-trial is not covered by the terms of the Article, and the right of appeal is nowhere in the Convention. It is now to be found in Article 2 of Protocol 7, signed in 1984 but not as yet ratified by all the Contracting States to the Convention. In the *Delcourt* case,[21] however, the Court said that:

> a state which does institute such courts [of appeal or cassation] is required to ensure that persons amenable to the law shall enjoy before these courts the fundamental guarantees contained in Article 6.

Where the possibility of appeal lies, Article 6 is applied to the proceedings in their entirety, so that deficiencies at one stage may be compensated at another.

---

[18] (1984) Series A, No. 80, and 7 *EHRR* 165.

[19] For example, *Guzzardi* v. *Italy.* See note 6 *supra;* Application 9174/80, *Zamir* v. *UK,* 29 *D&R* 153.

[20] (1984) Series A, No. 73, and 6 *EHRR* 409.

[21] *Delcourt* v. *Belgium,* (1970) Series A, No. 11, and 1 *EHRR* 355 at para. 25.

The determination of a criminal charge would also seem to include the determination of the sentence, and this brings the English procedure following a plea of "guilty" within the terms of the Article.

The criminal charge brought against the accused must always be one which constituted a criminal offence under national or international law at the time when it was committed. Similarly, the sentence imposed may not be heavier than that applicable when the crime was committed. An applicant against the Federal Republic of Germany was fined for having practised as a chartered accountant without having the requisite qualifications. By the time his appeal had been rejected the law had been repealed. He argued that Article 15 of the United Nations Civil and Political Covenant concludes: "If subsequent to the commission of the offence, provision is made by law for the imposition of a lighter penalty, the offender shall benefit thereby". Such a right, pointed out the Commission, is not contained in the Convention, and the applicant could rightly be found guilty of an offence which was contrary to the law when he committed it.

Sometimes statutes are vague and in recent years in this country we have seen the revival of Common Law crimes. Could an accused person argue that Article 7 of the Convention prevents a conviction of such Common Law crimes as conspiring to corrupt public morals, or public mischief? As we have seen, the Court in *The Sunday Times* case said that a citizen must have an adequate indication of the applicable rules, which must be formulated with sufficient precision to enable him to regulate his conduct. Before rejecting such a defence, therefore, the courts must at least be able to show that the defendant's conduct was such as could reasonably have been envisaged as illegal, but it may well be that even this is too vague to comply with the terms of Article 7.

Article 6 guarantees that when a judicial body is considering a case, its procedure shall be fair. Sydney Elmer Golder was serving a period of imprisonment in Parkhurst Prison on the Isle of Wight. Following prison disturbances he was accused of the assault of a prison officer. Although charges against him were dropped, the accusation remained on his prison record and jeopardized his chances of release on parole. As a result, he sought permission from the Home Secretary, as he was required to do, to consult a solicitor with a view to bringing an action for defamation against his accuser, in order to clear the record. Permission was refused and eventually Golder brought an application to the Commission, alleging violation of Article 6(1). The British Government, in its memorial, asserted that the provision guaranteed a fair trial once the court was seized of the matter, but that it did not expressly provide for a right of access to the courts. The Court of Human Rights, after examining the Preamble of the Convention, came to the conclusion that it would be inconceivable "... that Article 6(1) should describe in detail the procedural guarantees afforded to parties in a pending lawsuit and should not first protect that which alone makes it in fact possible to benefit from such guarantees, that is, access to a court. The fair, public and expeditious characteristics of judicial proceedings are of no value at all if there are no judicial proceedings". It held, therefore, that the right of access is inherent in Article 6(1) and denied that this was an extensive interpretation forcing new obligations on the Contracting States.[22] The Court went even further in the *Airey* case,[23] holding in effect that states were under a duty not merely not to obstruct access, but to ensure that it is effective and practical. Mrs Airey complained that the high costs involved in obtaining the necessary legal representation before the High Court in Ireland, pursuant to her action for judicial separation from her husband, amounted to denial of access under Article 6(1). In agreeing with her contention, and holding a violation of the provision, the Court said:

> The Convention is intended to guarantee not rights that are theoretical or illusory but rights that are practical and effective. This is particularly so of the right of access to the courts in view of the prominent place held in a democratic society by the right to a fair trial.[24]

In an application against the Federal Republic of Germany the applicant had signed an adjudication clause whereby he waived the operation of the normal court procedure. The Commission accepted that such a renunciation of the provisions of Article 6(1) was not prohibited by the Convention. In such a situation, however, the

---

[22] *Golder* v. *UK*, (1975) Series A, No. 18, and 1 *EHRR* 524 at para. 35.

[23] *Airey* v. *Ireland*, (1979) Series A, No. 32, and 2 *EHRR* 305.

[24] Para. 24. However, at para. 26 the Court pointed out that this did not mean the provision of legal aid for all cases. There may be other ways of ensuring access, such as reform of procedure etc.

circumstances surrounding the waiver clause must always be scrutinized with care by the Commission.[25]

In *Ashingdane* v. *UK*[26] the Court stated that the right of access is not absolute but may be subject to limitations such as are implied by the resources of individuals and of the community. It went on to say:

> Nonetheless the limitations applied must not restrict or reduce the access left to the individual in such a way or to such an extent that the very essence of the right is impaired. Furthermore, a limitation will not be compatible with Article 6(1) if it does not pursue a legitimate aim and if there is not a reasonable relationship of proportionality between the means employed and the aim sought to be achieved.

Once access to the tribunal has been achieved, Article 6 requires that the hearing should be held before "an independent and impartial tribunal established by law". Both the Commission and the Court have developed an extensive case law on Article 6, and the nature and structure of the many and varied tribunals set up within the Contracting States have frequently been matters of consideration. Here we should note briefly that the Convention requires that the body in question should have a judicial function, giving a binding decision according to a prescribed procedure. We saw earlier, in the case of *de Jong, Baljet and Van den Brink*,[27] that under Article 5 the advice of the *auditeur-militair*, although invariably followed, was not technically binding and was not therefore adequate as a judicial ruling. A court or tribunal must be independent both of the executive and of the parties, although the Court has ruled that it is not necessary that its role should be restricted to such judicial decision-making and that it may carry out other functions. For instance, in *Campbell and Fell* v. *UK*[28] the Court recognized that the disciplinary aspect of prison visitors was only part of their overall function. Indeed, the Strasbourg organs have accepted many diverse specialized tribunals as fulfilling the criteria. Needless to say, the broad applicability given to Article 6 has made this a necessary, and sometimes difficult,

---

[25] 1197/61 v. *Federal Republic of Germany,* 5 *YB* 88.
[26] See *supra,* note 10, at para. 57.
[27] (1984) Series A, No. 77, and 8 *EHRR* 20.
[28] (1984) Series A, No. 80, and 7 *EHRR* 165.

task.[29] The jurisprudence requires that the members of the tribunal be appointed in a manner and by such authority as guarantees their independence, and be free from outside pressures. Similarly, they must, in practice, have the security of knowing that they may not be removed.[30]

The impartiality of the tribunal requires that its members should be free from bias. In the *Boeckmans* application[31] the judge had uttered comments during the course of the trial which the Commission held were unacceptable. We have seen, in the *Schiesser* case, how the Court examined carefully the role of the District Attorney who ordered Schiesser's detention on remand because that official's function was usually involved with the Public Prosecutor's office. Similarly, in the *Delcourt* case,[32] the Advocat General had participated in the Cour de Cassation in a consultative capacity although he was a member of the Attorney General's Department. In both these cases, however, the Court was satisfied that impartiality had been maintained. In the applications by *Pataki* and *Dunshirn* against Austria,[33] the applicants complained that the sentences imposed upon them after their convictions were increased by the Court of Appeal sitting *in camera*, and that the Public Prosecutor was present in the Court of Appeal, whereas the accused and their lawyers were not given such an opportunity. The Austrian Government, shortly after these and similar cases were admitted, amended the Code of Criminal Procedure. In 1971, an applicant had complained that an English judge had allowed a prosecution witness to be called after both the Crown and defence had finished their cases. The Commission noted, however, that there had been exceptional circumstances, and since the applicant was not able to show that the judge had exercised his discretion unfairly, there was no violation of Article 6(1). As the Commission has often said, it is "... not called upon to decide whether or not the domestic courts have correctly assessed the evidence before them, but only whether evidence for and against the

---

[29] We have already encountered professional disciplinary bodies in *Le Compte, Van Leuven and De Mayere*. See *supra*, note 5, and also included, for instance, are arbitration bodies dealing with compensation for nationalization *Lithgow et al* v. *UK*, (1986) Series A, No. 102, and 8 *EHRR* 329. In *Benthem* v. *Federal Republic of Germany*, see note 7, *supra*, a Government department was held not to be a tribunal.

[30] See, for example *Campbell and Fell* and *Lithgow*, notes 28 and 29, *supra*.

[31] Application 1727/62, 8 *YB* 410.

[32] *Delcourt* v. *Belgium*, *supra*, note 21.

[33] Applications 596/59 and 789/60, 4 *YB* 736.

accused has been presented in such a manner, and the proceedings in general have been conducted in such a way, that he has had a fair trial."

The basic *procès contradictoire* is recognized as fundamental to Article 6(1). This is the right to put your own case or to have it put for you, the right to produce witnesses and examine those presented against you. The Convention does not secure the right of the individual to appear in person but this would seem to be necessary in some cases, where justice requires. The Commission has accepted also that the court must have the final discretion as to which witnesses may be called. Although an individual has certain procedural rights, if the court firmly believes that a particular witness will be irrelevant to the case it is deciding, it should be able to refuse to hear him. Similarly, the length of the court's hearings may become unreasonable if the parties insist on all the procedural rights which they are entitled to claim.

Pre-trial publicity may, of course, be relevant to the question of a fair trial. In such cases it must be decided whether the court has endeavoured to be fair. Jury-vetting is a topic which has not been brought to the Commission, although in the *Austria* v. *Italy*[34] case it was alleged that a majority of the jurors were of "Italian ethnic origin", and more likely to be adversely affected by the evidence. The Commission was not to decide that issue, however, because domestic remedies in relation to it had not been exhausted.

Article 6(1) by implication requires reasons to be given for a court's decision, especially if the opportunity of appeal is foreseen. An applicant cannot seek redress under the Article merely because the court has not given reasons for every important point, but where serious consequences follow from the decision, and where precision is important, reasons could be expected.[35]

It will be seen that in every case coming before a court or judicial body, the authorities have some discretion in determining the manner in which the hearing shall take place. The choice of judges may be a political one. The accused may be trying expressly to waste the court's time. It is necessary to recognize the immense amount of discretion vested in the authorities, and the Commission and Court

[34] Application 788/60, 6 *YB* 796.
[35] See, for example, *H.* v. *Belgium*, (1987) Series A, No. 127, and 10 *EHRR* 339.

must limit their roles to an examination of each case to determine, as well as they may, whether justice was done and was seen to be done. Interference with the substantive decisions of the courts must be avoided wherever possible, but so often procedure and substance are intimately combined.

Article 6(1) lays down that the public may be excluded from all or part of the trial in certain instances. These exceptions are wide, but it would be for the Court or Commission to decide if an applicant alleged that the public had been excluded for reasons not covered by the limitations laid down. Considerations of the private or professional lives of the parties to a dispute may, in some circumstances, mean that the hearing should not be held in public. Similarly, prison disciplinary hearings may be restricted from the public in the interests of security and public order. The objective of a public hearing is, however, to prevent the secret administration of justice without public scrutiny, and the presumption must always lie in favour of openness.

Judgment should be pronounced publicly, even where part of the proceedings have been held in private.

The fair and public hearing must take place within a reasonable time. As we have seen, this time period is not identical with that in Article 5(3), where the individual is detained, and which therefore requires "special diligence". The Commission said in the *Neumeister* case that the period of reasonable time commences at the moment from which the person concerned has been substantially affected as a result of the suspicion against him. In a civil case, this may in fact be before the issue of the writ which commences the proceedings. The Commission will examine the complexity of the case as a whole, as one factor in determining reasonableness. In the *Huber* application,[36] the proceedings took over twelve years and this was held to be unreasonable although, as we have seen, the failure of the Committee of Ministers to achieve a two-thirds majority prevented a final decision in this case. Sometimes a case's complexity will require special methods, and the Commission will then look at the way in which the authorities have handled the matter. For example, a complicated tax or fraud case may require a great deal of assistance from financial experts, and crimes which have taken place in several states may

---

[36] Application 4517/70, 38 *CD* 90 and 18 *YB* 324.

require co-operation between the police authorities in each of those states. Such circumstances may justifiably lengthen proceedings. As mentioned above, the applicant himself may in some cases be responsible for drawing out the time by unnecessary and excessive insistence upon all his procedural rights, or by failing to cooperate with the authorities or by being downright obstructive. As the Commission commented in the *Huber* case:

> ... any uncooperative or even obstructive attitude on the part of the applicant during the proceedings against him, although it cannot defeat his claim under Article 6(1) of the Convention, must nevertheless be taken into consideration in any examination of the question whether or not there has been a violation of his right to a hearing within a reasonable time as guaranteed by that provision. This follows clearly from the necessity to establish the causes of any delays which is an indispensable prerequisite to the examination of the question of violation.[37]

Even where a private party to proceedings is primarily responsible for inordinate delay, the authorities themselves may be required to show that appropriate steps were taken where necessary to expedite the proceedings. Similarly, where a state claims that there is a temporary back-log in the hearing of cases, it must show that it is using its best endeavours to overcome it.

An important aspect of fair hearing is that everyone shall be presumed innocent until proved guilty. In *Barberá, Messegué and Jabardo v. Spain*,[38] the Court amplified the meaning of the presumption of innocence:

> It requires, *inter alia*, that when carrying out their duties, the members of a court should not start with the preconceived idea that the accused has committed the offence charged; the burden of proof is on the prosecution, and any doubt should benefit the accused. It also follows that it is for the prosecution to inform the accused of the case that will be made against him, so that he may prepare and present his defence accordingly, and to adduce evidence sufficient to convict him.

The second Paragraph of Article 6 applies this to criminal trials but

---

[37] *Supra*, note 36, para. 111.
[38] (1988) Series A, No. 146, and 11 *EHRR* 360 at para. 77.

because of the extensive and autonomous interpretation of Article 6(1) this must be seen to be relevant across the board wherever some kind of penalty is a likely outcome of the hearing. Most European legal systems comply well with this requirement, and allegations of violation of the paragraph usually occur where some form of interruption of the proceedings has left behind an impression of guilt in the absence of formal findings. For example, in the case of *Adolf* v. *Austria*[39] the applicant was accused of throwing a key which hit an elderly lady, Mrs Proxauf. He denied the charge. Eventually the Austrian court terminated the proceedings against him, giving as reasons: "... the injury found is insignificant ... the fault of the accused may be described as insignificant and his character gives cause to expect that he will conduct himself properly in future". This unfortunate phraseology led the Commission to agree with the applicant that his guilt had been presumed. The Court found that although the decision could lead to such an implication there was not, ultimately, a violation of this part of the Convention.

It decided otherwise, however, in the *Minelli* case[40] against Switzerland. In that case Mr Minelli, a journalist, had made accusations of fraud against a company, *Télé-Répertoire S.A.* and its director Mr Vass, in a newspaper article he had written. Mr Vass and the Company filed a private prosecution against him for criminal defamation. Because of an almost identical case against another journalist elsewhere, the proceedings were suspended and eventually the period of limitation expired and the case was terminated. Under such circumstances costs were not payable out of public funds, and Mr Minelli was ordered to pay two-thirds of the court's costs, together with compensation for part of the private prosecutor's expenses. The basis of the apportionment was that in the case on account of which the prosecution had been suspended the accused had been found guilty, and that the present case would "very probably have led to the conviction" of the applicant. By contrast, however, where cases have been discontinued for various reasons and the applicant has been asked merely to pay his own expenses, the Court has been less willing to hold a violation

---

[39] See *supra*, note 16.
[40] (1983) Series A, No. 62, and 5 *EHRR* 554.

where it has been shown evidence that the accused was likely to have been convicted.[41]

Another situation where the presumption of innocence may be doubted exists where there is a presumption of law or fact which the accused is required to rebut. An applicant convicted of living on the immoral earnings of a prostitute complained of the British statutory provision, which read: "... a man who lives with or is habitually in the company of a prostitute ... shall be presumed to be knowingly living on the earnings of prostitution unless he proves the contrary". The Commission's view, however, was that since the provision was restrictively worded, was not unreasonable and could fairly easily be rebutted, it did not violate Article 6(2).[42]

Article 6(3) lists the minimum rights which can be expected by anyone when charged with a criminal offence. They must, however, be read with the provisions of Article 6(1) and may not of themselves be enough to guarantee a fair trial.

Everyone has the right to be informed promptly in a language he understands of the details of the charge against him, so that he may be able to prepare a defence.[43] The major requirement here would seem to be that the charge is elucidated in sufficient detail and clarity to enable the accused to answer the case and prepare a defence. Again, the charge must be made promptly, and particularly in time for the accused to take advantage of essential material evidential facts.

Adequate time and facilities must be allowed to prepare a defence, although the time will obviously vary according to the complexity and features of each case.[44] The accused must be given the opportunity to communicate with a lawyer and to discuss the matter in private,[45] unless there is evidence that the lawyer is abusing his position, and the right to privacy is thereby forfeited.[46]

Although in Application 5282/71 against the United King-

---

[41] For example, *Nölkenbockhoff* v. *Federal Republic of Germany*, *Lutz* v. *Federal Republic of Germany* and *Englert* v. *Federal Republic of Germany*, (1987) Series A, No. 123, and 10 *EHRR* 163, 13 *EHRR* 360.

[42] Application 5124/71, 42 *CD* 135. See also *Salabiaku* v. *France*, (1988) Series A, No. 141-A, and 13 *EHRR* 379.

[43] See *Brozicek* v. *Italy*, (1989) Series A, No. 167, and 12 *EHRR* 371.

[44] Cf *Campbell and Fell* v. *UK*, *supra*, note 28. *Albert and Le Compte* v. *Belgium*, (1983) Series A, No. 58, and 5 *EHRR* 533.

[45] *Can* v. *Austria*, (1985) Series A, No. 96, and 8 *EHHR* 121.

[46] *Campbell and Fell* v. *UK*, *supra*, note 28.

dom[47] it was held that this does not require the prosecuting authorities to give the accused notice of all the evidence which may be used during his trial, in *Jespers* v. *Belgium*[48] the Commission was of the view that the authorities should provide every opportunity for the accused "... to acquaint himself, for the purposes of preparing his defence, with the results of investigations carried out throughout the proceedings", no matter how, by whom, when or under whose authority. Practicability, however, would seem to rule out unlimited access.

Everyone has the right to a defence, but the Commission has decided that this means only that the defence shall have adequate representation, and not that the accused shall be allowed to decide whether to defend himself or to be legally represented. You may only defend yourself, it would seem, if the court decides that to allow you so to do would not be contrary to the interests of justice. In the same way, if you do not wish to defend yourself the court cannot stand in the way of recourse to legal assistance at your own expense.[49] If you choose legal representation then legal aid should be available if indicated in the "interests of justice".

Where the authorities decide that an accused person should be represented by a lawyer then they are required to provide legal aid where necessary. Where legal aid is granted, the accused loses the right to choose the lawyer himself.[50] On those occasions where the defence lawyer is chosen by the court, it has a special responsibility to ensure that there is a fair hearing, and the legal assistance must be "practical and effective" and not merely "theoretical or illusory".[51] Similarly where the legal aid lawyer proves incompetent or, for any reason, incapable of carrying out an adequate defence, the authorities should intervene.[52] Even where the accused is paying for legal representation, the national court must have the competence to decide on the necessary qualifications of persons appearing before it and whether they are suitable. In *Ensslin* v. *Federal Republic of*

---

[47] 42 *CD* 99.

[48] Application 8403/78, 27 *D&R* 61.

[49] *Pakelli* v. *Federal Republic of Germany*, (1983) Series A, No. 64, and 6 *EHRR* 1.

[50] Application 9728/82, *M.* v. *UK*, 36 *D&R* 155.

[51] *Artico* v. *Italy*, (1980) Series A, No. 37, and 3 *EHRR* 1, at para. 33.

[52] *Kamisinski* v. *Austria*, (1989) Series A, No. 168, and 13 *EHRR* 36. It may also be questioned whether those young lawyers required to contribute their services for little or no pay - as in *Gussenbauer* v. *Austria*, 4897/71 & 5219/71, 42 *CD* 41 and 94 and 15 *YB* 558 - could be relied upon to be conscientious.

Germany there was some suspicion that the lawyers chosen to represent the accused on terrorist charges had strong links with the terrorist organization itself.[53] Nevertheless, as the Commission has stated:

> In most cases a lawyer chosen by the accused himself is better equipped to undertake the defence. It follows that as a general rule an accused must not be deprived, against his will or without his knowledge, of the assistance of the defence counsel he has appointed.[54]

The question of whether the "interests of justice" point to free legal aid, is not always easy to answer. It must of course be left in the first instance, to the assessment of the national authorities, but will be subject to review by the Commission and Court. In *Granger* v. *UK* [55] legal aid had been refused for an appeal which, on the advice of counsel, was considered to have no prospect of success. When the case reached appeal, however, a difficult legal question arose. The Court held that it would have been in the interests of justice for legal aid to have been available from that point, and that the failure to review that original decision on legal aid gave rise to a violation of Article 6(3).

Every accused has the right to examine or have examined witnesses against him, and to present his own witnesses under the same conditions. This does not give the accused an unfettered right, as the court retains a final discretion as to whether particular witnesses are necessary. As we have already seen, the right to a fair hearing requires "equality of arms", and the Court decided in *Bönisch* v. *Austria* [56] that an expert witness called by the defence should be able to question witnesses and make comments to the same extent as one called by the prosecution. Where evidence is given beforehand by anonymous witnesses, or where witnesses refuse to appear before the court, with the result that the evidence cannot be effectively challenged, the Court has considered carefully the accused's rights under Article 6(3)(d) and has frequently found there to have been a violation.[57]

---

[53] Application 7572/76, *Ensslin* v. *Federal Republic of Germany*, 14 *D&R* 64 and 21 *YB* 470; See also Application 8295/78, *X* v. *UK*, 15 *D&R* 242.

[54] *Goddi* v. *Italy*, (1987) Series A, No. 76, at para. 64 (Report of the Commission).

[55] (1990) Series A, No. 174, and 12 *EHRR* 469.

[56] (1985) Series A, No. 92, and 9 *EHRR* 191.

[57] See, for example, *Kostovski* v. *Netherlands*, (1989) Series A, No. 166, and 12 *EHRR* 175; *Unterpertinger* v. *Austria*, (1986) Series A, No. 110, and 13 *EHRR* 434.

Finally, in Article 6(3)(e) everyone is given the free assistance of an interpreter if he cannot understand or speak the language used in court. This would probably include the provision of interpreters for the deaf or dumb.

Three applicants, Messrs. *Luedicke, Belkacem and Koç*,[58] complained to the Commission that this provision of Article 6 had been violated by the Federal Republic of Germany. In each case the applicant, being unable to understand German, was provided with an interpreter by the courts under provisions of the national law. Following conviction the applicants were called upon to pay the costs of the proceedings, which included the interpreters' fees. The German Government asserted that Article 6(3)(e) applied to accused persons but that exemption from payment of the interpreter's costs was forfeited on conviction. The Commission, and later the Court, held that all the costs of interpretation for anyone who cannot speak or understand the language of the court, including any translation necessary under Article 6(3)(a), must be borne by the Government in order to comply with the requirements of Article 6.

ARTICLE 13

While considering the position of the individual before the courts it may be useful to deal with Article 13. This Article, which has proved difficult both to interpret and apply, reads:

> Everyone whose rights and freedoms as set forth in this Convention are violated shall have an effective remedy before a national authority notwithstanding that the violation has been committed by persons acting in an official capacity.

A possible interpretation might be, that once a violation has been found by the Strasbourg machinery, the Respondent State is obliged to provide an effective remedy. This is an unlikely meaning, however, partly because any state which does not in practice remedy a violation would continue to be in breach of its obligations under Article 1 of the Convention, and partly because of the position of

---

[58] (1978) Series A, No. 29, and 2 *EHRR* 149.

Article 13 amongst other Articles of the Convention which are dealing with substantive rights.

If we adopt this interpretation – that is to say that an individual must be provided with an effective remedy which he may exhaust before bringing an application to the Commission – this must mean that such a remedy will be provided whenever a breach of one of the rights set forth in the Convention *may* have been violated and not, strictly, when they *are* found to have been violated. Both the Commission and the Court have found the Article difficult. In the *Klass* case[59] against Germany in 1978, however, the Court decided:

> Article 13 requires that where an individual considers himself to have been prejudiced by a measure allegedly in breach of the Convention, he should have a remedy before a national authority in order both to have his claim decided and, if appropriate, to obtain redress. Thus, Article 13 must be interpreted as guaranteeing an "effective remedy before a national authority" to everyone who *claims* that his rights and freedoms under the Convention have been violated.

Therefore, whenever an individual has an *arguable claim* to be the victim of a violation, an effective remedy before a national authority must be provided.[60] The Court has said that the issue of whether there is an "arguable claim" must be decided in the light of the distinctive facts of each application;[61] but in the later case of *Powell and Rayner* v. *UK* [62] it indicated, unsatisfactorily, that a case that is "manifestly ill-founded" cannot raise an arguable claim. In view of the nature of the Commission's enquiry before rejecting an application for such a cause, and particularly in light of the fact that this may include a determination of the justification of Government interference which may be considered ". . . necessary in a democratic society", it has been argued that the threshold of arguability and admissibility may not coincide.[63]

In the context of this Chapter it should be noted that the "effective

---

[59] (1978) Series A, No. 28 and 1 *EHRR* 214.

[60] See the Court's judgment in *Silver et al* v. *UK*, (1983) Series A, No. 61, and 5 *EHRR* 347.

[61] *Boyle and Rice* v. *UK*, (1988) Series A, No. 131, para. 55.

[62] (1990) Series A, No. 172 and 12 *EHRR* 355.

[63] See Françoise J. Hampson "The Concept of an 'Arguable Claim' under Article 13 of the European Convention on Human Rights", (1990) 39 *ICLQ* p. 891.

remedy" referred to in Article 13 is not restricted to a *judicial* remedy and indeed, in the *Leander* case,[64] the Court was prepared to accept an "aggregate of remedies". Article 6, we have seen, has been interpreted as giving a right of access to the courts when a "determination of civil rights and obligations" is called for. In such instances the consideration of Article 13 will usually be unnecessary. Article 13 will apply, however, to all the rights in the Convention over and above those referred to in Article 6(1).

[64] (1987) Series A, No. 116 and 9 *EHRR* 433.

CHAPTER EIGHT

Restrictions on the Rights and Freedoms

In the previous four chapters we have considered the major substantive rights secured by the Convention. It will have been noted that in deciding whether the Convention has been violated both the Commission and the Court are frequently called upon to arbitrate between the rights claimed by the individual and the broader interests of society as a whole. For example, my right to drive my motor car at high speed must necessarily be tempered by the rights and safety of other road users.

In the *Klass* judgment, which, it will be recalled, concerned the interception of telephones, the Court observed:

> ... some compromise between the requirements for defending democratic society and individual rights is inherent in the system of the Convention ... In the context of Article 8, this means that a balance must be sought between the exercise by the individual of the right guaranteed to him under paragraph 1 and the necessity under paragraph 2 to impose secret surveillance for the protection of the democratic society as a whole.[1]

It must be conceded, therefore, that on occasion the rights of the individual and those of the state may conflict. It is not reasonable that a state, with all the resources at its command, should reject its superior position and place itself, at all times, on an equal footing with each of its citizens. To do so would be to abrogate the responsibility which it has to its electorate. The European Convention is based on "effective political democracy", which presupposes the strength of the elected majority. The machinery set up by the Convention is there to see that the state does not abuse its position. Many of the Articles in the Convention outlining the rights and freedoms to be guaranteed contain exceptions, treatment according to which will not involve the state concerned in charges of violation of the Convention. Other clauses, too, including the general provision for

---

[1] *Klass* v. *Federal Republic of Germany*, Series A, No. 28, and 2 *EHRR* 214 at para. 59.

derogation in times of national emergency, are a common feature of human rights treaties. We should use a little space examining these exceptions in order to discover whether the Convention, or its application by the Strasbourg organs, has limited the rights and freedoms unreasonably.

The limitation clauses are there, in the first place, to protect the Convention itself. Rights are not absolute and to pretend that they are would, in a very short space of time, lead to the Convention being used to undermine the very rights it sets out to protect.

It must be remembered that the driving force behind the negotiations for the Council of Europe was the protection of democracy and the outlawing of totalitarianism and communism, which were seen as the major evils facing post-war Europe. Many states would not have signed and ratified, even at that time, a document which completely fettered independent action within domestic jurisdiction.

Again, few laws can withstand times of calamity and national emergency, and most domestic systems have special procedures for such occasions.

LIMITATIONS ON THE RIGHTS

Many of the Articles of the Convention, as we have seen in previous chapters, have built-in limitations. Article 5, for instance, while guaranteeing liberty, allows arrest and detention in certain circumstances. Forced labour may be imposed at times of national calamity, so that following an earthquake or other natural disaster it would be possible for the state to order all able-bodied men and women to participate in bringing the situation back to normal. Similarly, at times of riot or insurrection any action lawfully taken in the national interest, which results in death, will be excused. Article 12, whose object is to protect the right to marry, specifically conditions this upon the "national laws governing the exercise of this right".[2]

Articles 8 to 11, it will be recalled, together with Article 2 of Protocol 4,[3] and Article 1 of Protocol 7,[4] recognize that state intervention

---

[2] See the discussion in Chapter 4, *supra.*
[3] The right of liberty of movement and freedom of choice of residence.
[4] Freedom of aliens from arbitrary expulsion.

will be commonplace, and therefore set out to ensure that this interference is carefully controlled by including in each of their provisions a paragraph which lists restrictions and limitations on the rights to be guaranteed.

In every case, the paragraphs take a similar form. First of all, any interference by the authorities with the right in question must be "in accordance with the law", or "prescribed by law".[5] It will be recalled that in the *Sunday Times (No. 1)* case,[6] the Court was called upon to consider whether the UK law on contempt of court, as part of the Common Law, complied with this provision.

According to the judgment in that case,[7] there are two requirements that flow from the expression. The first is that the law must be adequately accessible:

> the citizen must be able to have an indication that is adequate in the circumstances of the legal rules applicable to a given case.

Secondly, there must be sufficient precision for the citizen to regulate his conduct:

> he must be able - if need be with appropriate advice - to foresee, to a degree that is reasonable in the circumstances, the consequences which a given action may entail.

In later cases the Court has gone on to add that the phrase does not merely refer back to domestic law but also relates to the quality of law, requiring it to be compatible with the rule of law, which is expressly mentioned in the Preamble to the Convention.[8] It would not be in keeping with the rule of law for a legal discretion to be conferred on the executive in terms of unfettered power.

> Consequently, the law must indicate the scope of any such discretion conferred on the competent authorities and the manner of its exercise with

---

[5] There appears to be no difference between these two phrases since they both appear in the official French version of the Convention as "prévue par la loi".

[6] (1979) Series A, No. 30, and 2 *EHRR* 245.

[7] *Supra*, note 6; para. 49 of the Judgment.

[8] See *Silver and others* v. *UK*, (1983) Series A, No. 61, and 5 *EHRR* 347 at para. 90, and *Malone* v. *UK*, (1984) Series A, No. 82, and 7 *EHRR* 14.

sufficient clarity, having regard to the legitimate aim of the measure in question.[9]

In the *Malone* case, the Court decided that the elements of the power in the United Kingdom to intercept communications were not laid down with sufficient precision in accessible legal rules, while in *Silver* the rules contained in unpublished practices similarly were not "in accordance with the law".

Where it is accepted that the interference with the right is "in accordance with the law", it must then be shown that it is "necessary in a democratic society" for the purpose of ensuring certain legitimate interests which are listed in the Articles. Although these interests vary, depending on the substantive right to which they are attached, they are similar, and cover the following: national security; public safety or the economic well-being of the country; public order; the prevention of crime; the protection of health and morals; the rights and freedoms or reputation of others; the prevention of the disclosure of information received in confidence; and the maintenance of the authority and impartiality of the judiciary.

It will be noted that the interests listed are wide, and that most Government interferences can be explained under one or other of them. The Commission and the Court have rarely attempted to define the scope of any particular one of them. The approach seems to have been rather to examine any interference to ascertain whether it is "necessary in a democratic society".

The Court's understanding of the term "necessary in a democratic society" has been developed through the cases, and is summarized in the judgment referred to above in *Silver et al v. UK*.[10] First of all, the adjective "necessary" is not synonymous with "indispensable", but neither does it have the flexibility allocated to such terms as "admissible", "ordinary", "useful", "reasonable" or "desirable". It should indicate, however, that there is a "pressing social need", although this must always be proportionate to the legitimate aim being pursued. A heavy-handed, unsympathetic approach or the blanket prohibition of an activity which could be more sensitively regulated, would not comply with the requirement. It may be that the rights of the

---

[9] *Malone* v. *UK, supra,* note 8, para. 68.
[10] See *supra,* note 6, at para. 97.

individual could have been granted without infringing the freedom of the community as a whole or without offending public opinion.

In a democracy, however, a government may be elected because it has indicated that it is prepared to take a tough stance or to introduce draconian measures. Who is to decide whether government interference is "necessary"; the Court of Human Rights, whose role is to implement the Convention, or the Government which has been mandated by the people? To allow the state authorities complete freedom would, of course, make a nonsense of the Convention and yet it is reasonable to suppose that in many matters a national government is in a better position than a group of international lawyers to respond to problems of this kind. As the Court said in the *Handyside* case:[11]

> By reason of their direct and continuous contact with the vital forces of their countries, state authorities are in principle in a better position than the international judge to give an opinion on the exact content of these requirements [for the protection of morals] as well as on the "necessity" of a "restriction" or "penalty" intended to meet them.

Both the Commission and the Court have gone towards solving this problem by granting states an area of discretion, which has been termed the "margin of appreciation". That is to say that they will recognize that the state has a certain margin of political and practical control within which it may operate. The "margin of appreciation" doctrine was introduced by the Commission as early as 1959, in the inter-state case between Greece and the United Kingdom, as a response to the latter's claim to derogation under Article 15 of the Convention. It was further elaborated in the *Lawless* case.[12] Since then, however, its use has not been confined to Article 15 cases and its principles have been applied in the consideration of all the limitations and restrictions that the Convention allows.

The difficulties with this notion are not with its existence – the Convention could not operate without some concept of this kind – but with the breadth of the margin of discretion which the Strasbourg organs should concede. The Court has reiterated on many occasions that the margin of appreciation is not unlimited, but that

[11] (1976) Series A, No. 24, and 1 *EHRR* 737 at para. 48.
[12] (1961) Series A, No. 3, and 1 *EHRR* 15.

the Court may always give a final ruling on whether restrictions are compatible with the Convention.

There is no space here to consider in detail the Court's jurisprudence on "margin of appreciation". Even if there were, it is submitted that no easy analysis would be forthcoming. It is undoubtedly true that the margin differs in accordance with the interest on which the restriction is being claimed. For example, in those cases concerning the nationalization of property and the economic policies of the state, a very wide margin has been allowed.[13] Cases concerning national security have been similarly treated. We have seen that in the *Sunday Times* case, concerning freedom of the press, little margin was allowed, while in other cases under Article 10 such as *Handyside* v. *UK* and *Müller* v. *Switzerland* - cases which concerned morals - the breadth of action allowed to the government was wide.

In the *Handyside* case[14] the offending book, which had been banned by the English courts, had been published in some form in other parts of the United Kingdom and, as a translation of a Danish original, had circulated freely in several other European states. The Court, in holding as we have already seen that the interference by the British courts was "necessary in a democratic society", stated at Paragraph 35:

> In particular, it is not possible to find in the domestic law of the various Contracting States a uniform European conception of morals. The view taken by their respective laws of the requirements of morals varies from time to time and from place to place, especially in our era which is characterized by a rapid and far-reaching evolution of opinions on the subject.

Although the attraction of such a view is apparent, it leaves open the question of whether, in view of the importance which is attached to the freedom of expression by the Strasbourg organs, those bodies charged with implementing a European standard of human rights should not feel compelled to play a part in its establishment. It is

---

[13] See, for instance, *James et al* v. *UK*, (1986) Series A, No. 98, and 8 *EHRR* 123, and *Lithgow et al* v. *UK*, (1986) Series A, No. 102, and 8 *EHRR* 329, *supra*, Chapter 5.

[14] See note 11, *supra* at para. 48. The same wording also appears in the judgment in the *Müller* case some twelve years later. (1988) Series A, No. 133, and 13 *EHRR* 212, para. 35.

submitted that the Court and, perhaps even more importantly, the Commission, should always strive to accept the narrowest possible margin of appreciation. Indeed, it might be argued that under the Convention they are obliged so to act. While this will not prove easy, either practically or politically, its long term effects in laying down European and international standards will be invaluable.

In general, subject to what has been said above on the "margin of appreciation", it may be stated that the Court and the Commission have established a rule of strict interpretation of restrictions and have rejected any criteria other than those mentioned in the exception clauses.

Since the Commission has held that certain rights are implicit in the Convention in such cases as *Golder*, can it not also claim that there are inherent limitations not expressly listed in the Convention's provisions? So, in *De Courcy* v. *United Kingdom*,[15] the Commission said:

> The limitation of the right of a detained person to conduct correspondence is a necessary part of his deprivation of liberty which is inherent in the punishment of imprisonment.

However, the Court disapproved of the idea of inherent limitations in the *Vagrancy* cases.[16] It may well be that the special conditions of one applicant will mean that his rights are limited more than another's. For instance, although the Commission and Court take the view that all restrictions have to pass the tests described above, and that the burden is on the Government concerned to show that particular interferences are "necessary", it is still possible, through the "margin of appreciation" doctrine for special categories of applicants such as prisoners, servicemen and civil servants to be treated differently. Care must be taken that inherent restrictions do not creep back into the jurisprudence.

---

[15] Application 2749/66, 24 *CD* 85 and 10 *YB* 388.
[16] *De Wilde, Ooms and Versyp* v. *Belgium*, (1971) Series A, No. 12, and 1 *EHRR* 374.

ARTICLE 17

Article 17 reads:

> Nothing in this Convention may be interpreted as implying for any state, group or person any right to engage in any activity or perform any act aimed at the destruction of any of the rights and freedoms set forth herein or at their limitations to a greater extent than is provided for in the Convention.

The aim of the Article is two-fold: first, to prevent applicants from invoking the Convention for their protection when their ultimate aim is the very destruction of all the Convention stands for; and secondly to prevent states from limiting the enjoyment of the Convention rights and freedoms in such a way as to destroy the very essence of those rights.

In 1957 members of the banned German Communist Party brought an application alleging violation of Articles 9–11 of the Convention. Their complaint was rejected by the Commission on the grounds of Article 17.[17] This has been criticized as an example of the over-cautiousness of the Commission in its early days, since Articles 9–11 contain their own limitations which, were they to have been examined with the diligence now paid by the Commission and Court to such interferences, would have rendered recourse to Article 17 unnecessary.

Mr Glimmerveen was President of the *Nederlandse Volks Unie*, a political party whose ideals included an ethnically homogeneous population, and which was against racial mixing. Having been found in possession of a leaflet inciting racial discrimination he was convicted of an offence by the Dutch courts. Furthermore, he and his co-applicant, Mr Hagenbeek, were prevented from standing in the election for the municipal council. They alleged a violation of, *inter alia*, Article 10 of the Convention.[18] The Commission rejected their application on the basis that the duties and responsibilities referred to in Article 10(2) found an even stronger expression in Article 17.

[17] Application 250/57, 1 *YB* 222.
[18] Applications 8348/78 and 8406/78, *Glimmerveen and Hagenbeek* v. *Netherlands*, 18 *D&R* 187, and 23 *YB* 366.

The Commission went on to say:

> The general purpose of Article 17 is to prevent totalitarian groups from exploiting in their own interests the principles enunciated by the Convention. To achieve that purpose, it is not necessary to take away every one of the rights and freedoms guaranteed from persons found to be engaged in activities aimed at the destruction of any of those rights and freedoms. Article 17 covers essentially those rights which, if invoked, will facilitate the attempt to derive therefrom a right to engage personally in activities aimed at the destruction of any of the rights and freedoms set forth in the Convention.

An applicant, therefore, is not deprived of all the rights contained in the Convention, but only of those which he or she is seeking to destroy. There may well be difficulties in deciding which rights so qualify but, for instance, the fact that Lawless was suspected of being a member of the IRA did not deprive him of the right not to be detained without trial.[19] It should also be noted that previous behaviour of a totalitarian nature does not necessarily deprive you of the Convention's protection if there is no evidence that your anti-Convention activities are likely to continue.[20]

ARTICLE 18

By its very nature this Article too can only be applied in conjunction with claims of violations of other substantive rights in the Convention where exceptions are allowed. It reads as follows:

> The restrictions permitted under this Convention to the said rights and freedoms shall not be applied for any purpose other than those for which they have been prescribed.

The rationale of the Article is, in general, to prevent mis-use of power by Governments who might impose restrictions on the right contained in the Convention for purposes other than those laid down in its provisions. Needless to say, in view of the broad interpretation which both the Commission and Court have given to the

---

[19] See *supra*, note 12.
[20] See *De Becker* v. *Belgium*, (1962) Series A, No. 4, and 1 *EHRR* 43.

legitimate interests listed in the Convention, and extensive application of the "margin of appreciation" doctrine, Article 18 has proved difficult to apply. It is not easy for the Commission or Court to raise the matter *ex officio* except in the most extreme of cases, while the burden of proof required of an applicant in establishing a violation of the Article is, in most cases, too heavy. Mr Handyside alleged that Government action against his "Little Red Schoolbook" was motivated not so much by the desire to protect morals as to prevent the development of modern teaching techniques, and was therefore outside the operation of Article 10(2) and should be set aside under Article 18. The Commission was not convinced, however, that there was any evidence to justify questioning the Government's motives and, considering that the interference was justified under Article 10(2), dismissed the Article 18 point fairly briefly. It is suggested that this illustrates a typical pattern, in normal circumstances, for the application of the Article.

ARTICLE 15:
THE RIGHT TO DEROGATE FROM THE CONVENTION

In times of national emergency it is agreed that Member States should be able to attempt to save the very existence of the nation by exercise of powers which would normally be outside the area of legality allowed by the Convention. For this purpose Article 15 was drafted as follows:

> In time of war or other public emergency threatening the life of the nation any High Contracting Party may take measures derogating from its obligations under this Convention to the extent strictly required by the exigencies of the situation, provided that such measures are not inconsistent with its obligations under international law.[21]

Nevertheless, no derogations are allowed from Article 2, except in respect of deaths resulting from lawful acts of war, or from Articles 3, 4(1) or 7. Both Articles 2 and 7 already have some limitation included in their second paragraphs, so in fact only the right not to

---

[21] Similar provisions are to be found in human rights treaties concluded since. See, for example, Article 4 of the International Covenant on Civil and Political Rights (1966), and Article 27 of the American Convention on Human Rights.

be subjected to torture or to inhuman or degrading treatment or punishment, and the right not to be held in slavery or servitude are without any limitation.

Several examples exist of derogation by states during the Convention's history, the most important of which are the early cases concerning Cyprus, *Greece* v. *UK*,[22] the *Lawless* case,[23] the *Greek* cases,[24] the case of *Ireland* v. *UK* [25] concerning events in Northern Ireland, and *Cyprus* v. *Turkey* [26]

Lawless, it will be recalled, had been detained under certain regulations made under the *Offences against the State (Amendment) Act* 1940. In a letter to the Secretary-General of the Council of Europe on 20 July 1957, the Irish Government stated that "... the detention of persons under the Act is considered necessary to prevent the commission of offences against public peace and order and to prevent the maintaining of military or armed forces other than those authorized by the Constitution". The question which the Commission, and later the Court, was called upon to answer was whether derogation claimed by the Government excused the action, which would otherwise have constituted a violation of the Convention. How far was the Commission to accept the word of the Irish Government, and to what extent was it able to question the motive of the derogation and hence challenge its validity? The Commission eventually held that the derogation was valid, and Professor Waldock, the President of the Commission at that time, summed up the duty of the Commission as he saw it:

> ... The question of whether or not to employ exceptional powers under Article 15 involves problems of appreciation and timing for a Government which may be most difficult, and especially difficult in a democracy ... [The Commission] recognizes that the Government has to balance the ills involved in a temporary restriction of fundamental rights against even worse consequences then for the people and perhaps larger dislocations then of fundamental rights and freedoms, if it is to put the situation right again ... Article 15 has to be read in the context of the

[22] Application 176/56, 2 *YB* 174.
[23] See *supra*, note 12.
[24] (1969) 12 *YB* 38.
[25] (1978) Series A, No. 25, and 2 *EHRR* 25.
[26] Applications 6780/74 and 6950/75, 2 *D&R* 125.

rather special subject-matter with which it deals: the responsibilities of a Government for maintaining law and order in a time of war or any other public emergency threatening the life of the nation. The concept of the margin of appreciation is that a Government's discharge of these responsibilities is essentially a delicate problem of appreciating complex factors and of balancing conflicting considerations of the public interest; and that, once the Commission or the Court is satisfied that the Government's appreciation is at least, on the margin of the powers conferred by Article 15, then the interest which the public itself has in effective Government and in the maintenance of order justifies and requires a decision in favour of the legality of the Government's appreciation.

The Commission decided in that case that the derogation was reasonable in the light of all the circumstances. This pattern of satisfying itself that the derogation under Article 15 is acceptable in the situation, has been generally followed.

The Commission has said a derogation under Article 15, subject to the margin of appreciation, must have the following characteristics:

(1) it must be actual or imminent;

(2) its effects must involve the whole nation;

(3) the continuance of the organized life of the community must be threatened;

(4) the crisis or danger must be exceptional, in that the normal measures or restrictions permitted by the Convention for the maintenance of public safety, health and order are plainly inadequate.

In the *Greek* case the Commission was again faced with the task of considering the validity of a derogation made by the Government, although some of the allegations were of violation of Article 3, to which derogation does not apply. The Commission stated that the burden was on the Government to show that the conditions justifying derogation had been, and were still, present. It found, in fact, that the displacement by force of the lawful Government by the Communists and their allies was not imminent on 21 April 1967, as the Greek Government had claimed. It also did not accept the Government's statement that street demonstrations and strikes in the first months of 1967 attained the magnitude of a public emergency, or that it was impossible for organized life to be carried on. The Commission therefore decided, but with five dissenting opinions, that there was no public emergency threatening the life of the nation in Greece justifying derogation.[27]

Under Paragraph 3 of Article 15 any High Contracting Party availing itself of the right of derogation "... shall keep the Secretary General of the Council of Europe fully informed of the measures which it has taken and the reasons therefor". In the *Greek* case the Commission took a strict line and held by a majority that the Greek Government had not kept the Secretary General informed, because it had not communicated the texts of certain legislative measures and the 1968 Constitution to him. It had not provided full information of administrative measures, in particular as regards the detention of persons without court order, and had not communicated its reasons for derogation until four months after such measures had been taken. This decision, it is submitted, is rather harsh since in the *Lawless* case it was implied that the important point was that the Secretary General's office should be aware of the situation and, as Mr Fawcett pointed out in his dissenting opinion on this aspect of the *Greek* case, since the first communication to the Secretary General notifying him of the constitutional crisis was in May, and since the Greek situation was being watched by the Parliamentary Assembly, there is strong argument for saying that the Secretary General should have sought information on those matters which he found unclear. However, since the Commission decided that there was no public emergency, the question as to whether Paragraph 3 had been complied with was no more relevant, in the long run, than whether the Greek measures outside the Convention were "strictly required by the exigencies of the situation". Nevertheless, it is interesting to note that the Commission seems inclined to place the whole burden of proving every part of Article 15 firmly on the shoulders of the respondent Government.

As we have seen above, the Commission and the Court have extended the doctrine of "margin of appreciation" to other Articles of the Convention, and in many instances they may be criticized for failing to meet their responsibilities. In the application of *Ireland* v. *United Kingdom* the Court had little difficulty in reaching agreement that the events in recent years in Northern Ireland constituted a

---

[27] Report of the Commission in 12 *YB*, "The Greek Case" (Special Volume) at para. 165.

threat to the life of the nation, and that the derogation from the Convention was valid. In its judgment the Court reiterated "the margin of appreciation" doctrine but seemed to recognize that there must necessarily be limits to its application. Paragraph 207 of the judgment concludes:

> It falls in the first place to each Contracting State, with its responsibility for "the life of [its] nation", to determine whether that life is threatened by a "public emergency" and, if so, how far it is necessary to go in attempting to overcome the emergency. By reason of their direct and continuous contact with the pressing needs of the moment, the national authorities are in principle in a better position than the international judge to decide both on the presence of such an emergency and on the nature and scope of derogations necessary to avert it. In this matter Article 15(1) leaves those authorities a wide margin of appreciation.
>
> Nevertheless, the states do not enjoy an unlimited power in this respect. The Court, which, with the Commission, is responsible for ensuring the observance of the states' engagements (Article 19), is empowered to rule on whether the states have gone beyond the "extent strictly required by the exigencies" of the crisis. The domestic margin of appreciation is thus accompanied by a European supervision.

The final effectiveness of this supervision might give rise to concern in the aftermath of the *Brogan* case.[28] It will be recalled that the Court in November 1988 decided that the *Prevention of Terrorism (Temporary Provisions) Act* 1984, by allowing prolonged detention of terrorist suspects, amounted to a violation by the United Kingdom of Article 5(3) of the Convention. A derogation under Article 15(1) with regard to Northern Ireland had been lodged in 1974 and, indeed, as we have just seen, had been accepted as valid in the interstate case brought by Ireland against Britain in 1978. In 1984 the United Kingdom Government informed the Secretary General of the Council of Europe that it was withdrawing this notice of derogation and that consequently "the provisions of the Convention are being fully executed".[29] Following the Court's decision of a violation the British Government was required to respond. It was not prepared to repeal the Act and was convinced that its provisions were

---

[28] *Brogan et al.* v. *UK*, Series A. No. 145-B and 11 *EHRR* 117.
[29] This was noted by the Court in its judgment - Series A, No. 145-B, and 11 *EHRR* 117 at para. 48.

necessary in the campaign against terrorism in Northern Ireland. Some three weeks later it informed the Secretary General that since the judgment it had continued to find it necessary to exercise the powers under the Act and therefore availed itself of the right of derogation under Article 15(1). How far this solution ought to have been accepted by the Committee of Ministers, whose task is to enforce the Court's finding, and how far the derogation can be retrospective and applicable to the Brogan case and others - particularly when it was not relied upon by the Government in that case - raises many questions for discussion.[30]

---

[30] The United Kingdon position has been challenged in the case of *Brannigan and McBride* v. *UK*, heard by the Court on 24 November 1992.

CHAPTER NINE

Procedural Limitations to the Guarantee

The machinery of the Convention is, by any account, cumbersome and long-winded, and we should examine whether this in itself deprives the victim of worthwhile relief. The relationship of the various bodies set up under the Convention is complex, and the interpretation adopted by the Commission, and accepted or rejected by the Court, has embellished this relationship with greater complications. The admissibility procedure is confusing to the man in the street and even to his lawyer and has been, at times, confused in itself. We must also examine the length of time which an application takes and the cost, both to the applicants and to the Governments. Are they getting value for money? Has its speedy drafting in any way affected the substantive rights contained in the Convention? We have already commented that many of the rights have "let-out" clauses, and have examined Article 15 which allows a state to derogate from the majority of these rights in times of emergency.

Has the Commission always considered the position of the individual or has it sometimes had at the back of its mind the paramount desire for self-survival?

THE ADMISSIBILITY DECISION

The vast majority of cases which go before the European Commission are rejected. This was always to be expected since, after all, the main function of the Commission, in the eyes of those who drafted the Convention, was to sift the cases and remove those which were obviously ill-founded. A human rights or civil liberties body, in seeking to find redress for those whose rights have genuinely been denied, also attracts madmen and cranks like a candle draws moths. Proportionally more cases have been admitted as lawyers have learned about the Commission and its jurisprudence. It cannot be denied, however, that the decision of the Commission on admissibility was, in the early years, the heart of the European human rights procedure, and that decisions on substantive rights have only during the last two decades begun to make any sort of impact on either international law or the domestic laws of the Contracting States. The European Commission was for a long time a body of interest more to academic lawyers than to individual victims. The lawyers have, as one of the original delegates to the Council of Europe put it to the present author, swarmed round the Convention like ants round jam.

However, we must look at the admissibility procedure of the European Commission in order to see the part that it plays in the international protection of human rights. There can be no doubt that in 1950 the machinery being set up in Strasbourg, however disappointing to some of its authors, was opening new areas of inter-state law which had not previously been explored. How perfectly correct it was of the statesmen of those days to fear that opening an international tribunal to individuals would lead to a deluge. How reasonable it was to place safeguards in the hands of a Commission. Similarly, one could expect the Commission not to put itself in a position where it could be accused of betraying the trust which had been placed in it, and to be, at times, rather timid in its decisions.

The Commission and the Court are now firmly established in a European setting. The Commission has from time to time examined its procedure, and has made changes to expedite the processing of applications,[1] but the States Parties too must be kept alive to the possibility that more major reforms might be made, in keeping with this responsible attitude which the Commission and the Court have maintained.

Before an application can be accepted for consideration as to whether there has been a violation of the Convention, there are virtually a dozen hurdles which it must clear, and should it fail at any one of these then it must be rejected.

1. EXHAUSTION OF LOCAL REMEDIES

Before the Commission proceeds to deal with an application from an individual, non-state agency or a state itself, it must be satisfied under the provisions of Article 26 that "all domestic remedies have

---

[1] See above, Chapter 3.

been exhausted, according to the generally recognized rules of international law".

For centuries it has been a rule of international law that before a case can be brought before an international tribunal it must be shown that all remedies in the courts of the Respondent State have been exhausted. The rule, in fact, appeared in Grotius's *De Jure Belli ac Pacis*. Especially in the last fifty years, with the tremendous increase in the number of international tribunals, the rule has achieved some prominence. Lord McNair, in *International Legal Opinions*, comes to the conclusion that the rule, which is "both ancient and commonplace . . . is so fundamental that it has become almost a cliché and it is difficult to find any real analysis of its meaning".

That the drafters of the Convention considered it to be a technical rule to be used to achieve their aims is obvious on examination. The rule, for the purposes of the Commission, is that no applicant can call upon the intervention of the Commission until all local means of redress have been tried. This rule is designed not only to prevent a flood of vexatious applications, but also to provide the state accused with every opportunity to make good any administrative or other mistakes prior to being brought before an international tribunal.

Article 26, however, requires remedies to have been exhausted, "according to the generally recognized rules of international law", yet there have been few occasions where the individual is left entirely alone to exhaust the remedies, and even fewer the times when he has been capable of bringing an action against his own state. The result is that it is doubtful whether at the time when the Convention was concluded, any general rules had been determined which were strictly applicable. The opinion of the European Commission in *Austria* v. *Italy*[2] was that the phrase "according to the generally recognized rules of international law" limits only the material content of the Article, and not its application *ratione personae*. When the rule is applied in international law it is frequently in respect of a dispute between private parties or in respect of an individual against an alien Government; in human rights proceedings it more often than not applies to an individual against his own Government. It refers not only to substantive law and normal legal proceedings, but also to

---

[2] Application 788/60, 4 *YB* 116.

administrative tribunals, where these exist. The drafters of the Convention seem to have been referring not to any specific rule but to the general concept as it appears in international law. The possibilities opened up by the concept in the sphere of human rights are (i) too strict an interpretation along the lines of international law without regard to the different situations involved, and (ii) the temptation to use the rule as one of convenience for dismissing claims of a doubtful nature which might become an embarrassment to the Commission itself, or to the signatory state concerned.

The Rule in Respect of Inter-State Applications

In examining the provisions of Article 26 the question arises as to whether the rule applies to inter-state applications. Under Article 24, any High Contracting Party may refer to the Commission any breach of the Convention by another Party. This comprises also the competence to complain to the Commission of any breach of the Convention's provisions, including its procedural terms or to complain, as has been the case, of legislative or administrative measures in conflict with the substantive provisions of the Convention. In either of these last two cases the "local remedies" rule cannot be applied, since there is rarely any action that can be brought in the courts and no individual "victim" exists who could commence litigation. This was illustrated by the first case brought by Greece against the United Kingdom in respect of Cyprus. In the *Austria* v. *Italy* case[3] the question of whether Article 26 applied to inter-state applications was discussed, and the Commission held that a state raising the defence of non-exhaustion has a duty to show that such remedies exist and that they have not been exhausted. In the second *Cyprus* case the exhaustion rule was not questioned but was automatically applied.[4] In this case the United Kingdom claimed that local remedies had not been exhausted. Although, the Government argued, no legal action was available against the state itself - either in the shape of the British Crown or the Government of Cyprus - it was possible to address a demand for compensation by petition either to the Governor of Cyprus or to the Queen. The Commission, however, dismissed this as

---

[3] *Supra,* note 2.
[4] Application 299/57, *Greece* v. *UK,* 2 *YB* 186.

an ineffective remedy, since it was a measure of grace outside the terms of Article 26. The United Kingdom Government further claimed that civil and criminal actions might have been instituted against any official alleged to be responsible for the acts of torture or ill-treatment. The Greek Government replied that the aim of the application was to establish the responsibility of the United Kingdom, and that actions against responsible individuals, rather than against the state itself, did not constitute effective and adequate remedies within Article 26. The Commission held that ". . . the said actions nevertheless make it possible for the Courts to find that the alleged facts are of a substantial and illegal character, as well as to fix compensation; and that the remedies in question are therefore, in principle, among those which must be tried before the Commission may be seized of the matter". In examining the facts of the application the Commission found that in 29 out of the 49 alleged cases of ill-treatment, the identity of the accused was unknown. Although in some cases no attempt had been made to discover the names from the United Kingdom Government, the Commission felt that the lack of readiness of that Government to reveal the names of the perpetrators, on request, was sufficient reason to group all 29 cases together, and to hold that all remedies had been exhausted. The Greek Government protested that in many of the 20 remaining cases, where the accused was identifiable, the person claiming to be a "victim" was at present in custody and thus prevented from instituting legal proceedings. The Commission did not feel, however, that the fact of detention had in itself been shown as preventing the individuals concerned from asserting their rights before the courts, and therefore rejected the 20 cases for non-exhaustion of local remedies.

In the 1967 applications against Greece by Denmark, Norway Sweden and Netherlands, it was alleged that Article 3 had been violated by the Greek Government. The Applicant States alleged that the violation of Article 3 related to an *administrative practice* of the respondent Government and hence that no exhaustion of local remedies was necessary, or that if it was then the remedies available were in fact inadequate and ineffective. All this was disputed by the Greek Government. The Commission, in its admissibility decision on this second part of the application, felt that the three applicant Governments had not offered substantial evidence to show the existence of an *administrative practice*, and that the rule of exhaustion could not be excluded on that ground. On the other hand, the measures taken by Greece with respect to the functioning and status of its courts of law persuaded the Commission that the domestic remedies indicated by the respondent Government were ineffective and insufficient. It therefore concluded that the application could not be rejected for non-exhaustion of domestic remedies.

The Commission's view is that *administrative practice* which may involve, for instance, a violation of Article 3, comprises two elements: repetition and tolerance. "Repetition" has been described by the Court as:

> ... an accumulation of identical or analogous breaches which are sufficiently numerous and inter-connected to amount not merely to isolated incidents or exceptions but to a pattern or system.[5]

The Commission reiterated in its Admissibility Report in the case brought by *France, Norway, Denmark, Sweden and Netherlands* v. *Turkey* the meaning of "official tolerance":[6]

> ... though acts of torture or ill-treatment are plainly illegal, they are tolerated in the sense that the superiors of those immediately responsible, though cognisant of such acts, take no action to punish them or to prevent their repetition; or that higher authority, in face of numerous allegations, manifests indifference by refusing any adequate investigation of their truth or falsity, or that in judicial proceedings a fair hearing of such complaints is denied.

At this admissibility stage, of course, there will have been no decision that a violation of the Convention has occurred; the opinion that there has been an administrative practice is merely *prima facie* and is reached in order to avoid the exhaustion of local remedies rule.

---

[5] *Ireland* v. *UK*, (1978) Series A, No. 25, and 2 *EHRR* 25 at para. 159.
[6] Applications 9940-9944/82, 35 *D&R* 143 and 26 *YB* 1, para. 19.

The Rule in Respect of Individual Applications

In general international law it is for the Respondent State to raise non-exhaustion of domestic remedies as a defence, and this, as we have seen, has been held to be the rule in the case of inter-state applications before the Commission. In the case of individual applications the Commission has said: "It is for the applicant to prove that he has exhausted every remedy available to him". However, the Commission does not appear to have stood by this strict burden of proof, and in the *De Becker* case it considered that there was a more positive duty upon it to make an *ex officio* examination in each case to verify that the rule had been complied with – that is to say, a duty incumbent upon it, in view of its position, to review each case thoroughly in the light of its own jurisprudence even where matters have not been raised by the parties. In the *De Becker* case[7] the Commission concluded:

> The Commission is *called upon to confirm*[8] . . . in every case whether all domestic remedies have in fact been exhausted, according to the generally recognized rules of international law.

This is perhaps more in keeping with the role which we might expect the Commission to adopt: that of *amicus curiae* of both parties. In 1960 certain changes were made in the Rules of Procedure of the Commission and the opportunity was then taken, it appears, to bring the Rules in line with the Commission's practice. Instead of requiring a party to provide evidence to show that all remedies have been exhausted, the Rule now says that the applicant shall "provide information enabling it to be shown that the conditions laid down in Article 26 of the Convention have been satisfied".[9] The *ex officio* examination by the Commission of the exhaustion question enables the Commission to calculate time limits for the purpose of the "six months rule" which we shall examine later, but does not preclude waiver of the exhaustion rule by the Government.

Normally, however, the objection of non-exhaustion may be

---

[7] Application 214/56, 2 *YB* 214 at para. 236.
[8] Emphasis added.
[9] Rules of the Commission. 44(2)(a).

raised by a Government at any time, and the fact that it has not been put forward in written observations does not prevent a state from raising it later at an oral hearing. For example, in a case in 1960, brought by *Retimag S.A.* against the Federal Republic of Germany,[10] the application was rejected for non-exhaustion of local remedies, yet this was not raised until the end of the oral proceedings, after all the other Government observations had been discussed. It is usual for the Commission to consider the exhaustion question first but often, although it finds a case inadmissible on grounds of non-exhaustion, it will state in its decision if it rejects the application for other reasons, such as its being incompatible with the terms of the Convention or manifestly ill-founded. The Court has taken the view that it can re-open the question of non-exhaustion of remedies,[11] although on several occasions there have been dissenting opinions by judges who believe that admissibility should be left entirely in the hands of the Commission.[12] The Court has ruled that exhaustion of local remedies does not apply to re-applications made under the provisions of Article 50.

In order properly to apply Article 26 the Commission, upon the researches and advice of its Secretariat, has had to become familiar with the judicial and legal systems of all the Member States. It is fair to say that the jurisprudence of international law in general, on the problems of applying the local remedies rule, has been greatly enhanced by the many decisions which the Commission has been called upon to make. Perhaps more importantly, the discussion and comparison of the court system in so many European states has proved useful in itself in increasing the understanding of lawyers and state authorities. The practice of closer legal and political co- operation called for in European integration, is well demonstrated at this point. To say that, however, is not to underestimate the difficulties which face the Commission in applying the rule. There are differences of approach within the Member States and common emphases such as

[10] Application 712/60, 4 *YB* 384.

[11] See *De Wilde, Ooms and Versyp* v. *Belgium,* (1971) Series A, No. 12 and 1 *EHRR* 373, and *Artico* v. *Italy,* (1980) Series A, No. 37 and 3 *EHRR* 1. and *Van Oosterwijck* v. *Belgium,* (1980) Series A, No. 40, and 3 *EHRR* 557.

[12] See, for example, the separate opinion of Judge Martens in *Brozicek* v. *Italy,* (1989) Series A, No. 167 and 12 *EHRR* 371, and again, consistently, in *Cardot* v. *France,* (1991) Series A, No. 200 and 13 *EHRR* 853.

efficiency, cost-awareness and availability of expertise are distributed variably throughout the legal systems. The Commission's approach, quite correctly, has been to recognize this and to ask the question whether, taking the case as a whole, the Respondent State has been given an opportunity to redress the wrongs complained of. It is for this reason not easy to draw up a concise jurisprudence.

The exhaustion of local remedies rule can best be examined under five headings.

(i) *The applicant must have exhausted all accessible remedies.*

The applicant must have exhausted all the remedies that the judicial system of the Defendant State puts at his disposal. He must exhaust not merely the remedies in the ordinary courts, but the whole range of legal remedies available. This point is well illustrated in the *Lawless* case.[13] Neither Lawless nor the Irish Government disputed that a person claiming to have been illegally detained in Ireland had available to him certain remedies before the ordinary courts, in particular, proceedings for *habeas corpus.* Even so he was informed by the Supreme Court of Ireland, on appeal, that the *Offences against the State (Amendment) Act* 1940, under which he had been detained without trial, was not in conflict with the Constitution (according to a previous decision) and that the European Convention of Human Rights, a violation of which he claimed, was not part of Irish law and could not therefore affect the right of the Government to invoke the 1940 Act. It appeared evident to the Commission that the grounds which led the High Court and the Supreme Court to dismiss Lawless's action for habeas corpus would have had equal force in proceedings by the applicant for false imprisonment, or in any other proceedings in the ordinary courts of the Republic of Ireland, and that therefore these other remedies were ineffective and not to be exhausted.

The Government pointed out that Lawless's claim was for compensation for detention from 12 July until his release. From 12 July until the early hours of the next day, he was held under powers contained in the 1939 *Offences Against the State Act.* On 13 July he was removed to a military detention camp. In the *habeas corpus* proceed-

---

[13] Application 332/57, 2 *YB* 308.

ings Lawless complained that he was not informed of the place to which he was being brought, and the Supreme Court had intimated that if these allegations were well-founded then that part of the applicant's arrest was illegal. The Government commented that in any case Lawless, though falsely imprisoned during the brief period covering his transfer to the internment camp, had brought no action in that regard. Lawless's counsel maintained that this period amounted to only two hours and that it was not felt worthwhile to bring an action which, since the space of time was so small compared to the whole period complained of, this could not constitute an effective remedy.

Section 8 of the 1940 Act set up an Internment Commission to examine detentions under the Act. A report from this Commission, recommending the release of a detained person, is binding upon the Government and effective to secure his release. Is this a domestic remedy, within the terms of Article 26? Unfortunately, since the application at the time of the decision was confined solely to compensation, and the Internment Commission could not award compensation, the European Commission did not feel itself called upon to answer this question.

Lawless had been informed that he could secure his release by giving an undertaking to respect the Constitution and laws of Ireland, and by agreeing not to be a member of an unlawful organization. The Commission held that this was not a procedure for which provision was made by law, and could not therefore be regarded as a domestic remedy within the generally recognized rules of international law.

The Commission has held that where several remedies are available to a potential applicant it is only necessary to exhaust those which are reasonably likely to prove effective.[14] Similarly, it has stated:

Where ... there is a choice of remedies open to the applicant to redress an alleged violation of the Convention, Article 26 of the Convention must be applied to reflect the practical realities of the applicant's position in

---

[14] See, for example, Application 5874/72, *Monika Berberich* v. *Federal Republic of Germany,* 46 *CD* 146 and 17 *YB* 386.

order to ensure the effective protection of the rights and freedoms guaranteed by the Convention.[15]

Some states, such as the Federal German Republic, have created a Supreme Court competent in constitutional matters. Where that is the case the applicant must have instituted a constitutional remedy, whenever this is possible, before he can be said to have exhausted domestic remedies. It is also to be noted that the Convention is *lex posterior* with regard to those provisions of the German Basic Law on human rights which are contradictory. Since such laws have been automatically superseded by the Convention, appeal against them before the Federal Constitutional Court cannot be necessary. A constitutional appeal is, however, required when the lower courts take no account of the Convention. Similarly, where the Convention guarantees rights exceeding in scope those of the German Basic Law, appeal to the Constitutional Court cannot be required.

In the *Guzzardi* case[16] the Commission held that where the terms of the Convention have been incorporated into national law it is sufficient that the applicant has sought a remedy in the courts, and he does not have to show that he has invoked the precise provision of the Convention.

Closely linked with the question of Constitutional Appeal is that of petition for a re-trial. The jurisprudence of the Commission, in general, points away from recognition of re-trial and similar "extraordinary" remedies for the purposes of exhaustion of local remedies, but always reserves the right to consider each application on its merits.

The problems were rehearsed in the application of Nielsen against Denmark. In the Danish judicial system there exists a Special Court of Revision, and in the *Nielsen* case[17] the Commission examined whether the right of recourse to this Court was a remedy according to the generally recognized rules of international law. The Danish Government's assertion was that the Supreme Court's judgment of two years before was the "final decision" for the purposes of calculating the six months

---

[15] Application 9118/80, *Allgemeine Gold-und Silberscheideanstalt A.G.* v. *UK*, 32 *D&R* 159. In that case the applicant was faced with a choice under German law of proceeding either *in rem* or *in personam.*
[16] Application 7367/76, 8 *D&R* 185 and 20 *YB* 462. This was re-affirmed in a recent case *Cardot* v. *France*, (1991), see *supra*, note 12.
[17] Application 343/57, 2 *YB* 412.

rule, and that the judgment given by the Special Court of Revision was not a local remedy under the terms of Article 26. The Special Court of Revision is an extraordinary court outside the usual system of the Danish Law Courts, and thus it was argued that "a petition to the Special Court of Revision cannot be described as an appeal and... in regard to the filing of petitions with that Court, the law does not impose any time limit; ... if the Commission was to consider that a petition to the Special Court is an ordinary remedy, criminal cases, dating back from many years, could be submitted to the Commission by the simple expedient of first petitioning the Special Court in this respect and then applying to the Commission within six months from the date of the decision of the Special Court". Similarly, the argument went on, to hold that the Special Court of Revision was an ordinary remedy would require all applicants to the Commission to petition it. The Commission, however, decided that the Special Court of Revision is manifestly an independent tribunal established by law, empowered to give binding decisions in law and capable of providing an effective remedy. It saw no grounds for excluding petitions to the Special Court from remedies which should be exhausted. The Government's complaints, that to accept the Court as a remedy to be exhausted would open the door to abuse, and that the Special Court was too limited in its scope, attracted the following comments from the Commission:

> These objections do not take account of the competence which the Commission has in every case to appreciate in the light of its particular facts whether any given remedy at any given date appeared to offer the applicant the possibility of an effective and sufficient remedy within the meaning of the generally recognized rules of international law in regard to the exhaustion of domestic remedies and, if not, to exclude it from consideration in applying the six-months time-limit.

In a later case concerning Denmark's Special Court of Revision, however, the Commission decided that the applicant's prospect of success in alleging procedural errors before the Special Court was so remote that it could not be regarded as an effective and sufficient remedy for the purposes of the rule.[18] Other cases have been similarly rejected.

---

[18] Application 4311/69, *X* v. *Denmark*, 37 *CD* 82 and 14 *YB* 280.

(ii) *The remedy must be adequate for the object of the application*

From the remedies that the judicial system of the state puts at his disposal, the applicant must introduce that one which most completely fulfils the objects of his application. One applicant complained, for instance, that the Public Prosecutor had submitted to the judges, without communicating with the defence, documents containing secret information unfavourable to him. The Commission held that it could not admit his application since the proper course for him to have taken was to have availed himself of hierarchical appeal (Dienstaufsichtsbeschwerde) against the magistrates concerned. In the *Lawless* case, as we have seen, the decision of the Internment Commission was not considered to be a remedy to be exhausted. Similarly, in the *De Becker* case the action for reinstatement was an inadequate remedy since it could not shield the applicant from the application of the Article of the Penal Code which prevented him from exercising his profession as a journalist.

Joseph Kaplan was chairman of the United Kingdom insurance company Indemnity Guarantee Assurance Ltd. In 1975 the Secretary of State, exercising powers conferred by the Insurance Companies Act 1974, decided that Mr Kaplan was not a fit and proper person to control an insurance company. In response to an application alleging that such a decision was contrary to Article 6(1) and should have been taken by an independent tribunal, the United Kingdom Government argued that local remedies, in the form of judicial review of the Minister's decision, had not been exhausted. The Commission correctly held that in an application for judicial review the courts could intervene only if the decision appeared to have been taken in error as to fact or law, unfairly, unreasonably or otherwise unlawfully and would not have provided a remedy to the complaint raised by the application.[19]

---

[19] Application 7598/76, *Kaplan* v. *UK*, 15 *D&R* 120 and 22 *YB* 190, 24 *YB* 460.

(iii) *The remedy must be effective*

In the *Nielsen* case the Commission refers to the need for domestic remedies to be able to furnish an effective and sufficient means of redressing the complaints. The notion of effectiveness seems to dominate the jurisprudence of the Commission. It reserves the right "...to appreciate in the light of its particular facts whether any given remedy at any given date appeared to offer the applicant the possibility of an effective and sufficient remedy".

The corollary of this is that an applicant is not bound to exhaust those remedies which, in the particular circumstances of the case, appear ineffective. Application *514/59* v. *Austria*[20] was made by a mother trying to regain guardianship of her daughter. Her original action in the District Court *(Bezirksgericht)* was dismissed, and this decision was confirmed on appeal. The applicant then seized the Court of first instance a second time, but her petition was rejected as containing no new facts. An appeal against this was pending before the *Landesgericht* when the application was made to the Commission. Normally an application in which a final decision is still to be made is rejected for non-exhaustion, at least until after that decision has been made. In this case, however, the Commission adopted the decision of the Permanent Court of International Justice in the *Panevezys-Saldutiskis* case, that it is not necessary to have recourse to domestic tribunals if the result must inevitably be a repetition of a decision already pronounced. As a result, the application was not rejected for non-exhaustion of local remedies. With regard to the exhaustion of domestic remedies in the *Cyprus* v. *Turkey* case, the Commission considered that such remedies as might be available could not be effective because of the circumstances prevailing following the military action by Turkey in Cyprus.

(iv) *The remedy must be sought in accordance with the requirements of the legal system.*

The applicant must seek the remedy which the judicial system makes available before the competent tribunals. So, where in one case an

---

[20] 3 *YB* 196.

applicant was involved in a dispute with a social assurance body in Germany, the Commission decided that this meant that he must exhaust all remedies before local social tribunals in order to comply with the rule. In those countries, such as the United Kingdom, where the system of administrative tribunals is complex, this rule of the Commission might form something of an obstacle. In the application by Yarrow plc. *et al* against the United Kingdom[21] the Commission was of the opinion that Yarrow's failure to take its compensation claim to the arbitration tribunal did not amount to non-exhaustion because that body provided only an *alternative* procedure for applying the compensation formula.

The remedy must be sought validly. For example, where a court has rejected a case because the plaintiff is of unsound mind and should have applied to the court through a tutor or guardian, the Commission cannot accept that local remedies have been exhausted unless special circumstances can be proved.

The remedy must have been sought within the time-limits of the municipal courts, where such limits exist. Every complaint made before the Commission must have been brought in substance before the local courts. This does not, of course, mean that the applicant is restricted to using only those arguments he has used in the lower courts, nor does it mean that the applicant is confined by any rules of court which existed there. It is enough that each complaint before the Commission has been part of the subject matter of previous court hearings.

(v) *Circumstances relieving the applicant from the obligation of exhausting local remedies.*

The Commission has built up a *jurisprudence constante* of certain conditions which can sometimes relieve an applicant of the obligation to exhaust local remedies. The dossier will be carefully examined, *ex officio* if need be, to discover if any of these special circumstances exist. When the applicant is complaining about certain legislative or administrative measures which are consistent with constitutional requirements, then it may be that no local remedies exist; or again, as in the *Alam and Khan* application against the

---

[21] Application 9266/81 30 *D&R* 155 and 26 *YB* 66.

United Kingdom,[22] the object of the application may be to question whether there is an effective remedy or not, in which situation the Commission may decide, as it did in that case, to join the question of non-exhaustion with the merits and admit the case without a full examination under Article 26.

The Commission concluded in the application of *Arthur Hilton* v. *United Kingdom*[23] that since access to the courts was involved, and since Mr Hilton had shown that he had sought permission to institute legal proceedings, the requirements under Article 26 had been fulfilled.

The Commission has adopted and expanded the general international law rule that there will be times when an individual is not required, because of special circumstances, to exhaust all the remedies. We have already seen that where the decision is bound to be a repetition of an earlier one or where there is a well-established jurisprudence of the municipal tribunal, the applicant is relieved of the duty of exhaustion. Presumably the rules of judicial precedent in the United Kingdom could provide examples of this.

It is obvious that where a complaint concerns a dispute over facts, and an appeal court cannot review matters of fact, the applicant is excused from going to such a superior court. On the other hand, where the appeal court could review the case but leave to apply must be made, an applicant will fall foul of the non-exhaustion rule if no application for leave is made. In Application 10789/84 against the United Kingdom,[24] the applicants had been refused leave to apply to the House of Lords by the Court of Appeal, but had failed to apply directly to the House of Lords for leave. The fact that they had been advised by counsel that, in his opinion, they stood little chance of success did not, in the Commission's view, absolve them of their obligation. In another case, however, counsel's unequivocal opinion that there could be no successful outcome was accepted.[25]

Slowness of procedure and long delays pending a decision have been held by the Commission to be other circumstances absolving an applicant from the exhaustion rule, but the Commission has laid

[22] Application 2991/66, 24 *CD* 116 and 11 *YB* 788.
[23] Application 5613/72, 4 *D&R* 177 and 19 *YB* 256.
[24] 40 *D&R* 298.
[25] Application 10000/82, 33 *D&R* 247.

down that it must consider the delay "abnormal" before it will waive compliance with Article 26. Ignorance as to the existence of a remedy cannot be a special circumstance, and it was to no avail that an applicant excused herself from the six months rule on the ground that she had only recently heard of the existence of the European Commission. Financial incapacity is no excuse. Similarly, the Commission cannot take cognisance of an applicant's own opinion as to the chance of success. The Commission spent little time with the applicant who stated that the judges lacked integrity, or with the lady who gave up attempts to settle the question of her nationality because she was "disgusted by German justice". The Commission has also rejected as not being special circumstances: police threats to the applicant; failure to exhaust because of a lawyer's negligence or because of a procedural mistake; bad health; and the raising of issues on appeal prejudicial to the interests of the applicant. This last instance is illustrated by Application 627/59, when the applicant complained that his case was conducted without regard to his religion, but did not appeal on this point since he contended that the question of respect for Jewish religious holidays and rites might, if raised, have been prejudicial to his appeal, in view of the alleged influence in the German courts of persons once closely connected with the Nazi régime.

We saw when examining the rule in relation to inter-state applications that an *administrative practice* absolved the applicant Government from establishing that local remedies had been pursued. The same exception was shown in the case of *Donnelly et al* v. *United Kingdom*[26] to apply to individual applications. It will be recalled that in that case, concerning allegations of violation of Article 3 by ill-treatment of detainees in Northern Ireland, the applicants asserted that since the ill-treatment was an *administrative practice* the requirement of exhaustion of domestic remedies was excluded. The Commission, while rejecting the particular application, commented:

> ... an administrative practice in violation of the Convention may be of such a nature as to render the available domestic remedies ineffective or inadequate. However, not every practice in violation of the Convention will necessarily have such an effect. Thus where no tolerance of ill-treatment by

---

[26] Applications 5577/72–5583/72, 43 *CD* 122 and 19 *YB* 84.

the higher authorities of the state has been shown to exist but the possibility exists that ill-treatment has been tolerated at the middle or lower level of the chain of command, the Commission must ascertain whether, having regard to matters such as possible difficulty in obtaining probative evidence, the remedies available were effective in practice and whether, having regard to the steps taken by the higher authorities to carry out their duty towards the individuals concerned to prevent the occurrence of repetition of acts of ill-treatment, they can be considered adequate.

2. THE SIX MONTHS TIME-LIMIT

Following the exhaustion of domestic remedies an intending applicant must, according to the concluding provisions of Article 26, submit his application to the Commission within a period of six months either from the date on which the final decision was taken or from when it was notified to him. The idea of a time-limit was introduced to minimize uncertainty for the Contracting States. Periods of limitation are to be found within the municipal law of several of the signatory states, but few precedents exist within the realm of international law. It is true that similar limits existed in international agreements such as the General Act of Geneva of 1928, and the European Convention for the Pacific Settlement of Disputes of 1957, but these are inter-state agreements and do not directly affect individuals.

The important question here is: what can be considered a final decision for the purposes of the rule? To answer it we must encroach on the previous subsection, where we considered what constituted an effective remedy. As we saw there, a *recours en grâce* cannot be considered as such. Similarly, petitions to the Procurator-General, Attorney-General or Public Prosecutor, for a plea of nullity, have been ignored by the Commission in calculating the rule. We saw in the *Nielsen* case that in so far as the position in a re-trial is concerned, the Commission will consider each application carefully and decide whether a petition for revision or re-trial is an effective remedy, but will not hold that this constitutes a final decision for the purposes of the six months rule unless there is sufficient chance of success. It is to be commented that where an applicant applies for revision proceedings and these are flatly refused, he runs the risk that the Commission will not accept this as a final decision, as a consequence of which the original decision may fall outside the time-limit. His preferred course would appear to be an application to the Commission in the first place, with pleadings to the effect that further recourse to local courts would be pointless. If the Commission refuses to consider the case at this point on account of non-exhaustion, then it would later be estopped from holding the application for revision an ineffective remedy.

The Commission held in the *De Becker* case, and in later applications, that the six months time-limit is not relevant to applications complaining about legislation which creates a continuing situation, when there is no domestic remedy, within the meaning of Article 26 of the Convention, whereby such legislation can be attacked. In Application 7379/76 against United Kingdom, the applicant complained that the 1968 *British Railways Act* deprived him of land which he would have obtained, according to an 1839 Act, following the closure of a railway line. The Commission held that this did not amount to a continuing violation, and that since the Act could not be challenged in the courts, the date of enactment and bringing into effect of the 1968 Act should be taken as the "final decision".[27] Similarly, in Application 8440/78 *Christians against Racism and Fascism* v. *UK*,[28] where a two month ban on public processions in the Metropolitan Police District was proclaimed under the 1936 Public Order Act, the relevant date, for the purposes of the rule, was deemed by the Commission to be the date on which the proscribed procession was due to take place.

3. ARTICLE 27 (1) (A): ANONYMOUS APPLICATIONS

The question of anonymity has not been raised often in the discussions of the Commission. One decision which did cover this point is Application 361/58, against the Republic of Ireland. In that case the applicant signed himself "Lover of tranquillity". The application was duly dismissed as anonymous, but the Commission stated that it considered that an application should be rejected as anonymous only if

---

[27] 8 *D&R* 211. The same applicant re-applied later purporting to have new information - Application 8206/78, 25 *D&R* 147 - but the Commission saw no reason to change its view.

[28] 21 *D&R* 138 and 24 *YB* 178.

the file contains no element enabling identification of the applicant to be made.

4. ARTICLE 27(1)(B): APPLICATIONS SUBSTANTIALLY THE SAME

The Commission will reject any application which it has already considered, unless the applicant can show that there is relevant new information. Similarly, it will not re-hear an application which has previously been before another international tribunal or subject to another procedure of international investigation or settlement. The Commission has therefore held inadmissible a case which repeated the former complaints but advanced fresh legal arguments. It has admitted, however, an application which was substantially the same but which contained "new information" and it has, in several cases, defined what it considers this phrase to mean. It does not reject re-applications from individuals who return, having exhausted those local remedies on account of which the application was originally held to be inadmissible.

It is interesting here to mention Application 493/59,[29] which was brought against Ireland. The facts were similar to those of the *Lawless* case in that they concerned Ireland's derogation from the Convention under Article 15. As a result of this, when the respondent Government was invited to make written observations the Commission recommended that it should do so in the light of the Commission's decision on admissibility in the *Lawless* case. The section of those written observations which is of especial interest for present purposes is the reason given by the Irish Government as to why it considered the case inadmissible, which was as follows:

> The Application being substantially the same as the Application 332/57, Gerard Lawless against the Respondent Government, and containing no relevant new information, the Commission should refuse to pursue further the consideration of the Application which must be found to be similarly covered by the provision of Article 15, paragraph (1) of the Convention, and should accordingly declare it inadmissible under the terms of Article 27, paragraph (1)(b).

[29] 4 *YB* 302.

One feels that this objection on the part of the Irish Government, if taken seriously, can only demonstrate the lengths to which the Government felt it should go in legal argument to prevent a case being successfully brought against it. It cannot be disputed that Article 27(1)(b) does not apply. These were two separate applications, with *different parties*, and the facts of the *Lawless* case could not preclude a separate and thorough examination of each of the applications by the Commission. The Commission has rejected all notions of *res judicata*, so that Governments should not rely on the maxim *ne bis in idem* in an effort to impose any form of precedent on the Commission.

5. APPLICATIONS INCOMPATIBLE WITH THE PROVISIONS OF THE CONVENTION (ARTICLE 27(2))

The first of three concepts embodied in the second paragraph of Article 27 allows the Commission to reject any application which it considers incompatible with the provisions of the Convention. In its jurisprudence under this heading the Commission has distinguished six types of inadmissibility. An application cannot be accepted:

(a) when it claims violation of a right not guaranteed by the Convention *(ratione materiae);*

(b) if the applicant or respondent are persons or states incompetent to appear before the Commission *(ratione personae);*

(c) when it is properly covered by a reservation of a Contracting Party;

(d) when it deals with an Article which is the subject of a valid derogation made under Article 15 (although derogation has usually been dealt with as a separate issue);

(e) if it falls under the heading of Article 17, in that it claims the right to engage in activities which could destroy other rights granted in the Convention;

(f) if it attempts to use the Commission as a Court of fourth instance.

(a) *Ratione materiae*

Article 1 states that the Contracting Parties shall secure to everyone within their jurisdiction the "rights and freedoms defined in Section 1 of this Convention". In consequence, it follows that the Commission cannot consider allegations of violations of rights which do not appear in the Convention. Numerous applications have been made to the Commission, particularly in the early days, alleging violation of rights not guaranteed, and these have always been rejected by the Commission. It is common for applicants to cite in their applications Articles of the Universal Declaration which do not exist in the European Convention. The right to work is a provision in point, and the rights claimed in other applications at times make interesting if not humorous reading. They include: the right to carry on a trade; the right to profit on the sale of goods; the right to practise as a nature healer; the right to holidays with pay (again in the Universal Declaration); the right to free hospital treatment; the right to be considered a person having been persecuted for political opinions; the right to leave a country or to return; to claim nationality or a passport; or to reside in one's own country. Some of these last rights, however, may be covered by the protection of other provisions such as the rights of family and private life. Similarly, the right to asylum, although not included in the Convention and having been rejected as incompatible in some cases, in other cases has been recognized by the protection of other rights; for example, the right to freedom of expression and the right not to be subjected to inhuman treatment. Other rights, such as the right of prisoners to holidays, show the romance which has attached itself to the phrase "human rights".

Strictly speaking, inter-state applications do not come within Paragraphs 1 and 2 of Article 27. However, it is to be assumed that these may be rejected under the generally recognized rules of international law *ratione materiae* and as outside the competence of the Commission.

According to Article 24 "Any High Contracting Party may refer to the Commission ... any alleged breach of the provisions of the Convention by another Contracting Party". This must be interpreted to refer to all the provisions of the Convention, and not merely to the rights set forth in the Convention. It must include, for instance, the obligation of a state to "furnish all necessary facilities" under Article 28, and the obligation in Article 31(2) not to publish the report of the Committee of Ministers. Since no applications of this kind have been received by the Commission, it is not possible to make any comment on that body's attitude towards them. It must be assumed, however, that faced with such an application the Commission would take great pains to ensure that it was admissible *ratione materiae* not only in respect of the substantive material, but of all the provisions of the Convention.

(b) *Ratione personae*

We have already seen[30] that under Article 25(1) only "victims" of an alleged violation may bring an application before the Commission, and that this itself is conditional upon a state's declaration. It is also the case, of course, that the obligations in the Convention only bind states and that they alone can be brought before the Strasbourg organs.

Many applications have been rejected by the Commission because they have been brought against states not party to the Convention. The Commission may hear applications brought against Contracting Parties only, and will reject all others, such as Application 262/57, which amounted to an action against Czechoslovakia which was not at that time a Party to the Convention. Again, any application complaining of the actions of an institution can only be accepted if the Contracting Party is answerable for that institution. Needless to say, this question is not easy to answer in the context of the wide variety of quasi-governmental organizations which exist throughout the European states. In general, the Commission will examine the question of state responsibility: under the principles of international law a state may incur responsibility if it encourages or consents to violations of the Convention by its citizens, or fails to punish or exact redress from those perpetrating such acts. Nevertheless, the principles of international law in such cases are not always easy to apply. Not only must the state complained of be a Member of the Council of Europe, it must also have signed and ratified the Convention and have made a declaration that it will recognize individual applications.

An application was brought by the French Trade Union, *La Confédération Française Démocratique du Travail*, against the European Communities, or alternatively their Member States, jointly and severally.[31] The Commission rejected the application, in so far as it

---

[30] *Supra*, Chapter 3.
[31] Application 8030/77, 13 *D&R* 231.

was directed against the European Communities, on the grounds that the European Communities were not a Contracting Party. The fact that France had not yet deposited a declaration under Article 25 recognising individual petitions also deprived the Commission of the opportunity to admit this application.

While dealing with complaints incompatible with the terms of the Convention, we should mention two other headings which have been reasons for rejection of applications, but which are rarely called upon by the Commission now that the Convention is better known. First is inadmissibility *ratione loci*, where the alleged violation took place within territory to which the Convention does not apply; for example, there have been applications concerning East Berlin and the former Belgian Congo. Under the provisions of Article 1 the Contracting States are to secure the rights and freedoms to anyone within their jurisdiction. The Commission has indicated that this is not limited to territorial jurisdiction. It also held, however, that the United Kingdom's participation in the Four Power agreement, whereby that state was involved in the supervision of the prisoner Rudolf Hess in Spandau prison in Berlin, did not mean that Hess was "within the jurisdiction" of the United Kingdom.[32] Secondly, the Commission received many applications in its early days concerning events which took place before the coming into force of the Convention with respect to the state concerned, such as complaints about Nazi atrocities. These have been rejected as incompatible with the Convention *ratione temporis.*

(c) *Applications covered by reservations*

Reservations to human rights treaties, because of the nature of the legal obligations involved, fit uneasily into the scheme of international law. The question of derogation to the European Convention was subjected to long and difficult debate at the drafting stage. The result was Article 64 of the Convention, which seeks to restrain any profligate use of powers of reservation. That Article allows reservations (which must be taken to include interpretative declarations)[33] to be made at the time of signature or ratification

---

[32] Application 6231/73, *Ilse Hess* v. *UK*, 2 *D&R* 72 and 18 *YB* 146.
[33] Application 9116/80, *Temeltasch* v. *Switzerland,* 26 *D&R* 217.

with respect to particular provisions of the Convention to the extent that any law in force in the particular state is not in conformity with the provisions of the Convention.[34] Reservations of a general character are not permitted.

The power to make a reservation would seem to be limited to the substantive rights laid down in the Convention and its Protocols.[35] This view is reinforced by Pararaph 2 of Article 64 which requires any reservation to contain a brief statement of the law concerned. Reservations purporting to limit the exercise of the supervisory functions of the Strasbourg organs would seem to be outside the terms of the Article so that a reservation lodged by France, subjecting the validity of any derogation made under Article 15 of the Convention to provisions of the French Constitution, might prove to be unacceptable. Restrictions on the right to individual petition and the jurisdiction of the Court contained in the Turkish declarations of 1987 under Articles 25 and 46 are, in the same way, of dubious legality.[36] Since prior acceptance of a reservation by the other Contracting Parties is not a requirement, the Commission and the Court have held themselves entitled to pronounce upon validity and to determine whether the exact scope of the reservation is apparent from its terms.[37] There would appear to be no other way of challenging a reservation and the Commission and Court may do so, of course, only when seized of an application in which validity is challenged.

Where a state has made a reservation in respect of a provision of the Convention under Article 64, however, any application brought against that state which falls within the scope of the reservation will be rejected by the Commission, using the formula of incompatibility with the Convention.

[34] In practice the re-enactment of similar laws by a Contracting State after ratification has not elicited disapproval.

[35] An exception is Protocol 6, which abolishes the death penalty, and does not allow reservations.

[36] See, Iain Cameron "Turkey and Article 25 of the European Convention on Human Rights", (1988) 37 *ICLQ* 887.

[37] *Belilos* v. *Switzerland* (1988) Series A, No. 132.

(d) *Applications covered by derogations*

By the same reasoning, any application concerning provisions already the subject of a derogation under Article 15 would be rejected as incompatible under Article 27(2). The majority of cases in which Article 15 has been invoked, however, have been inter-state applications to which Article 27(2) does not apply.

(e) *Applications inadmissible under Article 17*

It was realized that it would be possible for an applicant to claim rights under the Convention which would enable him to carry out activities, the ultimate aim of which was the destruction of the rights and freedoms guaranteed. Article 17, as we have seen, was designed to preclude such eventualities. It is under this Article that the Commission has rejected applications from communist, racist and extreme right-wing groups and individuals. Here again, the incompatibility formula under Article 27(2) has been used as grounds of inadmissibility.

(f) *Applications inadmissible as being appeals of "fourth instance"*

The Commission's role, according to Article 19, is "to ensure the observance of the engagements undertaken by the High Contracting Parties in the present Convention". The Commission is not, therefore, a court of appeal, in the sense that it will reassess the judgments given by local courts, and will only examine allegations that a specific provision of the Convention has been violated. Any application using the Commission as a "fourth instance", will be rejected under Article 27(2). In some cases however, especially where the Convention has been made a part of the municipal law, this distinction, it is submitted, may not be easy to make.

6. APPLICATIONS MANIFESTLY ILL-FOUNDED

In its decision on admissibility in the *Lawless* case the Commission stated:[38]

> ... at this stage of the proceedings, the Commission's task in deciding whether the application is inadmissible under Article 27, paragraph 2, as manifestly ill-founded, is limited to determining whether a *prima facie* examination of the facts of the case and the statements of the Parties does or does not disclose any possible ground on which a breach of the Convention could ultimately be found to be established; ... it cannot be concluded from a *prima facie* examination of the facts and statements of the Parties in the present case that there is no possible ground on which a breach of the Convention could ultimately be found to be established.

It went on to reject the Government's contention that the application was inadmissible as being manifestly ill-founded. This same definition has subsequently appeared in numerous cases and is now referred to as "well-established jurisprudence of the Commission". Thus, where the Commission cannot decide whether a case is admissible without making an examination of the facts, it has often reported that the application cannot be manifestly ill-founded. A common formula adopted by the Commission is exemplified by the *Klass* case against the Federal Republic of Germany where the Commission, in deciding on admissibility said:[39]

> With regard to the question whether under Article 27(2) the application is inadmissible as being "manifestly ill-founded", the Commission finds that it raises complex questions of law and fact, which are also of general interest for the application of the Convention. Having carried out a preliminary examination of the information and arguments submitted by the parties the Commission considers that the determination of these questions must depend upon an examination of the merits. It follows that the application cannot be regarded as manifestly ill-founded within the meaning of Art 27(2) of the Convention ...

The term "manifestly ill-founded" was not to be found in the

---

[38] See *supra*, note 13 at para. 336.

[39] Application 5029/71, *Klass* v. *Federal Republic of Germany*, 17 *YB* 178 at 208.

draft Convention of the European Movement, but was added by the Legal Committee to the first draft Convention presented to the Consultative Assembly in 1949. Quite obviously, the main reason for the insertion of the Article in its present form was to reassure Governments that their surrender of sovereignty would not be abused by permitting frivolous applications. The phrase "manifestly ill-founded" was left undefined during the debates. As a legal maxim it does not exist in English or French law. The phrase "offensichtlich unbegründet", which translates literally, is to be found in an old section of the German Penal Code, and has since been adopted by the Federal Constitutional Court. It must be remembered, however, that Germany was not a member of the Council of Europe when the phrase was first introduced into the draft Convention. With such a lack of definition it was to be expected that "manifestly ill-founded" would become a "catch-all" clause, allowing the rejection of all obviously unacceptable applications that could not be fitted into any other category. It is perhaps the Commission's final reason for not accepting an application.

The word "manifestly", it has been argued, implies that an application should be admitted if a reasonable doubt exists. If an application does need more than a preliminary examination to show that it is ill-founded, there is a strong case for admitting it, since any further investigation will necessitate a consideration of the facts by the Commission. If the Commission eventually found, in such a case, that the application was without foundation, it could still reject it on the grounds of non-violation.

If an application is not serious, or is politically inspired, it should be possible in most cases to ascertain this almost immediately. Any ill-founded applications which are admitted could also be rejected later under the provision laid down in Article 29.

7. APPLICATIONS ABUSIVE OF THE RIGHT OF PETITION

The Commission's jurisprudence reveals three types of case where it will reject applications as being abusive of the right of petition. The most usual is illustrated by Application 244/57,[40] where the Commission stated that a persistent and negligent disregard for the

---

[40] 1 YB 196.

rules laid down to enable the Secretariat to prepare applications for presentation was an abuse of the right of petition. A second instance of the use of this formula is where the Commission has decided that the facts so obviously do not indicate a violation as to render an application abusive. This was illustrated by the application of Ilse Koch against the Federal Republic of Germany.[41] The Commission decided that the applicant had presented a series of allegations and complaints unsupported by the Convention, merely to escape the consequences of a prison sentence. It would, however, seem better that such cases were rejected as manifestly ill-founded. In the *Lawless* and *Iversen* cases the respondent Governments alleged that the applications had been lodged for political reasons, and were hence abusive and to be rejected on that ground. This argument was not accepted by the Commission. The third example where abuse has been the cause of inadmissibility is illustrated by the case of *Rafael* v. *Austria*,[42] and is a little disturbing. In that case, which concerned complaints of prolonged detention on remand, the prisoner made defamatory remarks concerning the Government and in particular repeated these statements about the Government's agent before the Commission. The Commission held that this abuse was a ground for the inadmissibility of the application as a whole, irrespective of the fact that there was *prima facie* evidence of a violation of the Convention. Whereas prolonged delay and general non-cooperation can validly be seen as misuses of the Convention machinery, abuse in the form of objectionable phraseology should only be a ground for rejection under Article 27 when it can be shown to impede the decision of the Commission. The European Agreement relating to Persons Participating in Proceedings of the European Commission and Court of Human Rights, signed in 1969, and which came into force in April 1971, allows something akin to "privilege" to those appearing before the Commission and Court, but this would not be relevant in instances of abusive behaviour, particularly since the Commission can waive the terms of the agreement.

---

[41] Application 1270/61, 5 *YB* 126.
[42] Application 2424/65, 26 *CD* 54 and 9 *YB* 426.

CHAPTER TEN

Conclusions

The critic trying to gauge the success of the European Convention on Human Rights is faced with difficulties. First of all, it is essential to take account of the limitations which beset the Convention simply on the grounds that it is a regional treaty drawn up to serve some twenty-six geographically associated states.

The Convention, as we saw in chapter two, is deeply embedded in the concept of European integration; it was a reaction to the Second World War, and to this extent should perhaps be viewed as a political, as much as a legal, instrument. The lawyer, however, cannot easily distinguish between the two, and must examine the aims of the Convention as stated within its provisions and, in particular, by reference to the means which it lays down for carrying these out. The Convention derives a great deal of strength from the fact that it is a European agreement between states sharing cultural, political and economic similarities. Nonetheless this must colour the Convention in the general picture of international human rights protection. We have seen, in fact, that attempts by the Strasbourg organs to create "European" standards have been fraught with difficulties. While it is agreed that there is, on the whole, a common heritage of traditions within Europe, there is also a broad panoply of social, cultural and religious ideals. The need to respect these, and at the same time ensure that they are acceptable within the larger frame of human rights norms, has often proved challenging and has led to some perhaps unwarranted criticism of the Commission and Court. A large school of thought holds that regional protection of human rights which prevents ethnic and cultural differences from being suffocated is the pattern for the future, and for this reason the European model has attracted a great deal of attention.

Twenty-six "like-minded" states are eligible at present to sign and ratify the European Convention and all have taken this step.[1] Others,

---

[1] Czechoslovakia, before it divided into two states, was a Member of the Council of Europe and a Party to the European Convention.

newly initiated into the "democratic club", have been left in little doubt that they are expected to become full Contracting Parties as soon as possible.[2] It is also now expected that the right of individual petition will be accepted, and that all the Parties will recognize the compulsory jurisdiction of the Court. It is worth pointing out again that the ability to accept the Convention and its implementing machinery has been taken as the benchmark of democratic respectability.

In evaluating the contribution which the Convention has made to international law, the right of the individual to petition an international tribunal, limited though it may be, must take prominence. Only a few minor examples exist in the history of international law where the *locus standi* of individuals has been recognized, and no matter what the eventual fate of the Convention may be, it would appear to have established the feasibility of such a course of action for the future. On the question of its contribution to the law of human rights, there is no doubt that many of the decisions given under it will be referred to in future by other bodies as standard-setting and, as far as European integration is concerned, the pre-eminence accorded to the rights of the individual is recognized as an important feature in the process of harmonization of laws. Again, the European Commission's rules and practice concerning exhaustion of local remedies appear to be adding greatly to the jurisprudence of international law on this topic.

Nevertheless, certain questions remain. What do we expect a human rights treaty like the European Convention to do? What is its function? Is it to relieve, directly, the plight of the individual citizen, or to raise points of a humanitarian nature, by means of consideration of specific complaints, with a view to the eventual homogenization of European law?

Of course, the answer is bound to lie in both of these, since they cannot be exclusive. Judge Fitzmaurice, in the *Tyrer* case, was perturbed that a Convention conceived in response to the atrocities perpetrated in the Second World War should be used to challenge corporal punishment in general. Human rights standards cannot remain static and must bear a close relationship with the decisions of

---

[2] Poland is a Contracting Party to the Convention but has not yet lodged optional declarations under Articles 25 and 46. Polish membership of the Council of Europe was delayed by the organization until democratic elections had been held.

national courts, with public opinion and with the law and standard-setting debates of the national legislators. In the majority of Member States the Convention has the status of national law, and it is also deemed by the European Court of Justice in Luxembourg to embody the fundamental principles of law to be applied with respect to the treatment of individuals within the Community. To this extent, therefore, it must be considered to be "Constitutional" in nature and be a final recourse for the injured individual. Nevertheless, the refusal by states such as the United Kingdom to give the Convention the status of national law, and the decision by the Luxembourg Court that it is not Community law as such, seem to stress that parallel to its constitutionality lies a deeper political and ethical imperative. The increased use of the Court in the last ten years or so may be explained by a recognition, on the part of all involved – the Commission and its Secretariat, the States Parties and the lawyers within the national territories – that there are difficult *legal* questions to be answered which should be decided judicially.

A prominent initial feature in our study, however, was that the Commission, quite understandably, trod very carefully and timidly in its early days. As a consequence many important decisions on matters of fundamental freedom were able to be avoided. This is not to suggest that the Commission was to be blamed, or was in any way intentionally shirking its responsibilities. By taking refuge in legalism and procedural nicety, the Commission could have sacrificed the respect of states, civil rights workers, lawyers and applicants. This respect was essential for the Convention's success, be it as a political treaty within the pattern of European integration, or as a Bill of Rights for the individual victim. Recent decisions seem to show that the Commission and Court have finally realized that their function in controlling the discretion of states is the chief way in which they are able to raise the standards of human rights from levels based on the history and complacency of the nineteenth and early twentieth centuries.

It is also true, of course, that the European Convention may be looked upon primarily as a weapon in the armoury of law reform, where the individual is merely the catalyst enabling the falling short of the standard by individual states to be revealed. In many instances the Court is not called upon, or does not deem it necessary, to award compensation because the decision that the Convention has been violated is often enough reward for the individual victim or, more likely, the pressure group which has adopted the cause. Often applicants have been no better off, except in peace of mind, after applying to the European Commission, although in fact the presence of the Convention and the existence of its machinery has improved the quality of life of many other European citizens. Indeed, application to the Commission can bring with it, if one so desires, a great deal of publicity: Stein Andreas Iversen, in his application in 1962, alleged that the Norwegian Government was attempting to "socialize" dentistry, and gained newspaper space in his own country and in the rest of Europe for his allegations. In like manner, youthfully recruited sailors brought the attention of the public and Parliament to their plight. Pat Arrowsmith, a seasoned campaigner, did not hesitate to use the Convention to get publicity for her causes.

One cannot accept this altruistic view of the Convention entirely. How many victims of oppression are prepared to sacrifice time and expense, and risk the notoriety which application to the Convention brings, in order to gain true relief for others in like circumstances, but not for themselves? A majority of serious applications to the Commission have concerned Articles 5 and 6 of the Convention, the right to liberty and the right to a fair trial, and many of these applications do in fact contain sad stories of specific and sometimes unique deprivation of freedom. It is, at the same time, noticeable that many applications come in waves. Word is passed around prisons that here is another pastime which might bring about release or relief, and so the Commission's Secretariat is snowed under with applications on topics such as those revealed by the "equality-of-arms" cases against Austria in the sixties, or the series of UK prisoners' rights cases decided by the Court, or the Article 6 length of proceedings cases brought during the last few years against Italy.

It must be an inescapable conclusion, however, that the successes of the European Convention have in many cases been indirect, and that the individual has benefited either because of the mere presence of the treaty and its machinery, or through the application by someone else in a similar position. The Prison Rules were changed by the British Government to avoid the possibility of another case, such as that brought by Knechtl, in the future.

Inter-state petition does not seem to have resulted in much

improvement in the rights and freedoms of the individual, but has had the desired effect of bringing the situation prevailing in any one state to the attention of the other European states and the world. One might, however, question whether it should stop there. Greece left the Council of Europe and denounced the Convention and its Commission; United Kingdom mistreatment in Cyprus was forgotten after a political settlement had soothed the inter-state enmity. The *Irish* v. *United Kingdom* case extracted from the British Government the promise that the five techniques of interrogation would not be used again, but otherwise served merely to fuel Irish-British enmity.

If inter-state petitions are to be successful it would seem that they need to be backed by similar moves in the Parliamentary Assembly, as happened in the Greek cases. This could point to a lessening of the value of the Commission's function in inter-state cases for which, in general, it might expect to provide an adequate solution. The view of the Committee of Ministers in the *Cyprus* v. *Turkey* case that the infringement of human rights could only be remedied by the re-establishment of peace between the communities, emphasizes the point. The Human Dimension aspects of the CSCE raise the question of its overlap with the Council of Europe's activities. As the states of Eastern and Central Europe strive to enter the Western European arena, the requirement for democracy and the guarantee of human rights has been articulated. The Council of Europe sees itself as playing an important role in this process, but at the same time has recognized a certain weakness in its political and enforcement procedures. The CSCE security arrangements relieve the Council of Europe from many of the more difficult re-organizational problems, while at the same time bringing non-European powers such as the US, Canada and the Republics of the Commonwealth of Independent States into what is primarily a political operation.

The increasing number of applications to the Commission and the greater use of the Court have led to a back-log of cases before the Strasbourg organs. Protocol 8, as we have seen, was an attempt to improve the efficiency of the Commission by providing for its operation by means of Chambers and Committees. Although the figures indicate that this is having the desired effect of speeding-up cases, it is important to remember that the number of Contracting States has recently increased, and that as more states become eligible to join the Council of Europe[3] the potential number of applicants will increase. It is estimated that within the space of a few years membership could number over thirty-five states.

We should consider, therefore, how efficient the Strasbourg organs are, and are likely to remain, in carrying out their tasks.

One notable aspect of international adjudication is the slowness with which cases achieve settlement. There are obvious reasons for this: the distance, geographically and otherwise, between the parties; the delays involved in transporting witnesses and experts; the difficulties of assembling together, at one time, all the judges of the various nations. In addition to this, there is the fact that Governments traditionally take a good deal of trouble in defending their actions by consulting highly qualified lawyers, and neither governments nor highly qualified lawyers can be hurried. Rarely can a law student, during his course, follow an international case through all the stages of its procedure to its conclusion; the same, it appears, can be said of the cases before the European Commission and Court of Human Rights. In one case, *The Inhabitants of Mol* v. *Belgium*, fifteen years elapsed between the application and the termination of the proceedings.

It does, however, seem more important that human rights cases should be dealt with speedily. Even if the object of the decision is only to act as a warning, to awaken the European states to what is going on, then there would seem ample reason for speed. If the European Commission and Court are to guarantee the rights and freedoms of the individual, and to bring relief and an end to undue suffering, then a prompt solution is of the very essence of the international machinery.

The Kenyan and East African Asians who were not allowed to land in Britain but were returned and so shuttled back and forth from London, applied to the European Commission in February 1970. Although a relatively speedy decision was produced in that case, it was not until October of that year that the Commission was able to admit the application, and then, failing to achieve a friendly settlement, adopted its report on this case in December 1973. Only in October 1977 did the Committee of Ministers adopt its resolution, although it is true that one of the reasons for delay in this case was

---

[3] Or, sadly, as more states divide into national or religious units.

that the United Kingdom was reviewing its voucher system for immigrants. If the Commission is to work as a conciliatory body then unquestionably it must be given time to operate, but two important factors must be borne in mind. First, the claim of the applicant must at all times remain the predominant issue and secondly, it is important that if time is to be spent in consideration of an application, then this should be after the admissibility decision. The *Stögmüller* case, concerning over-lengthy detention, took just over seven years to get through the Convention's process. Two years were spent in considering admissibility, although admittedly the facts of the case were complex. Two years and eight months were taken up with attempts to achieve a friendly settlement, while from the date of adoption of its report by the Commission to the date of the Court's judgment, over two and a half years passed. The *Wemhoff* case took four and a half years to decide that there was no violation of the Convention, but there the admissibility decision was given in six months. This seems to be the shortest time that a case of any importance takes to get through the Commission's admissibility procedure, even where the case is given precedence. The later trend adopted by the Commission - of postponing the admissibility decision, where the facts are complex, until discussion of the merits - does help to speed up the progress of an application.

Nevertheless, we must also give full credit to the scheme which the Commission has put in place, and recognize that by undertaking a more extensive consideration of the facts at the admissibility stage and often venturing into the area of the merits, the Commission may, in fact, be improving efficiency. For example, where Government interference is allowed under the second Paragraphs of Articles 8 to 11 the admissibility stage may well be an appropriate moment to apply a *jurisprudence constante,* with the consequences that each case gets consideration at some depth, and yet the longer, and obviously fruitless, procedures which would otherwise follow, are bypassed.

In the Inter-American Commission the admissibility decision is treated virtually as administration and, similarly, the Human Rights Committee of the United Nations has not found admissibility questions too demanding. It is submitted, however, that the procedures of the Strasbourg organs are legally much more significant than those of either of these bodies.

The procedures introduced under Protocol 8 have been in operation for two years, and seem to be having a noticeable effect on the processing of applications. Nevertheless, it is likely that very little improvement can be achieved under present circumstances by changing the Convention further, short of fundamental reform of the whole machinery. The members of the Commission are at the moment part-time, and are otherwise lawyers, academics and judges of some repute in their own countries. They are all continuously in touch with the municipal law of their own states and, more importantly, cognisant of the political situation pertaining in Europe at any given time. A full-time Commission might get out of touch much more easily and become a body of anonymous international civil servants.

The stages of procedure after admissibility must also be kept as short as possible when not involving actual negotiation for a friendly settlement. Governments should not be given overlong extensions of time-limits in producing pleadings and memorials, preliminary issues must be disposed of by the Court as expeditiously as possible and, most of all, it is important that the administration of a case before the Commission and, especially, the Court, should be run as efficiently as modern methods of communications allow. Indeed, during the last sixteen years most cases submitted to the Court have been dealt with in less than two years, and the majority in just over one year.

In the same way that a human rights charter must necessarily guarantee rights without undue delay, it must also set up machinery which is available to all, irrespective of wealth. Human rights are not the privilege of the rich, nor should they be that of the poor. Human rights should not be bought and hence any tribunal must be open to all without regard to income. In 1963 the Commission therefore set up a system of free legal aid for impecunious applicants. This scheme is set out in an Addendum to the Rules of Procedure of the Commission, paragraph 1 of which reads:

The Commission may, either at the request of an applicant lodging an application under Article 25 of the Convention or *proprio motu,* grant free legal aid to that applicant for the representation of his case:

(a) where observations in writing on the admissibility of that application have been received from the High Contracting Party concerned in pursuance of Rule 42, paragraph 2b, or where the time limit for their submission has expired, or

(b) where the application has been declared admissible.

The Addendum to the rules goes on to lay down that free legal aid shall be granted only where the Commission is satisfied that it is essential for the proper discharge of its duties and that the applicant has insufficient means to meet all or part of the costs involved. The applicant is required to submit a statement of his financial position, certified by the appropriate domestic authorities, and the comments of the Government are also sought. After this, the Commission decides whether aid should be given. Grants may cover travelling, subsistence and other necessary out-of-pocket expenses and lawyer's fees, but fees to such a representative will only be paid to a barrister, solicitor or professor of law, or a professionally qualified person of similar status. Aid is normally paid according to an agreement between the lawyer and the Secretary to the Commission, and now normally follows a scale of payment which the Secretary has drawn up according to practice. The Commission can revoke the legal aid granted. The Secretary General of the Council of Europe is notified of the fees paid and this is provided from the Council budget. A similar scheme of legal aid is appended to the Rules of Court.

It is of course extremely satisfactory that a free legal aid scheme should have been introduced by the Secretariat, moreover the cost to the Council of Europe and to the Member States concerned has been negligible. The United Kingdom Supply Estimates for 1991–92 reveal that the British share of general expenses of the Council of Europe for the period in question was to be 16.71 per cent of the Council's *total* budget and amount to £9,800,000. A point which should not go unmentioned, therefore, is that it would seem that the Member States of the Council are paying at a very moderate rate.

A noticeable feature of the Strasbourg human rights process is the number of persons involved in it. If all the states who are members of the Council of Europe ratify the Convention, there will be 26 Commissioners, 26 Judges and the same number of Ministers involved in each case decided by the Court. The summary procedure introduced by Article 8 reduces this number, but only for the simpler or less deserving cases. The European Court of Human Rights in plenary session is the largest international court ever to have deliberated. It is most likely that as it increases in size its decision-making powers will, in practice, be stretched, leading to a diminution in its authority. It must also not be forgotten that each of the bodies must be fully provided with legal, administrative, secretarial and linguistic facilities. The essence of efficiency, seen from the eyes of the individual applicant, is that a fair decision should emanate with the shortest possible delay. The dual procedure - first before the Commission and then the Court - undoubtedly leads to a duplication of work and effort. Are there, therefore, reforms which might improve the Strasbourg procedure?

The Council of Europe Directorate of Human Rights is not unaware that improvements need to be made and, as part of its continuous mandate to oversee and develop the human rights within the organization, has set up a Committee of Experts for the improvement of procedures for the protection of human rights.

Various proposals have been made for streamlining the Strasbourg procedures. Protocol 8 is now in force and being applied, a draft Protocol 10, which will reduce the two thirds majority of the Committee of Ministers to a simple majority, awaits signature and will, if accepted, strengthen the judicial nature of the guarantee. It will be recalled that the Convention is the result of a series of compromises made in 1950. Many of these are no longer appropriate, while the respect which has been earned by the Commission and the Court means that some of the provisions agreed originally to protect the sovereignty of states are no longer deemed necessary.[4]

Where the Commission has failed to achieve a friendly settlement and has drawn up its report expressing an opinion as to a violation, the suggestion has been made that if, within the three month period laid down in Article 32, the case is not referred to the Court, then the Commission's report should be published and be considered binding. This would indeed speed up the final decision and avoid duplication of work. In the eyes of many it would also have the advantage of avoiding the political ramifications of referral to the Committee of Ministers. Such a procedure would probably allow for an appeal to the Court by any of the parties. It is questionable, however,

---

[4] For instance, the proscription of individual invocation of the Court will be bypassed when Protocol 9 comes into force.

whether appeals should be contemplated. The Convention machinery, in almost every case, follows a long process within the national courts, and a final answer from a Strasbourg body, without room for appeal, is probably preferable. Such a solution would not decrease the personnel involved, whereas, if a procedure for appeal were instituted, it would be very likely to increase and complicate the workload of the Secretariat and Registry. Similar proposals to divide the Commission and Court into smaller groups would be equally more expensive.

Present thinking on ways to expedite the Strasbourg decision envisages some kind of merger of the Commission and the Court. A proposal to this effect is likely to be made shortly.[5] The great advantage of merger would not only be to speed up the final decision but also to avoid the duplication of effort and administration which the present system entails. This includes not only the work carried out by the Secretariat and Registry but also that of the applicants' legal advisors. The present procedure involves the preparation of written and oral submissions to the Commission and the presentation of oral arguments before the Court. Not only is this time consuming, it is also expensive and detracts from the working of the Convention. As barrister Anthony Lester has written:

> The level of legal aid is so low as to render a lawyer's services virtually voluntary which restricts the development of a pool of lawyers with the expertise and willingness to take such cases.[6]

Although a merged Court would, at one stroke, halve the number of personnel involved in the decision-making process, the need would remain to ensure that the safeguards built into the original treaty are maintained. It would seem to be important, even if the present Parties are content with the way in which the Convention machinery is working, to prevent possible abuses in future.

The original conception of the Commission was that it should act as a filter, mainly to protect the states from unwarranted and abusive

---

[5] Ideas of this kind have long been discussed. See, for example, the Second Seminar on International Law and European Law at the University of Neuchatel 14-15 March 1986. *Merger of the European Commission and Court of Human Rights* 8 H.R.L.J. (1987), part 1.

[6] *Op. cit.* 8 *HRLJ* at p. 35.

applications. It is noticeable that all human rights procedures have such filters built into them, although not all are as complex and large-scale as the European Commission. Anthony Lester points out,[7] as we have seen elsewhere in this study, that the Commission's Secretariat has developed a role for itself of assisting applicants, advising them of procedural difficulties and even encouraging them to apply. The Commission has become, as he puts it, "user-friendly". In the case of merger the admissibility stage, which, as shown by the numbers rejected, is still essential, would have to be carried out by the Court, presumably by means of small Chambers or delegated judges. It would seem unlikely that the Court's Registry would be equipped or inclined to dispense the service which the Secretariat now provides. Since the admissibility stage has loomed large in the process so far, it probably could not be down-graded and any attempts to reduce it to an administrative decision would be resisted. A summary decision by a small Chamber or by a judge sitting alone might arouse calls for appeal of the admissibility decision – a procedure which, it is submitted, should be avoided. Legal costs would probably remain much as they are at the moment.

At present the Commission's second and major task is that of fact-finding. This it does with the help of its Secretariat, and by occasionally delegating Commissioners to carry out on-the-spot, fact-finding missions. There is, of course, no reason why the Court should not engage in this task itself. National courts, it is to be noted, assume such responsibilities. It is also true, however, that most superior or Constitutional courts are seized of cases once the facts have been established and are required only to reach a decision on the law. Fact-finding by a merged Court would need to be done by means of small Chambers, thereby increasing the risk of dragging out the procedure, or by introducing into the Strasbourg procedure the concept of Advocates General, familiar in many European legal systems and also in the European Court of Justice.

Closely allied to the establishment of the facts in the Strasbourg machinery is the possibility of conciliation and the negotiation of a friendly settlement. This is an important feature of the present procedures. Settlement out-of-court is, of course, a common occurrence in most jurisdictions, and the requirement that the Court

---

[7] *Op. cit.*

should approve the settlement would not seem an impediment. Nevertheless, a Court cannot give its blessing to a settlement until the facts of the complaint have been established. Under the present procedures the Commission is conversant with the facts by the time negotiations for a friendly settlement begin. It can therefore easily act as a third party, using the President of the Commission or a member of the Secretariat as a "go-between". The Commission may also be able to exert pressure by advising the parties what its opinion is likely to be, failing a friendly settlement. It is submitted that a settlement negotiated by the Court would be more formally pursued. It must also be admitted that in those cases where a friendly settlement is unlikely, because of the entrenched position of the parties, the Court could proceed to a judicial determination more quickly. A merged Court is likely to establish a more judicial trend, but conciliation must always remain an important option as long as the human rights principles laid down in the Convention are respected.

The chief advantage of merger of the Commission and the Court would be felt at the adjudication stage. One binding decision would avoid duplication, delay and cost. Protocol 9, giving direct access to the Court, has set the scene for a one-body procedure. The adjudicatory role of the Committee of Ministers would be eliminated in the case of individual applications, although there may need to be further thought given to inter-state petitions. We have seen that such applications between states are in most cases political in nature, and rarely susceptible to judicial procedures. A Committee of Ministers' presence might be justified for such cases.

At the present time the Commission takes part in the proceedings before the Court, acting not on behalf of the applicant but more as a kind of *amicus curiae*, representing the Convention and the other Contracting Parties. It would seem useful for the Court to retain such a representation since each of the opposing parties might have an interest over and beyond the Convention or the human rights embodied in it. How this is to be done will depend on the method of fact-finding selected. It could be a *rapporteur* delegated from the fact-finding Chamber or some kind of Advocate-General.

It is to be hoped that if the Commission and Court are amalgamated the opportunity will be taken to extend the jurisdiction of the merged court to the execution and supervision of judgments. The elimination of the Commission and the Committee of Ministers from the early part of the process may arouse an unwillingness on the part of Contracting States to dispense with the participation of the Committee of Ministers altogether. Nevertheless its role should be subject to the scrutiny of the Court. Anthony Lester, who has appeared as counsel before the Court on numerous occasions, points out that success before the Court may be minimized by a subsequent response accepted by the Committee:[8]

> There seems to be an operational assumption that altered legislation equals compliance. The correctness of that assumption may thus have to be tested by subsequent litigants.

We have seen throughout our study disappointments and challenges at every stage. The Council of Europe itself was less exciting than the idealists at its conception would have liked, the European Convention was based on a series of compromises which disappointed many of its champions, the Commission of Human Rights, for reasons which have now proved correct, approached its task in the early days gingerly and slowly. Similarly, the Court has proved on occasion to be timid and conservative. Through all this, however, the Strasbourg machinery has built for itself an important pedestal in international human rights law. It has brought about the acceptance of an individual's complaint against the state, it has established a role for judicial determination in international human rights law and has demonstrated that human rights law does not stand still but takes succeeding generations' manners and morals in its stride.

For various understandable reasons the Council of Europe has been much more successful than the United Nations in providing machinery to which Members can allow embarrassing human rights problems to be taken. Once an international tribunal is seized of the matter, a state can then continue with less interruption to seek for a solution while benefiting from the automatic delay which such a procedure grants. Neither the Council of Europe nor the Commission of Human Rights nor the Committee of Experts on Human Rights may become complacent. Even with the best will in the world, compromise rights, accepted by the disappointed Parliamentary Assembly in 1950, might still be watered down to a level where they

---

[8] *Op. cit.*, p. 40.

are completely ineffectual unless a vigilant watch is maintained. The answer to the question *sed quis custodiet ipsos custodes* is that the ultimate guardians must be the Parliamentary Assembly, the politicians and lawyers of the Member States and, even more, the European Commission and the applicants and lawyers appearing before them.

APPENDIX

THE EUROPEAN CONVENTION FOR THE PROTECTION OF HUMAN RIGHTS AND FUNDAMENTAL FREEDOMS

Rome, 4 November 1950

Entry into force: 3 September 1953, in accordance with Article 66.[1]

The governments signatory hereto, being members of the Council of Europe,

Considering the Universal Declaration of Human Rights proclaimed by the General Assembly of the United Nations on 10 December 1948;

Considering that this declaration aims at securing the universal and effective recognition and observance of the rights therein declared;

Considering that the aim of the Council of Europe is the achievement of greater unity between its members and that one of the methods by which that aim is to be pursued is the maintenance and further realisation of human rights and fundamental freedoms;

Reaffirming their profound belief in those fundamental freedoms which are the foundation of justice and peace in the world and are best maintained on the one hand by an effective political democracy and on the other by a common understanding and observance of the human rights upon which they depend;

Being resolved, as the governments of European countries which are like minded and have a common heritage of political traditions, ideals freedom and the rule of law, to take the first steps for the collective enforcement of certain of the rights stated in the Universal Declaration,

Have agreed as follows:

Article 1

The High Contracting Parties shall secure to everyone within their jurisdiction the rights and freedoms defined in Section I of this Convention.

---

[1] Text amended according to the provisions of Protocol No. 3, which entered into force on 21 September 1970, of Protocol No. 5, which entered into force on 20 December 1971 and of Protocol No. 8, which entered into force on 1 January 1990, and comprising also the text of Protocol No. 2 which, in accordance with Article 5, paragraph 3, thereof, has been an integral part of the Convention since its entry into force on 21 September 1970.

Section I

Article 2

1. Everyone's right to life shall be protected by law. No one shall be deprived of his life intentionally save in the execution of a sentence of court following his conviction of a crime for which this penalty is provided by law.

2. Deprivation of life shall not be regarded as inflicted in contravention of this Article when it results from the use of force which is no more than absolutely necessary:

    (a) in defence of any person from unlawful violence;

    (b) in order to effect a lawful arrest or to prevent the escape of a person lawfully detained;

    (c) in action lawfully taken for the purpose of quelling a riot or insurrection.

Article 3

No one shall be subjected to torture or to inhuman or degrading treatment or punishment.

Article 4

1. No one shall be held in slavery or servitude.

2. No one shall be required to perform forced or compulsory labour.

3. For the purpose of this article the term "forced or compulsory labour" shall not include:

    (a) any work required to be done in the ordinary course of detention imposed according to the provisions of Article 5 of this Convention or during conditional release from such detention;

    (b) any service of a military character or, in case of conscientious objectors in countries where they are recognised, service exacted instead of compulsory military service;

    (c) any service exacted in case of an emergency or calamity threatening the life or well-being of the community;

    (d) any work or service which forms part of normal civic obligations.

Article 5

1. Everyone has the right to liberty and security of person. No one shall be deprived of his liberty save in the following cases and in accordance with a procedure prescribed by law:

    (a) the lawful detention of a person after conviction by a competent court;

    (b) the lawful arrest or detention of a person for non-compliance with the lawful order of a court or in order to secure the fulfilment of any obligation prescribed by law;

(c) the lawful arrest or detention of a person effected for the purpose of a bringing him before the competent legal authority on reasonable suspicion of having committed an offence or when it is reasonably considered necessary to prevent his committing an offence or fleeing after having done so;

(d) the detention of a minor by lawful order for the purpose of educational supervision or his lawful detention for the purpose of bringing him before the competent legal authority;

(e) the lawful detention of persons for the prevention of the spreading of infectious diseases, of persons of unsound mind, alcoholics or drug addicts or vagrants;

(f) the lawful arrest or detention of a person to prevent his effecting an unauthorised entry into the country or of a person against whom action is being taken with a view to deportation or extradition.

2. Everyone who is arrested shall be informed promptly, in a language which he understands, of the reasons for his arrest and of any charge against him.

3. Everyone arrested or detained in accordance with the provisions of paragraph 1(c) of this Article shall be brought promptly before a judge or other officer authorised by law to exercise judicial power and shall be entitled to trial within a reasonable time or to release pending trial. Release may be conditioned by guarantees to appear for trial.

4. Everyone who is deprived of his liberty by arrest or detention shall be entitled to take proceedings by which the lawfulness of his detention shall be decided speedily by a court and his release ordered if the detention is not lawful.

5. Everyone who has been the victim of arrest or detention in contravention of the provisions of this Article shall have an enforceable right to compensation.

Article 6

1. In the determination of his civil rights and obligations or of any criminal charge against him, everyone is entitled to a fair and public hearing within a reasonable time by an independent and impartial tribunal established by law. Judgment shall be pronounced publicly but the press and public may be excluded from all or part of the trial in the interests of morals, public order or national security in a democratic society, where the interests of juveniles or the protection of the private life of the parties so require, or to the extent strictly necessary in the opinion of the court in special circumstances where publicity would prejudice the interests of justice.

2. Everyone charged with a criminal offence shall be presumed innocent until proved guilty according to law.

3. Everyone charged with a criminal offence has the following minimum rights:

(a) to be informed promptly, in a language which he understands and in detail, of the nature and cause of the accusation against him;

(b)   to have adequate time and facilities for the preparation of his defence;

(c)   to defend himself in person or through legal assistance of his own choosing or, if he has not sufficient means to pay for legal assistance, to be given it free when the interests of justice so require;

(d)   to examine or have examined witnesses against him and to obtain the attendance and examination of witnesses on his behalf under the same conditions as witnesses against him;

(e)   to have the free assistance of an interpreter if he cannot understand or speak the language used in court.

Article 7

1.   No one shall be held guilty of any criminal offence on account of any act or omission which did not constitute a criminal offence under national or international law at the time when it was committed. Nor shall a heavier penalty be imposed than the one that was applicable at the time the criminal offence was committed.

2.   This article shall not prejudice the trial and punishment of any person for any act or omission which, at the time when it was committed, was criminal according to the general principles of law recognised by civilised nations.

Article 8

1.   Everyone has the right to respect for his private and family life, his home and his correspondence.

2.   There shall be no interference by a public authority with the exercise of this right except such as is in accordance with the law and is necessary in a democratic society in the interests of national security, public safety or the economic well-being of the country, for the prevention of disorder or crime, for the protection of health or morals, or for the protection of the rights and freedoms of others.

Article 9

1.   Everyone has the right to freedom of thought, conscience and religion; this right includes freedom to change his religion or belief and freedom either alone or in community with others and in public or in private, to manifest his religion or belief, in worship, teaching, practice and observance.

2.   Freedom to manifest one's religion or beliefs shall be subject only to such limitations as are prescribed by law and are necessary in a democratic society in the interests of public safety, for the protection of public order, health or morals, or for the protection of the rights and freedoms of others.

Article 10

1.   Everyone has the right to freedom of expression. This right shall include freedom to hold opinions and to receive and impart information and ideas without interference by public authority and regardless of frontiers. This

article shall not prevent States from requiring the licensing of broadcasting, television or cinema enterprises.

2. The exercise of these freedoms, since it carries with it duties and responsibilities, may be subject to such formalities, conditions, restrictions or penalties as are prescribed by law and are necessary in a democratic society, in the interests of national security, territorial integrity or public safety, for the prevention of disorder or crime, for the protection of health or morals, for the protection of the reputation or rights of others, for preventing the disclosure of information received in confidence, or for maintaining the authority and impartiality of the judiciary.

Article 11

1. Everyone has the right to freedom of peaceful assembly and to freedom of association with others, including the right to form and to join trade unions for the protection of his interests.

2. No restrictions shall be placed on the exercise of these rights other than such as are prescribed by law and are necessary in a democratic society in the interests of national security or public safety, for the prevention of disorder or crime, for the protection of health or morals or for the protection of the rights and freedoms of others. This Article shall not prevent the imposition of lawful restrictions on the exercise of these rights by members of the armed forces, of the police or of the administration of the State.

Article 12

Men and women of marriageable age have the right to marry and to found a family, according to the national laws governing the exercise of this right.

Article 13

Everyone whose rights and freedoms as set forth in this Convention are violated shall have an effective remedy before a national authority notwithstanding that the violation has been committed by persons acting in an official capacity.

Article 14

The enjoyment of the rights and freedoms set forth in this Convention shall be secured without discrimination on any ground such as sex, race, colour, language, religion, political or other opinion, national or social origin, association with a national minority, property, birth or other status.

Article 15

1. In time of war or other public emergency threatening the life of the nation any High Contracting Party may take measures derogating from its obligations under this Convention to the extent strictly required by the exigencies of the situation, provided that such measures are not inconsistent with its other obligations under international law.

2. No derogation from Article 2, except in respect of deaths resulting from

lawful acts of war, or from Articles 3, 4 (paragraph 1) and 7 shall be made under this provision.

3. Any High Contracting Party availing itself of this right of derogation shall keep the Secretary General of the Council of Europe fully informed of the measures which it has taken and the reasons therefor. It shall also inform the Secretary General of the Council of Europe when such measures have ceased to operate and the provisions of the Convention are again being fully executed.

Article 16

Nothing in Articles 10, 11 and 14 shall be regarded as preventing the High Contracting Parties from imposing restrictions on the political activity of aliens.

Article 17

Nothing in this Convention may be interpreted as implying for any State, group or person any right to engage in any activity or perform any act aimed at the destruction of any of the rights and freedoms set forth herein or at their limitation to a greater extent than is provided for in the Convention.

Article 18

The restrictions permitted under this Convention to the said rights and freedoms shall not be applied for any purpose other than those for which they have been prescribed.

Section II

Article 19

To ensure the observance of the engagements undertaken by the High Contracting Parties in the present Convention, there shall be set up:

(a) a European Commission of Human Rights, hereinafter referred to as "the Commission";

(b) a European Court of Human Rights, hereinafter referred to as "the Court".

Section III

Article 20

1. The Commission shall consist of a number of members equal to that of the High Contracting Parties. No two members of the Commission may be nationals of the same State.

2. The Commission shall sit in plenary session. It may, however, set up chambers, each composed of at least seven members. The chambers may examine petitions submitted under Article 25 of this Convention which can be dealt with on the basis of established case-law or which raise no serious question affecting the interpretation or application of the Convention. Subject to this restriction and to the provisions of paragraph 5 of this Article, the chambers

shall exercise all the powers conferred on the Commission by the Convention.

The member of the Commission elected in respect of a High Contracting Party against which a petition has been lodged shall have the right to sit on a chamber to which that petition has been referred.

3. The Commission may set up committees, each composed of at least three members, with the power, exercisable by a unanimous vote, to declare inadmissible or strike from its list of cases a petition submitted under Article 25, when such a decision can be taken without further examination.

4. A chamber or committee may at any time relinquish jurisdiction in favour of the plenary Commission, which may also order the transfer to it of any petition referred to a chamber or committee.

5. Only the plenary Commission can exercise the following powers:

   (a) the examination of applications submitted under Article 24;

   (b) the bringing of a case before the Court in accordance with Article 48(a);

   (c) the drawing up of rules of procedure in accordance with Article 36.

Article 21

1. The members of the Commission shall be elected by the Committee of Ministers by an absolute majority of votes, from a list of names drawn up by the Bureau of the Consultative Assembly; each group of the representatives of the High Contracting Parties in the Consultative Assembly shall put forward three candidates, of whom two at least shall be its nationals.

2. As far as applicable, the same procedure shall be followed to complete the Commission in the event of other States subsequently becoming Parties to this Convention, and in filling casual vacancies.

3. The candidates shall be of high moral character and must either possess the qualifications required for appointment to high judicial office or be persons of recognised competence in national or international law.

Article 22

1. The members of the Commission shall be elected for a period of six years. They may be re-elected. However, of the members elected at the first election, the terms of seven members shall expire at the end of three years.

2. The members whose terms are to expire at the end of the initial period of three years shall be chosen by lot by the Secretary General of the Council of Europe immediately after the first election has been completed.

3. In order to ensure that, as far as possible, one half of the membership of the Commission shall be renewed every three years, the Committee of Ministers may decide, before proceeding to any subsequent election, that the term or terms of office of one or more members to be elected shall be for a period other than six years but not more than nine and not less than three years.

4. In cases where more than one term of office is involved and the Committee of Ministers applies the preceding paragraph, the allocation of the terms of office shall be effected by the drawing of lots by the Secretary General, immediately after the election.

5. A member of the Commission elected to replace a member whose term of office has not expired shall hold office for the remainder of his predecessor's term.

6. The members of the Commission shall hold office until replaced. After having been replaced, they shall continue to deal with such cases as they already have under consideration.

Article 23

The members of the Commission shall sit on the Commission in their individual capacity. During their term of office they shall not hold any position which is incompatible with their independence and impartiality as members of the Commission or the demands of this office.

Article 24

Any High Contracting Party may refer to the Commission, through the Secretary General of the Council of Europe, any alleged breach of the provisions of the Convention by another High Contracting Party.

Article 25

1. The Commission may receive petitions addressed to the Secretary General of the Council of Europe from any person, non-governmental organisation or group of individuals claiming to be the victim of a violation by one of the High Contracting Parties of the rights set forth in this Convention, provided that the High Contracting Party against which the complaint has been lodged has declared that it recognises the competence of the Commission to receive such petitions. Those of the High Contracting Parties who have made such a declaration undertake not to hinder in any way the effective exercise of this right.

2. Such declarations may be made for a specific period.

3. The declarations shall be deposited with the Secretary General of the Council of Europe who shall transmit copies thereof to the High Contracting Parties and publish them.

4. The Commission shall only exercise the powers provided for in this Article when at least six High Contracting Parties are bound by declarations made in accordance with the preceding paragraphs.

Article 26

The Commission may only deal with the matter after all domestic remedies have been exhausted, according to the generally recognised rules of international law, and within a period of six months from the date on which the final decision was taken.

Article 27

1. The Commission shall not deal with any petition submitted under Article 25 which:

    (a) is anonymous, or

    (b) is substantially the same as a matter which has already been examined by the Commission or has already been submitted to another procedure of international investigation or settlement and if it contains no relevant new information.

2. The Commission shall consider inadmissible any petition submitted under Article 25 which it considers incompatible with the provisions of the present Convention, manifestly ill-founded, or an abuse of the right of petition.

3. The Commission shall reject any petition referred to it which it considers inadmissible under Article 26.

Article 28

1. In the event of the Commission accepting a petition referred to it:

    (a) it shall, with a view to ascertaining the facts, undertake together with the representatives of the parties an examination of the petition and, if need be, an investigation, for the effective conduct of which the States concerned shall furnish all necessary facilities, after an exchange of views with the Commission;

    (b) it shall at the same time place itself at the disposal of the parties concerned with a view to securing a friendly settlement of the matter on the basis of respect for human rights as defined in this Convention.

2. If the Commission succeeds in effecting a friendly settlement, it shall draw up a report which shall be sent to the States concerned, to the Committee of Ministers and to the Secretary General of the Council of Europe for publication. This report shall be confined to a brief statement of the facts and of the solution reached.

Article 29

After it has accepted a petition submitted under Article 25, the Commission may nevertheless decide by a majority of two-thirds of its members to reject the petition if, in the course of its examination, it finds that the existence of one of the grounds for non-acceptance provided for in Article 27 has been established. In such a case, the decision shall be communicated to the parties.

Article 30

1. The Commission may at any stage of the proceedings decide to strike a petition out of its list of cases where the circumstances lead to the conclusion that:

    (a) the applicant does not intend to pursue his petition, or

    (b) the matter has been resolved, or

    (c) for any other reason established by the Commission, it is no longer justified to continue the examination of the petition. However, the Commission shall continue the examination of a petition if respect for human rights as defined in this Convention so requires.

2. If the Commission decides to strike a petition out of its list after having accepted it, it shall draw up a report which shall contain a statement of the facts and the decision striking out the petition together with reasons therefor. The report shall be transmitted to the parties, as well as to the Committee of Ministers for information. The Commission may publish it.

3. The Commission may decide to restore a petition to its list of cases if it considers that the circumstances justify such a course.

Article 31

1. If the examination of a petition has not been completed in accordance with Article 28 (paragraph 2), 29 or 30, the Commission shall draw up a report on the facts and state its opinion as to whether the facts found disclose a breach by the State concerned of its obligations under the Convention. The individual opinions of members of the Commission on this point may be stated in the report.

2. The report shall be transmitted to the Committee of Ministers. It shall also be transmitted to the States concerned, who shall not be at liberty to publish it.

3. In transmitting the report to the Committee of Ministers the Commission may make such proposals as it thinks fit.

Article 32

1. If the question is not referred to the Court in accordance with Article 48 of this Convention within a period of three months from the date of the transmission of the report to the Committee of Ministers, the Committee of Ministers shall decide by a majority of two-thirds of the members entitled to sit on the Committee whether there has been a violation of the Convention.

2. In the affirmative case the Committee of Ministers shall prescribe a period during which the High Contracting Party concerned must take the measures required by the decision of the Committee of Ministers.

3. If the High Contracting Party concerned has not taken satisfactory measures within the prescribed period, the Committee of Ministers shall decide by the majority provided for in paragraph (1) above what effect shall be given to its original decision and shall publish the report.

4. The High Contracting Parties undertake to regard as binding on them any decision which the Committee of Ministers may take in application of the preceding paragraphs.

Article 33

The Commission shall meet in camera.

Article 34

Subject to the provisions of Articles 20 (paragraph 3) and 29, the Commission shall take its decisions by a majority of the members present and voting.

Article 35

The Commission shall meet as the circumstances require. The meetings shall be convened by the Secretary General of the Council of Europe.

Article 36

The Commission shall draw up its own rules of procedure.

Article 37

The secretariat of the Commission shall be provided by the Secretary General of the Council of Europe.

Section IV

Article 38

The European Court of Human Rights shall consist of a number of judges equal to that of the members of the Council of Europe. No two judges may be nationals of the same State.

Article 39

1. The members of the Court shall be elected by the Consultative Assembly by a majority of the votes cast from a list of persons nominated by the members of the Council of Europe; each member shall nominate three candidates, of whom two at least shall be its nationals.

2. As far as applicable, the same procedure shall be followed to complete the Court in the event of the admission of new members of the Council of Europe, and in filling casual vacancies.

3. The candidates shall be of high moral character and must possess the qualifications required for appointment to high judicial office or be jurisconsults of recognised competence.

Article 40

1. The members of the Court shall be elected for a period of nine years. They may be re-elected. However, of the members elected at the first election the terms of four members shall expire at the end of three years and the terms of four more members shall expire at the end of six years.

2. The members whose terms are to expire at the end of the initial periods of three and six years shall be chosen by lot by the Secretary General immediately after the first election has been completed.

3. In order to ensure that, as far as possible, one third of the membership of the Court shall be renewed every three years, the Consultative Assembly may decide, before proceeding to any subsequent election, that the term or terms

of office of one or more members to be elected shall be for a period other than nine years but not more than twelve and not less than six years.

4. In cases where more than one term of office is involved and the Consultative Assembly applies the preceding paragraph, the allocation of the terms of office shall be effected by the drawing of lots by the Secretary General immediately after the election.

5. A member of the Court elected to replace a member whose term of office has not expired shall hold office for the remainder of his predecessor's term.

6. The members of the Court shall hold office until replaced. After having been replaced, they shall continue to deal with such cases as they already have under consideration.

7. The members of the Court shall sit on the Court in their individual capacity. During their term of office they shall not hold any position which is incompatible with their independence and impartiality as members of the Court or the demands of this office.

Article 41

The Court shall elect its President and one or two Vice-Presidents for a period of three years. They may be re-elected.

Article 42

The members of the Court shall receive for each day of duty a compensation to be determined by the Committee of Ministers.

Article 43

For the consideration of each case brought before it the Court shall consist of a chamber composed of nine judges. There shall sit as an *ex officio* member of the chamber the judge who is a national of any State Party concerned, or, if there is none, a person of its choice who shall sit in the capacity of judge; the names of the other judges shall be chosen by lot by the President before the opening of the case.

Article 44

Only the High Contracting Parties and the Commission shall have the right to bring a case before the Court.

Article 45

The jurisdiction of the Court shall extend to all cases concerning the interpretation and application of the present Convention which the High Contracting Parties or the Commission shall refer to it in accordance with Article 48.

Article 46

1. Any of the High Contracting Parties may at any time declare that it recognises as compulsory *ipso facto* and without special agreement the jurisdiction of the Court in all matters concerning the interpretation and application of the present Convention.

2. The declarations referred to above may be made unconditionally or on condition of reciprocity on the part of several or certain other High Contracting Parties or for a specified period.

3. These declarations shall be deposited with the Secretary General of the Council of Europe who shall transmit copies thereof to the High Contracting Parties.

Article 47

The Court may only deal with a case after the Commission has acknowledged the failure of efforts for a friendly settlement and within the period of three months provided for in Article 32.

Article 48

The following may bring a case before the Court, provided that the High Contracting Party concerned, if there is only one, or the High Contracting Parties concerned, if there is more than one, are subject to the compulsory jurisdiction of the Court or, failing that, with the consent of the High Contracting Party concerned, if there is only one, or of the High Contracting Parties concerned if there is more than one:

(a) the Commission;

(b) a High Contracting Party whose national is alleged to be a victim;

(c) a High Contracting Party which referred the case to the Commission;

(d) a High Contracting Party against which the complaint has been lodged.

Article 49

In the event of dispute as to whether the Court has jurisdiction, the matter shall be settled by the decision of the Court.

Article 50

If the Court finds that a decision or a measure taken by a legal authority or any other authority of a High Contracting Party is completely or partially in conflict with the obligations arising from the present Convention, and if the internal law of the said Party allows only partial reparation to be made for the consequences of this decision or measure, the decision of the Court shall, if necessary, afford just satisfaction to the injured party.

Article 51

1. Reasons shall be given for the judgment of the Court.

2. If the judgment does not represent in whole or in part the unanimous opinion of the judges, any judge shall be entitled to deliver a separate opinion.

Article 52

The judgment of the Court shall be final.

Article 53

The High Contracting Parties undertake to abide by the decision of the Court in any case to which they are parties.

Article 54

The judgment of the Court shall be transmitted to the Committee of Ministers which shall supervise its execution.

Article 55

The Court shall draw up its own rules and shall determine its own procedure.

Article 56

1. The first election of the members of the Court shall take place after the declarations by the High Contracting Parties mentioned in Article 46 have reached a total of eight.

2. No case can be brought before the Court before this election.

Section V

Article 57

On receipt of a request from the Secretary General of the Council of Europe any High Contracting Party shall furnish an explanation of the manner in which its internal law ensures the effective implementation of any of the provisions of this Convention.

Article 58

The expenses of the Commission and the Court shall be borne by the Council of Europe.

Article 59

The members of the Commission and of the Court shall be entitled, during the discharge of their functions, to the privileges and immunities provided for in Article 40 of the Statute of the Council of Europe and in the agreements made thereunder.

Article 60

Nothing in this Convention shall be construed as limiting or derogating from any of the human rights and fundamental freedoms which may be ensured under the laws of any High Contracting Party or under any other agreement to which it is a Party.

Article 61

Nothing in this Convention shall prejudice the powers conferred on the Committee of Ministers by the Statute of the Council of Europe.

Article 62

The High Contracting Parties agree that, except by special agreement, they will not avail themselves of treaties, conventions or declarations in force between them for the purpose of submitting, by way of petition, a dispute arising out of the interpretation or application of this Convention to a means of settlement other than those provided for in this Convention.

Article 63

1. Any State may at the time of its ratification or at any time thereafter declare by notification addressed to the Secretary General of the Council of Europe that the present Convention shall extend to all or any of the territories for whose international relations it is responsible.

2. The Convention shall extend to the territory or territories named in the notification as from the thirtieth day after the receipt of this notification by the Secretary General of the Council of Europe.

3. The provisions of this Convention shall be applied in such territories with due regard, however, to local requirements.

4. Any State which has made a declaration in accordance with paragraph 1 of this Article may at any time thereafter declare on behalf of one or more of the territories to which the declaration relates that it accepts the competence of the Commission to receive petitions from individuals, non-governmental organisations or groups of individuals in accordance with Article 25 of the present Convention.

Article 64

1. Any State may, when signing this Convention or when depositing its instrument of ratification, make a reservation in respect of any particular provision of the Convention to the extent that any law then in force in its territory is not in conformity with the provision. Reservations of a general character shall not be permitted under this Article.

2. Any reservation made under this article shall contain a brief statement of the law concerned.

Article 65

1. A High Contracting Party may denounce the present Convention only after the expiry of five years from the date on which it became a Party to it and after six months' notice contained in a notification addressed the Secretary General of the Council of Europe, who shall inform the other High Contracting Parties.

2. Such a denunciation shall not have the effect of releasing the High Contracting Party concerned from its obligations under this Convention in respect of any act which, being capable of constituting a violation of such obligations, may have been performed by it before the date at which the denunciation became effective.

3. Any High Contracting Party which shall cease to be a member of the Council of Europe shall cease to be a Party to this Convention under the same conditions.

4. The Convention may be denounced in accordance with the provisions of the preceding paragraphs in respect of any territory to which it has been declared to extend under the terms of Article 63.

Article 66

1. This Convention shall be open to the signature of the members of the Council of Europe. It shall be ratified. Ratifications shall be deposited with the Secretary General of the Council of Europe.

2. The present Convention shall come into force after the deposit of ten instruments of ratification.

3. As regards any signatory ratifying subsequently, the Convention shall come into force at the date of the deposit of its instrument of ratification.

4. The Secretary General of the Council of Europe shall notify all the members of the Council of Europe of the entry into force of the Convention, the names of the High Contracting Parties who have ratified it, and the deposit of all instruments of ratification which may be effected subsequently.

Done at Rome this 4th day of November 1950, in English and French, both texts being equally authentic, in a single copy which shall remain deposited in the archives of the Council of Europe. The Secretary General shall transmit certified copies to each of the signatories.

PROTOCOL 1

Paris, March 1952. [2]

The governments signatory hereto, being members of the Council of Europe,

Being resolved to take steps to ensure the collective enforcement of certain rights and freedoms other than those already included in Section I of the Convention for the Protection of Human Rights and Fundamental Freedoms signed at Rome on 4 November, 1950 (hereinafter referred to as "the Convention"),

Have agreed as follows:

Article 1

Every natural or legal person is entitled to the peaceful enjoyment of his possessions. No one shall be deprived of his possessions except in the public interest and subject to the conditions provided for by law and by the general principles of international law.

The preceding provisions shall not, however, in any way impair the right of a State to enforce such laws as it deems necessary to control the use of property in accordance with the general interest or to secure the payment of taxes or other contributions or penalties.

[2] Entry into force: 18 May 1954, in accordance with Article 6.

Article 2

No person shall be denied the right to education. In the exerciseof any functions which it assumes in relation to education and to teaching the State shall respect the right of parents to ensure such education and teaching in conformity with their own religious and philosophical convictions.

Article 3

The High Contracting Parties undertake to hold free elections at reasonable intervals by secret ballot, under conditions which will ensure the free expression of the opinion of the people in the choice of the legislature.

Article 4

Any High Contracting Party may at the time of signature or ratification or at any time thereafter communicate to the Secretary General of the Council of Europe a declaration stating the extent to which it undertakes that the provisions of the present Protocol shall apply to such of the territories for the international relations of which it is responsible as are named therein.

Any High Contracting Party which has communicated a declaration in virtue of the preceding paragraph may from time to time communicate a further declaration modifying the terms of any former declaration or terminating the application of the provisions of this Protocol in respect of any territory.

A declaration made in accordance with this Article shall be deemed to have been made in accordance with paragraph 1 of Article 63 of the Convention.

Article 5

As between the High Contracting Parties the provisions of Articles 1, 2, 3 and 4 of this Protocol shall be regarded as additional articles to the Convention and all the provisions of the Convention shall apply accordingly.

Article 6

This Protocol shall be open for signature by the members of the Council of Europe who are the signatories of the Convention; it shall be ratified at the same time as or after the ratification of the Convention. It shall enter into force after the deposit of ten instruments of ratification. As regards any signatory ratifying subsequently, the Protocol shall enter into force at the date of the deposit of its instrument of ratification.

The instruments of ratification shall be deposited with the Secretary General of the Council of Europe, who will notify all members of the names of those who have ratified.

Done at Paris, this 20th day of March 1952, in English and French, both texts being equally authentic, in a single copy which shall remain deposited in the archives of the Council of Europe. The Secretary General shall transmit certified copies to each of the signatory governments.

PROTOCOL 2

Strasbourg, 6 May 1963.[3]

The member States of the Council of Europe signatory hereto,

Having regard to the provisions of the Convention for the Protection of Human Rights and Fundamental Freedoms signed at Rome on 4 November 1950 (hereinafter referred to as "the Convention") and, in particular, Article 19 instituting, among other bodies, a European Court of Human Rights (hereinafter referred to as "the Court");

Considering that it is expedient to confer upon the Court competence to give advisory opinions subject to certain conditions,

Have agreed as follows:

Article 1

1. The Court may, at the request of the Committee of Ministers, give advisory opinions on legal questions concerning the interpretation of the Convention and the Protocols thereto.

2. Such opinions shall not deal with any question relating to the content or scope of the rights or freedoms defined in Section I of the Convention and in the Protocols thereto, or with any other question which the Commission, the Court or the Committee of Ministers might have to consider in consequence of any such proceedings as could be instituted in accordance with the Convention.

3. Decisions of the Committee of Ministers to request an advisory opinion of the Court shall require a two-thirds majority vote of the representatives entitled to sit on the Committee.

Article 2

The Court shall decide whether a request for an advisory opinion submitted by the Committee of Ministers is within its consultative competence as defined in Article 1 of this Protocol.

Article 3

1. For the consideration of requests for an advisory opinion, the Court shall sit in plenary session.

2. Reasons shall be given for advisory opinions of the Court.

3. If the advisory opinion does not represent in whole or in part the unanimous opinion of the judges, any judge shall be entitled to deliver a separate opinion.

4. Advisory opinions of the Court shall be communicated to the Committee of Ministers.

[3] Entry into force: 21 September 1970, in accordance with Article 5.

Article 4

The powers of the Court under Article 55 of the Convention shall extend to the drawing up of such rules and the determination of such procedure as the Court may think necessary for the purposes of this Protocol.

Article 5

1. This Protocol shall be open to signature by member States of the Council of Europe, signatories to the Convention, who may become Parties to it by:

    (a) signature without reservation in respect of ratification or acceptance;

    (b) signature with reservation in respect of ratification or acceptance followed by ratification or acceptance.

    Instruments of ratification or acceptance shall be deposited with the Secretary General of the Council of Europe.

2. This Protocol shall enter into force as soon as all States Parties to the Convention shall have become Parties to the Protocol, in accordance with the provisions of paragraph 1 of this Article.

3. From the date of the entry into force of this Protocol, Articles 1 to 4 shall be considered an integral part of the Convention.

4. The Secretary General of the Council of Europe shall notify the member States of the Council of:

    (a) any signature without reservation in respect of ratification or acceptance;

    (b) any signature with reservation in respect of ratification or acceptance;

    (c) the deposit of any instrument of ratification or acceptance;

    (d) the date of entry into force of this Protocol in accordance with paragraph 2 of this Article.

In witness whereof, the undersigned, being duly authorised thereto have signed this Protocol.

Done at Strasbourg, this 6th day of May 1963, in English and French both texts being equally authoritative, in a single copy which shall remain deposited in the archives of the Council of Europe. The Secretary General shall transmit certified copies to each of the signatory States.

PROTOCOL 4

Strasbourg, 16 September 1963.[4]

The governments signatory hereto, being members of the Council of Europe,

Being resolved to take steps to ensure the collective enforcement of certain rights and freedoms other than those already included in Section 1 of the

---

[4] Entry into force: 2 May 1968, in accordance with Article 7.

Convention for the Protection of Human Rights and Fundamental Freedoms signed at Rome on 4 November 1950 (hereinafter referred to as "the Convention") and in Articles 1 to 3 of the First Protocol to the Convention, signed at Paris on 20 March 1952,

Have agreed as follows:

Article 1

No one shall be deprived of his liberty merely on the ground of inability to fulfil a contractual obligation.

Article 2

1. Everyone lawfully within the territory of a State shall, within that territory, have the right to liberty of movement and freedom to choose his residence.

2. Everyone shall be free to leave any country, including his own.

3. No restrictions shall be placed on the exercise of these rights other than such as are in accordance with law and are necessary in a democratic society in the interests of national security or public safety, for the maintenance of *ordre public*, for the prevention of crime, for the protection of health or morals, or for the protection of the rights and freedoms of others.

4. The rights set forth in paragraph 1 may also be subject, in particular areas, to restrictions imposed in accordance with law and justified by the public interest in a democratic society.

Article 3

1. No one shall be expelled, by means either of an individual or of a collective measure, from the territory of the State of which he is a national.

2. No one shall be deprived of the right to enter the territory of the State of which he is a national.

Article 4

Collective expulsion of aliens is prohibited.

Article 5

1. Any High Contracting Party may, at the time of signature or ratification of this Protocol, or at any time thereafter, communicate to the Secretary General of the Council of Europe a declaration stating the extent to which it undertakes that the provisions of this Protocol shall apply to such of the territories for the international relations of which it is responsible as are named therein.

2. Any High Contracting Party which has communicated a declaration in virtue of the preceding paragraph may, from time to time, communicate a further declaration modifying the terms of any former declaration or terminating the application of the provisions of this Protocol in respect of any territory.

3. A declaration made in accordance with this Article shall be deemed to have been made in accordance with paragraph 1 of Article 63 of the Convention.

4. The territory of any State to which this Protocol applies by virtue of ratification or acceptance by that State, and each territory to which this Protocol is applied by virtue of a declaration by that State under this Article, shall be treated as separate territories for the purpose of the references in Articles 2 and 3 to the territory of a State.

Article 6

1. As between the High Contracting Parties the provisions of Articles 1 to 5 of this Protocol shall be regarded as additional articles to the Convention, and all the provisions of the Convention shall apply accordingly.

2. Nevertheless, the right of individual recourse recognised by a declaration made under Article 25 of the Convention, or the acceptance of the compulsory jurisdiction of the Court by a declaration made under Article 46 of the Convention, shall not be effective in relation to this Protocol unless the High Contracting Party concerned has made a statement recognising such right, or accepting such jurisdiction, in respect of all or any of Articles 1 to 4 of the Protocol.

Article 7

1. This Protocol shall be open for signature by the members of the Council of Europe who are the signatories of the Convention; it shall be ratified at the same time as or after the ratification of the Convention. It shall enter into force after the deposit of five instruments of ratification. As regards any signatory ratifying subsequently, the Protocol shall enter into force at the date of the deposit of its instrument of ratification.

2. The instruments of ratification shall be deposited with the Secretary General of the Council of Europe, who will notify all members of the names of those who have ratified.

In witness whereof, the undersigned, being duly authorised thereto, have signed this Protocol.

Done at Strasbourg, this 16th day of September 1963, in English and in French, both texts being equally authoritative, in a single copy which shall remain deposited in the archives of the Council of Europe. The Secretary General shall transmit certified copies to each of the signatory States.

PROTOCOL 6

Strasbourg, 28 April 1983.[5]

The member States of the Council of Europe, signatory to this Protocol to the Convention for the Protection of Human Rights and Fundamental Freedoms, signed at Rome on 4 November 1950 (hereinafter referred to as "the Convention"),

[5] Entry into force: 1 March 1985, in accordance with Article 8.

Considering that the evolution that has occurred in several member States of the Council of Europe expresses a general tendency in favour of abolition of the death penalty,

Have agreed as follows:

Article 1

The death penalty shall be abolished. No one shall be condemned to such penalty or executed.

Article 2

A State may make provision in its law for the death penalty in respect of acts committed in time of war or of imminent threat of war; such penalty shall be applied only in the instances laid down in the law and in accordance with its provisions. The State shall communicate to the Secretary General of the Council of Europe the relevant provisions of that law.

Article 3

No derogation from the provisions of this Protocol shall be made under Article 15 of the Convention.

Article 4

No reservation may be made under Article 64 of the Convention in respect of the provisions of this Protocol.

Article 5

1. Any State may at the time of signature or when depositing its instrument of ratification, acceptance or approval, specify the territory or territories to which this Protocol shall apply.

2. Any State may at any later date, by a declaration addressed to the Secretary General of the Council of Europe, extend the application of this Protocol to any other territory specified in the declaration. In respect of such territory the Protocol shall enter into force on the first day of the month following the date of receipt of such a declaration by the Secretary General.

3. Any declaration made under the two preceding paragraphs may, in respect of any territory specified in such declaration, be withdrawn by a notification addressed to the Secretary General. The withdrawal shall become effective on the first day of the month following the date of receipt of such notification by the Secretary General.

Article 6

As between the States Parties the provisions of Articles 1 to 5 of this Protocol shall be regarded as additional Articles to the Convention and all the provisions of the Convention shall apply accordingly.

Article 7

This Protocol shall be open for signature by the member States of the Council of Europe, signatories to the Convention. It shall be subject to ratification, acceptance or approval. A member State of the Council of Europe may not ratify, accept or approve this Protocol unless it has simultaneously or previously, ratified the Convention. Instruments of ratification, acceptance or approval shall be deposited with the Secretary General of the Council of Europe.

Article 8

1. This Protocol shall enter into force on the first day of the month following the date on which five member States of the Council of Europe have expressed their consent to be bound by the Protocol in accordance with the provisions of Article 7.

2. In respect of any member State which subsequently expresses its consent to be bound by it, the Protocol shall enter into force on the first day of the month following the date of the deposit of the instrument of ratification, acceptance or approval.

Article 9

The Secretary General of the Council of Europe shall notify the member States of the Council of:

(a) any signature;

(b) the deposit of any instrument of ratification, acceptance or approval;

(c) any date of entry into force of this Protocol in accordance with Articles 5 and 8;

(d) any other act, notification or communication relating to this Protocol.

In witness whereof the undersigned, being duly authorised thereto, have signed this Protocol.

Done at Strasbourg, this 28th day of April 1983, in English and French, both texts being equally authentic, in a single copy which shall be deposited in the archives of the Council of Europe. The Secretary General of the Council of Europe shall transmit certified copies to each member State of the Council of Europe.

PROTOCOL 7

Strasbourg, 22 November 1984.[6]

The member States of the Council of Europe signatory hereto,

Being resolved to take further steps to ensure the collective enforcement of certain rights and freedoms by means of the Convention for the Protection of Human Rights and Fundamental Freedoms signed at Rome on 4 November 1950 (hereinafter referred to as "the Convention"),

---

[6] Entry into force: 1 November 1988, in accordance with Article 9.

Have agreed as follows:

Article 1

1. An alien lawfully resident in the territory of a State shall not be expelled therefrom except in pursuance of a decision reached in accordance with law and shall be allowed:

    (a) to submit reasons against his expulsion;

    (b) to have his case reviewed; and

    (c) to be represented for these purposes before the competent authority or a person or persons designated by that authority.

2. An alien may be expelled before the exercise of his rights under paragraph l(a), (b) and (c) of this Article, when such expulsion is necessary in the interests of public order or is grounded on reasons of national security.

Article 2

1. Everyone convicted of a criminal offence by a tribunal shall have the right to have his conviction or sentence reviewed by a higher tribunal. The exercise of this right, including the grounds on which it may be exercised shall be governed by law.

2. This right may be subject to exceptions in regard to offences of a minor character, as prescribed by law, or in cases in which the person concerned was tried in the first instance by the highest tribunal or was convicted following an appeal against acquittal.

Article 3

When a person has by a final decision been convicted of a criminal offence and when subsequently his conviction has been reversed, or he has been pardoned, on the ground that a new or newly discovered fact shows conclusively that there has been a miscarriage of justice, the person who has suffered punishment as a result of such conviction shall be compensated according to the law or the practice of the State concerned, unless it is proved that the non-disclosure of the unknown fact in time is wholly or partly attributable to him.

Article 4

1. No one shall be liable to be tried or punished again in criminal proceedings under the jurisdiction of the same State for an offence for which he has already been finally acquitted or convicted in accordance with the law and penal procedure of that State.

2. The provisions of the preceding paragraph shall not prevent the reopening of the case in accordance with the law and penal procedure of the State concerned, if there is evidence of new or newly discovered facts, or if there has been a fundamental defect in the previous proceedings, which could affect the outcome of the case.

3. No derogation from this Article shall be made under Article 15 of the Convention.

Article 5

Spouses shall enjoy equality of rights and responsibilities of a private law character between them, and in their relations with their children, as to marriage, during marriage and in the event of its dissolution. This Article shall not prevent States from taking such measures as are necessary in the interests of the children.

Article 6

1. Any State may at the time of signature or when depositing its instrument of ratification, acceptance or approval, specify the territory or territories to which this Protocol shall apply and state the extent to which it undertakes that the provisions of this Protocol shall apply to such territory or territories.

2. Any State may at any later day, by a declaration addressed to the Secretary General of the Council of Europe, extend the application of this Protocol to any other territory specified in the declaration. In respect of such territory the Protocol shall enter into force on the first day of the month following the expiration of a period of two months after the date of receipt by the Secretary General of such declaration.

3. Any declaration made under the two preceding paragraphs may, in respect of any territory specified in such declaration, be withdrawn or modified by a notification addressed to the Secretary General. The withdrawal or modification shall become effective on the first day of the month following the expiration of a period of two months after the date of receipt of such notification by the Secretary General.

4. A declaration made in accordance with this Article shall be deemed to have been made in accordance with paragraph 1 of Article 63 of the Convention.

5. The territory of any State to which this Protocol applies by virtue of ratification, acceptance or approval by that State, and each territory to which this Protocol is applied by virtue of a declaration by that State under this Article, may be treated as separate territories for the purpose of the reference in Article 1 to the territory of a State.

Article 7

1. As between the States Parties, the provisions of Articles 1 to 6 of this Protocol shall be regarded as additional Articles to the Convention and all the provisions of the Convention shall apply accordingly.

2. Nevertheless, the right of individual recourse recognised by a declaration made under Article 25 of the Convention, or the acceptance of the compulsory jurisdiction of the Court by a declaration made under Article 46 of the Convention, shall not be effective in relation to this Protocol unless the State concerned has made a statement recognising such right, or accepting such jurisdiction in respect of Articles 1 to 5 of this Protocol.

Article 8

This Protocol shall be open for signature by member States of the Council of Europe which have signed the Convention. It is subject to ratification, acceptance or approval. A member State of the Council of Europe may not ratify, accept or approve this Protocol without previously or simultaneously ratifying the Convention. Instruments of ratification, acceptance or approval shall be deposited with the Secretary General of the Council of Europe.

Article 9

1.   This Protocol shall enter into force on the first day of the month following the expiration of a period of two months after the date on which seven member States of the Council of Europe have expressed their consent to be bound by the Protocol in accordance with the provisions of Article 8.

2.   In respect of any member State which subsequently expresses its consent to be bound by it, the Protocol shall enter into force on the first day of the month following the expiration of a period of two months after the date of the deposit of the instrument of ratification, acceptance or approval.

Article 10

The Secretary General of the Council of Europe shall notify all the member States of the Council of Europe of:

(a) any signature;

(b) the deposit of any instrument of ratification, acceptance or approval;

(c) any date of entry into force of this Protocol in accordance with Articles 6 and 9;

(d) any other act, notification or declaration relating to this Protocol.

In witness whereof the undersigned, being duly authorised thereto, have signed this Protocol.

Done at Strasbourg, this 22nd day of November 1984, in English and French, both texts being equally authentic, in a single copy which shall be deposited in the archives of the Council of Europe. The Secretary General of the Council of Europe shall transmit certified copies to each member State of the Council of Europe.

PROTOCOL 9

Rome, 6 November 1990.[7]

The member States of the Council of Europe, signatories to this Protocol to the Convention for the Protection of Human Rights and Fundamental Freedoms, signed at Rome on 4 November 1950 (hereinafter referred to as "the Convention"),

---

[7] At the beginning of January 1993 the Protocol had been ratified by six states - Austria, Finland, Malta, Netherlands, Norway and Sweden.

Being resolved to make further improvements to the procedure under the Convention,

Have agreed as follows:

Article 1

For Parties to the Convention which are bound by this Protocol, the Convention shall be amended as provided in Articles 2 to 5.

Article 2

Article 31, paragraph 2, of the Convention, shall read as follows:

> "2. The report shall be transmitted to the Committee of Ministers. The report shall also be transmitted to the States concerned and, if it deals with a petition submitted under Article 25, the applicant. The States concerned and the applicant shall not be at liberty to publish it."

Article 3

Article 44 of the Convention shall read as follows:

> "Only the High Contracting Parties, the Commission, and persons, non-governmental organisations or groups of individuals having submitted a petition under Article 25 shall have the right to bring a case before the Court."

Article 4

Article 45 of the Convention shall read as follows:

> "The jurisdiction of the Court shall extend to all cases concerning the interpretation and application of the present Convention which are referred to it in accordance with Article 48."

Article 5

Article 48 of the Convention shall read as follows:

> "1. The following may refer a case to the Court, provided that the High Contracting Party concerned, if there is only one, or the High Contracting Parties concerned, if there is more than one, are subject to the compulsory jurisdiction of the Court or, failing that, with the consent of the High Contracting Party concerned, if there is only one, or of the High Contracting Parties concerned if there is more than one:
>
> (a) the Commission;
>
> (b) a High Contracting Party whose national is alleged to be a victim;
>
> (c) a High Contracting Party which referred the case to the Commission;
>
> (d) a High Contracting Party against which the complaint has been lodged;
>
> (e) the person, non-governmental organisation or group of individuals having lodged the complaint with the Commission.
>
> 2. If a case is referred to the Court only in accordance with paragraph

1 (e), it shall first be submitted to a panel composed of three members of the Court. There shall sit as an *ex officio* member of the panel the judge elected in respect of the High Contracting Party against which the complaint has been lodged, or, if there is none, a person of its choice who shall sit in the capacity of judge. If the complaint has been lodged against more than one High Contracting Party, the size of the panel shall be increased accordingly.

If the case does not raise a serious question affecting the interpretation or application of the Convention and does not for any other reason warrant consideration by the Court, the panel may, by a unanimous vote decide that it shall not be considered by the Court. In that event, the Committee of Ministers shall decide, in accordance with the provisions of Article 32, whether there has been a violation of the Convention."

Article 6

1. This Protocol shall be open for signature by member States of the Council of Europe signatories to the Convention, which may express their consent to be bound by:

   (a) signature without reservation as to ratification, acceptance or approval; or

   (b) signature subject to ratification, acceptance or approval, followed by ratification, acceptance or approval.

2. The instruments of ratification, acceptance or approval shall be deposited with the Secretary General of the Council of Europe.

Article 7

1. This Protocol shall enter into force on the first day of the month following the expiration of a period of three months after the date on which ten member States of the Council of Europe have expressed their consent to be bound by the Protocol in accordance with the provisions of Article 6.

2. In respect of any member State which subsequently expresses its consent to be bound by it, the Protocol shall enter into force on the first day of the month following the expiration of a period of three months after the date of signature or of the deposit of the instrument of ratification acceptance or approval.

Article 8

The Secretary General of the Council of Europe shall notify member States of the Council of Europe of:

   (a) any signature;

   (b) the deposit of any instrument of ratification, acceptance or approval;

   (c) any date of entry into force of this Protocol in accordance with Article 7;

(d) any other act, notification or declaration relating to this Protocol.

In witness whereof, the undersigned, being duly authorised thereto, have signed this Protocol.

Done at Rome, this 6th day of November 1990, in English and French, both texts being equally authentic, in a single copy which shall be deposited in the archives of the Council of Europe. The Secretary General of the Council of Europe shall transmit certified copies to each member State of the Council of Europe.

PROTOCOL 10

Strasbourg, 25 March 1992

The member States of the Council of Europe, signatories to this Protocol to the Convention for the Protection of Human Rights and Fundamental Freedoms, signed at Rome on 4 November 1950 (hereinafter referred to as "the Convention"),

Considering that it is advisable to amend Article 32 of the Convention with a view to the reduction of the two-thirds majority provided therein,

Have agreed as follows:

Article 1

The words "of two-thirds" shall be deleted from paragraph 1 of Article 32 of the Convention.

Article 2

1. This Protocol shall be open for signature by member States of the Council of Europe signatories to the Convention, which may express their consent to be bound by:

    (a) signature without reservation as to ratification, acceptance or approval, or

    (b) signature subject to ratification, acceptance or approval, followed by ratification, acceptance or approval.

2. Instruments of ratification, acceptance or approval shall be deposited with the Secretary General of the Council of Europe.

Article 3

This Protocol shall enter into force on the first day following the expiration of a period of three months after the date on which all Parties to the Convention have expressed their consent to be bound by the Protocol in accordance with the provisions of Article 2.

Article 4

The Secretary of the Council of Europe shall notify the member States of the Council of

(a)   any signature;

(b)   the deposit of any instrument of ratification, acceptance or approval;

(c)   the date of entry into force of this Protocol in accordance with Article 3;

(d)   any other act, notification or communication relating to this Protocol.

Index